Insurance Law in the United Kingdom

Insurance Law in the United Kingdom

Fourth Edition

John Birds

This book was originally published as a monograph in the International Encyclopaedia of Laws/Insurance Law.

Founding Editor: Roger Blanpain
General Editor: Frank Hendrickx
Volume Editor: Herman Cousy

Wolters Kluwer

Published by:
Kluwer Law International B.V.
PO Box 316
2400 AH Alphen aan den Rijn
The Netherlands
E-mail: international-sales@wolterskluwer.com
Website: lrus.wolterskluwer.com

Sold and distributed in North, Central and South America by:
Wolters Kluwer Legal & Regulatory U.S.
7201 McKinney Circle
Frederick, MD 21704
United States of America
Email: customer.service@wolterskluwer.com

Sold and distributed in all other countries by:
Air Business Subscriptions
Rockwood House
Haywards Heath
West Sussex
RH16 3DH
United Kingdom
Email: international-customerservice@wolterskluwer.com

Printed on acid-free paper

ISBN 978-94-035-0301-1

e-Book: ISBN 978-94-035-0215-1
web-PDF: ISBN 978-94-035-0261-8

This title is available on www.kluwerlawonline.com

Printed in the United Kingdom.

The Author

John Birds is Emeritus Professor in the School of Law, University of Manchester and Honorary Professor in both the School of Law, University of Sheffield and the School of Law, University of Exeter. He was Professor of Commercial Law at Manchester from 2006 to 2010, having previously been Professor of Commercial Law and Head of the Department of Law at the University of Sheffield. He taught at Sheffield from 1978 after six years as a lecturer at Queen Mary College, University of London. His interests lie in Insurance Law and Company Law, and he has lectured and written widely on these topics. Among other things, he is the author of *Modern Insurance Law*, the tenth edition of which was published in 2016, has been for several editions one of the editors of *MacGillivray on Insurance Law*, the thirteenth edition being published in 2015, is one of the editors of *The Principles of European Insurance Contract Law* and is General Editor of the *Encyclopedia of Insurance Law*. He is a contributor to *Gore-Browne on Companies* (forty-fifth edition, 2004) and co-editor of *Boyle and Birds' Company Law* (ninth edition, 2014). He has been on the editorial board of a number of journals and is the editor of the Insurance section the *Journal of Business Law*. He has also written numerous articles in the fields of insurance and company law, was a consultant to the UK Law Commissions concerning their project on insurance law reform and a member of the Project Group and Drafting Committee of the Project for the Restatement of European Insurance Contract Law.

The Author

Table of Contents

Table of Contents

List of Abbreviations

BILA	British Insurance Law Association
CGT	Capital Gains Tax
CII	Critical Illness Insurance
COBS	Conduct of Business Sourcebook
ECJ	European Court of Justice
FCA	Financial Conduct Authority
FOS	Financial Ombudsman Service
FSA	Financial Services Authority
FSCS	Financial Services Compensation Scheme
ICC	Institute Cargo Clauses
ICOB	Insurance Conduct of Business Rules
ICOBS	Insurance Conduct of Business Sourcebook
ILU	Institute of London Underwriters
ITC	Institute Time Clauses
IVC	Institute Voyage Clauses
MIB	Motor Insurers' Bureau
PET	Potentially Exempt Transfer
PHI	Permanent Health Insurance
PRA	Prudential Regulation Authority
SSP	Statutory Sick Pay
UNCTAD	United Nations Commission on Trade and Development

List of Abbreviations

General Introduction

§1. General Background Information

1. The United Kingdom (UK) consists, strictly speaking, of four countries, namely England, Wales, Scotland and Northern Ireland.[1] England and Wales, which have been ruled as one country for many centuries, were united with Scotland in 1707. For well over a decade, Scotland has had its own Parliament with many domestic legislative powers devolved to it. The Welsh Assembly has more limited law-making powers. In 1800, the whole of Ireland became part of the Kingdom, but on its partition in 1922, only the six counties in the North, the predominantly Protestant part, remained part of the UK. Great Britain is the island which contains the first three countries, while the term 'British Isles' is merely a geographical description of all the islands which lie off the north-west coast of continental Europe.[2]

The UK occupies about 242,432 square kilometres and has a population of some 62.5 million people (about 257 inhabitants per square kilometre). It is about the same size as New Zealand and about half the size of France.

I. Political and Legal System

2. Notwithstanding the union of England and Wales with Scotland, the Scottish legal system has always quite been separate from that applying in England and Wales. The law of the latter is based on the Common Law which, indeed, was formulated in the English courts from medieval times and now applies to a large number of countries in the world. These are primarily countries, which were once part of the British Empire and include the United States of America as well as those countries such as Australia, Canada and New Zealand which are part of the British Commonwealth. Because of the common base of the Common Law, and because British insurance contract law is still very much based on case law, decisions of the courts of the Commonwealth and of the United States remain persuasive authority in the British courts.[3] In contrast, Scots Law is still based on Roman Law rather than the Common Law, although in

1. Notwithstanding the presence of the latter, the common adjective, derived from geography and which is generally used in this work, is British.
2. The British Isles therefore includes the Isle of Man and the Channel Islands which, although they have very close ties with the UK, are not part of it.
3. For this reason, such decisions are sometimes cited in this work, and texts published in these countries can be a useful source of reference on matters of British insurance law.

respect of the law of insurance this has relatively few consequences.[4] Northern Ireland also has a separate legal system, although it is based on the common law. However, final appeals in both Scotland and Northern Ireland, as well as in England and Wales, are to the Supreme Court of the UK, which replaced the House of Lords as the ultimate Court of Appeal within the UK from August 2009.

3. The UK does not have a written constitution, except to the extent that the Human Rights Act 1998 incorporates the European Convention on Human Rights. Its constitution is said to depend on a series of rules and conventions which have grown up over the centuries and have been modified from time to time by Act of Parliament. The Parliament, which is the Parliament of the whole of the UK and, subject to the statute governing devolution, has power to pass laws applying to the whole or any part thereof, is comprised of the sovereign, the House of Lords and the House of Commons.[5] The development of the British Constitution over the years was from a totalitarian monarchy to a modern day constitutional monarchy in which the sovereign, currently Queen Elizabeth II, is the Head of State but, by convention, with very few real powers. The House of Commons is the only part of the constitution elected by the people, and the political party which commands a majority of that House is the one which conventionally forms the government of the day. There are some 650 elected members of the House of Commons, each elected by a single constituency under a 'first past the post' voting system. The result is that a majority of members of this House is almost always elected by less than 50% of the electorate. There is a very strong party political system, the two major parties being the Conservative Party (of the right) and the Labour Party (of the left) and each having traditional strength in certain parts of the country and hence in particular constituencies. The third, centre, party, which is now the Liberal Democratic Party, has strength in a limited number of areas but has never, hitherto, been able to command sufficient general support to win more than relatively few seats in the House of Commons. A General Election for members of the House of Commons must be held every five years. Subject to qualifications laid down by the Parliament Acts of 1911 and 1947, the House of Lords, which consists of both hereditary peers and appointed life peers, as well as some bishops of the Established Church of England, has in theory equal legislative status with the House of Commons. In practice, the House of Lords has very little legislative power and is mainly a debating and revising chamber. There have been government plans to revise the membership and limit the formal powers of the House of Lords. The absence of a written constitution means that, subject to constraints imposed by accession to membership of what is now the

4. Sometimes therefore Scottish cases are cited as good authority throughout the UK, although the reader should be warned that there are some differences.
5. Conventionally Acts of Parliament applied to Scotland only if they expressly so declared and some separate provision is often made because of the different origins of Scots law. *A fortiori* this remains the position under devolution. For many years Northern Ireland had its own Parliament with power to make statute law; this was suspended during the troubles there but now some law-making powers have reverted to Northern Ireland.

European Union,[6] the Parliament is supreme, and the courts have no right to invalidate any law properly passed through the correct Parliamentary procedures.

4. The British electoral system, briefly described above, has for many years resulted in traditionally 'strong' government in the sense of one political party having a sufficiently large majority in the House of Commons to govern without effective opposition for up to five years, although that pattern changed in 2010 when no one party commanded a majority and the government was made up of the Conservative and Liberal Democratic parties acting in coalition. The Conservative government subsequently elected in 2015 lost its overall majority following the general election in 2017 and at the time of writing commands only a majority with the support of the Northern Irish Democratic Unionist Party. The leader of the largest party is the Prime Minister and he or she chooses the Cabinet, which forms the inner core of the executive. This body is strengthened against the legislature by the convention of Cabinet collective responsibility, under which Cabinet ministers are not permitted to criticize Cabinet decisions in public, unless they are prepared to resign. The Prime Minister and his or her Cabinet wield considerable executive power and, by convention, can carry out many major acts of state, such as the making of war and the signing of international treaties, without reference to Parliament.[7] In the administration of government, the Cabinet is assisted by the Civil Service, divided into many government departments each of which is headed by a Cabinet member known as a Minister or Secretary of State. The most important government departments are the Home Office (similar to a Ministry of the Interior) headed by the Home Secretary, the Treasury headed by the Chancellor of the Exchequer, the Foreign and Commonwealth Office headed by the Foreign Secretary, the Ministry of Justice (headed by the Lord Chancellor) and the Ministry of Defence headed by the Defence Secretary. The one which has responsibility for the regulation of insurance business is the Treasury, although these powers have been vested in the Bank of England, the Prudential Regulation Authority (PRA) and the Financial Conduct Authority (FCA) which together have control of the whole of the financial services sector.

5. Notwithstanding what has been said above, there are in fact a number of ways in which the British government is controlled. The electoral system already described means that a fairly moderate swing of public opinion against the government will be sufficient to unseat it at a general election. Government ministers are subject to questioning in Parliament, particularly by the increasingly powerful specialized House of Commons committees. The backbench members of the governing party do occasionally revolt and require the government to pay attention to their views and public pressure groups, and the press can mobilize public opinion in a manner which persuades government to change its mind. Most important, under the informal British Constitution, is the position of the judiciary. This has always regarded itself as strongly independent of government and increasingly is prepared to accede to challenges against government power, particularly by way of judicial review of government action. Under this procedure, for example, secondary legislation (*see infra*) has been struck down as *ultra*

---

6. This membership, of course, now seems to be coming to an end as a result of the UK's giving notice to leave. Exactly what this will mean is at the time of writing unclear, as will be explained further later.
7. Historically this derives from the power of the monarch.

vires the primary legislation (the Act of Parliament) under which it was made, and in other ways the actions of government departments have sometimes been declared unlawful. The incorporation of the European Convention on Human Rights also gives some powers to the courts to strike down legislation contrary to its terms.

6. UK law[8] consists of both Acts of Parliament (and secondary legislation made thereunder)[9] and of rules laid down by the courts (the 'common law'). Much of insurance law is common law in this sense. Acts are introduced into either the House of Commons or the House of Lords as Bills, which go through a series of procedures known as readings and committees during which they are subject to scrutiny, debate and, occasionally, amendment. The majority of legislation is introduced by the Government of the day, but any member of either House can introduce a Bill, and this procedure is sometimes used for purely law reforming measures which command general assent. An increasing volume of legislation these days becomes law as secondary or delegated legislation, as already described. These arise when an Act of Parliament confers authority on the Government to act in this way. This sort of legislation is in practice subject to very little scrutiny.

7. The legal system consists of a hierarchy of courts, in which courts lower in the hierarchy are bound by decisions of the higher courts, and in general, courts at any level are bound by their own previous decisions. This case law based system of 'precedent' is inherent to the Common Law system (as compared with systems based on Roman law). As already indicated, the Supreme Court is the ultimate court for all the countries of the Kingdom. Below it, in England and Wales, is the Court of Appeal, which hears appeals from the courts of first instance. The latter comprise the High Court, which has three Divisions,[10] and the County Courts, the latter being inferior to the High Court.[11] Apart from certain areas of law (not including insurance law) which are reserved to the High Court, the principal factor which determines in which Court of First Instance a case is heard is the amount of money at stake.[12] In Scotland, the Court of Session is the equivalent of the Court of Appeal.

8. The history of the court system which produced the common law is highly complex, but there is one aspect of it which needs brief mention here. This is the separate development in separate courts of common law and equity (the term 'common law' being used here, confusingly, in a narrower sense than to describe the system as a whole as compared to, say, Roman law). For reasons which do not need elaboration here, there grew up two systems of courts, the common law courts, which tended to become extremely technical, and the courts of equity, which were much more flexible

8. This account is concerned solely with civil law as opposed to criminal law.
9. These are statutory instruments or Orders in Council, which have a title, the year of their passing and a number.
10. The Queen's Bench Division, the Chancery Division and the Family Division. Insurance disputes involving a commercial insured will almost always be heard in the Queen's Bench Division and generally in the Commercial Court which is a part of that Division.
11. The High Court sits in London and at a few other major cities. There are county courts in towns of any real size.
12. Legislation has increased the jurisdiction of the county courts considerably, so that it is now mandatory to use them in respect of ordinary contract disputes when the amount involved is up to Pound Sterling (GBP) 25,000. Disputes involving amounts between GBP 25,000 and GBP 50,000 can be tried therein if the parties agree.

in terms of both legal principles and remedies. Eventually the systems were 'merged' in 1875, but the distinction still matters considerably for some parts of British law where it is proper to talk of rules of equity as opposed to rules of common law; in these instances, where there is any conflict, the rules of equity prevail. This distinction does not have very many consequences for insurance law (or for contract law generally), but there are some consequences as will be seen in the text that follows.

II. Commerce and Industry

9. The UK was one of the first industrialized nations, using its power and the British Empire to achieve its status as one of the wealthiest countries in the world. Although its power and wealth has declined in relative terms, it is still regarded as among the leading industrialized countries. Its historical strength in manufacturing industry has, however, declined somewhat and been replaced by strength in commerce and finance. Its balance of payments depends very heavily these days on its 'export' of so-called invisibles such as insurance, and it is probably proper to describe it as one of the leading centres in the world for insurance, banking and other financial services.

III. Financial Institutions

10. The UK's financial institutions are dominant in a number of ways. In particular, as already explained, they account for a substantial part of the modern economy. They are made up of the insurance organizations and banking and other financial institutions. Insurance companies and pension funds are the major investors in the shares of public companies and thus in a position to wield enormous influence in the economy as a whole. All the UK financial institutions are also major employers of people.

IV. Currency Legislation and Monetary Regulations

11. Until 1979, there were strict exchange controls governing the flow of money into and out of the UK, but these were suspended in that year and have since been abolished. There are thus no controls relevant at this time to this work.

V. Insurance Business, General Organization and Special Features

12. A brief general description of the UK insurance industry is given in Chapter 1 of Part I below. One particular feature worth highlighting at this stage is the power wielded by the industry, which stems from the factors already mentioned, namely its position of power in the economy and its contribution to UK exports. The industry is generally represented by the Association of British Insurers, a trade association to which almost the entire UK insurance company market belongs. There is no doubt that this body has a considerable influence with government.

§2. Historical Background of Insurance and Insurance Legislation

13. The origins of the insurance contract in the UK are to be found when London merchants in the sixteenth century adopted the practices carried out by Italian merchants for some years previously. Given the times, the original type of insurance was marine insurance, effected by groups of merchants agreeing that each would bear the risks attaching to the others' ships and cargoes. Only from the late seventeenth century did the business of insurance in its modern sense grow up, originally when insurers gathered to offer their services at a coffee house owned by a man called Edward Lloyd.[13] Types of insurance other than marine followed rather later, often stimulated by particular events. Thus, it seems that it was the Great Fire of London in 1666, which stimulated the growth of fire insurance, and increasing industrialization in the nineteenth century that was the impetus for very many types of insurance ranging from personal accident insurance to workmen's compensation and liability insurances. Life insurance predated the Industrial Revolution and indeed was regulated in certain respects by an Act of 1774.[14]

14. In the early days of the marine insurance contract, disputes were decided according to the law merchant, and indeed in 1601, merchants secured the establishment by statute of a Chamber of Assurance outside the normal legal system. The common law took a relatively late interest in insurance, the instigator of that interest being Lord Mansfield, Lord Chief Justice in the latter part of the eighteenth century. He applied principles derived from the law merchant as well as more traditional common law concepts to produce what are still the foundations of modern insurance law.

15. Parliament has traditionally only relatively rarely intervened to pass legislation in the insurance field and, except in a few cases, has been concerned merely to check isolated abuses. However, there was a notable change in 2012 and in 2015 when the Consumer Insurance (Disclosure and Representations) Act and the Insurance Act, respectively, were enacted; these are considered in Part II, Chapter 5. Otherwise, the principal cases of Parliamentary intervention are:

(1) control of abuses where policies disguised as insurance policies were in effect wagering contracts;[15]
(2) the codification of marine insurance law in the Marine Insurance Act 1906;[16]
(3) the regulation of industrial life assurance[17] in a series of statutes;

13. The start of Lloyd's of London, the basis of operation of which is still the same. *See* para. 38.
14. *See* para. 73.
15. As to these, *see* Part II, Ch. 2, *infra* .
16. As to this, *see* Part III, Ch. 3, *infra* .
17. Industrial life assurance is life insurance where the premiums are paid to collectors at less than two monthly intervals; the amounts involved, both premiums and sums insured, are usually small. It has rapidly declined in importance in recent years.

(4) legislation to secure the financial solvency of the providers of insurance;[18]
(5) legislation making compulsory certain types of insurance, principally motor vehicle insurance[19] and employers' liability insurance;[20] and
(6) legislation to control the selling of insurance.[21]

§3. Sources of Insurance Law

I. Legislation

16. As already indicated, legislation is not an important source of insurance law in the UK except in specific instances. In particular, there is no general insurance code governing the law applying to the insurance contract. With qualifications, the real sources of insurance contract law outside of marine insurance,[22] aspects of consumer insurance law and related areas,[23] are the common law principles developed by the judges since the time of Lord Mansfield and, in part, the standard documents of insurance. Proposal forms and policies have for so long been drafted in a fairly uniform way by insurers that it can almost be said that certain things are law because they will be found in any insurance contract. The voluminous legislation that does exist is concerned primarily with the regulation of insurance business and the selling of insurance. It consists of parts of the Financial Services and Markets Act 2000 and rules made under that Act, and is described later.[24]

II. Government Regulations

17. As indicated, the above-mentioned legislation is supplemented by regulations made by statutory instrument. Such regulations can only be made pursuant to an Act of Parliament and with the approval of Parliament.[25]

---

18. *See* Part I, *infra* .
19. *See* Part IV, *infra* .
20. *See* Part V, Ch. 1, *infra* .
21. *See* Part V, Ch. 4, *infra* .
22. As already indicated, marine insurance law was codified in the Marine Insurance Act 1906.
23. Under the Consumer Insurance (Disclosure and Representations) Act 2012 and the Insurance Act 2015.
24. *See* especially Part I and Part V, Ch. 4, *infra* .
25. Sometimes approval is required in terms of a resolution of both House of Parliament (the affirmative resolution procedure); sometimes approval is deemed unless there is a resolution refusing it (the negative resolution procedure).

III. Regulation by Government Agencies

18. The PRA and the FCA are the bodies authorized to make rules under the 2000 Act and do so by means of their Handbooks.[26] Until recently, self-regulation by the insurance industry was an important source of insurance practice, but this has declined recently for reasons described below.

IV. Private International Law and Jurisdiction

19. Where an insurance transaction has links with more than one country,[27] it will be necessary to use the rules of private international law, or conflict of laws, to determine by which system of law any disputes are to be resolved (the proper law) and to ascertain which system of courts has jurisdiction to decide this and enforce a judgment given in a third country.[28] It remains to be seen whether or to what extent the UK's departure from the European Union will affect what is described here.

20. As far as jurisdiction is concerned, within the European Union, this is primarily governed by EC Council Regulation No. 44/2001, which replaced in this respect the Civil Jurisdiction and Judgments Act 1982.[29] If an action is brought against or by an insurer not domiciled in any of the Contracting States,[30] the jurisdiction of the courts is governed by the traditional principle that the court has jurisdiction if the defendant can be served with a claim in England or with notice of proceedings abroad.[31] In respect of actions against insurers domiciled in any of the Contracting States,[32] the English courts will have jurisdiction if the defendant submits to the jurisdiction or in a number of instances, the most important of which can be summarized as follows:

(1) If the insurer or policyholder is domiciled in England.
(2) In cases of liability insurance or insurances of immovable property, if the harmful event occurred in England.
(3) In cases of liability insurance concerning claims by the insured, where the injured third party has brought proceedings against the insured in England.

26. *See* further below and Part V, Ch. 4.
27. Within the UK, this will be so where, e.g., a policy is issued by a Scottish insurer to someone resident in England. Given the number of insurers registered in Scotland, this is quite a common occurrence.
28. For detail to supplement this very brief account, the reader is referred to Ch. 13 of *MacGillivray on Insurance Law*, 13th ed., and Ch. 2 of Clarke, *The Law of Insurance Contracts*, and the detailed reference sources referred to therein.
29. This Act gave effect to the Brussels Convention on Jurisdiction and the Enforcement of Judgments in Civil and Commercial Matters. It is possible to contract out of the basic rules laid down by the Act only if the requirements specified in Sch. 1, Art. 17 are complied with. The Brussels convention and hence the 1982 Act still apply to determine jurisdiction between the UK and Denmark.
30. The EC Member States except Denmark.
31. The latter is possible if, among other things, the proper law of the contract is English.
32. There are special rules limiting the jurisdiction of the English courts in respect of insurers domiciled in Scotland or Northern Ireland.

(4) In the case of a counterclaim, if the insurer has commenced proceedings in England based on the same contract or facts. In respect of actions by insurers against a defendant domiciled in any of the Contracting States, such proceedings may in general be brought in the English courts only if the defendant is domiciled in England or has a branch, agency or establishment in England out of the operations of which the dispute arises.

21. The question of the proper law of the insurance contract depends on whether or not the risks are situated in the UK or another Member State of the EC. If they are, then as far as general insurance is concerned,[33] the matter is governed by the Financial Services and Markets Act 2000 (Law Applicable to Contracts of Insurance) Regulations 2001.[34] Under these provisions, in brief, where the policyholder has his habitual residence or central administration within the territory of the Member State where the risk is situated, the law applicable to the contract is the law of that State. Where the latter law allows, the parties may choose the law of another country, but this choice must be expressed or demonstrated with reasonable certainty by the terms of the contract or the circumstances of the case. If this is not so, or if no choice has been made, the contract is governed by the law of the country with which it is most closely connected (rebuttably presumed to be the Member State where the risk is situated). Where the policyholder does not have his habitual residence or central administration within the territory of the Member State where the risk is situated, the parties may choose to apply either the law of the State where the risk is situated or the law of the country where the policyholder has his habitual residence or central administration.

22. Contracts covering risks outside the EEA, long-term contracts and reinsurance contracts are governed by the common law and the Contracts (Applicable Law) Act 1990.[35] These usually produce the result that the law of the insurer's country applies and in any event allows a much freer choice of law than the other provisions.[36]

§4. Dispute Settlement and Arbitration

23. The formal court system briefly described earlier will be used to settle insurance disputes but in general only as a last resort. Disputes concerning commercial insurances are often referred to arbitration pursuant to a provision to that effect in the contract.[37] Such arbitrations are usually conducted under the auspices of the Chartered Institute of Arbitrators with a leading practising lawyer appointed as arbitrator. As far as consumer insurances are concerned, from 1981 to 2001, there were two mechanisms available as an alternative to the courts, although it was not compulsory for a private policyholder to use either. These two were the Insurance Ombudsman Bureau (IOB) and Personal Insurances Arbitration Service (PIAS). Both arose out of the insurance

33. The common law rules (*see infra*) still apply to long-term insurance and reinsurance.
34. SI 2635, implementing Art. 7 of EC Directive 88/357.
35. Implementing the Rome Convention on the Law Applicable to Contractual Obligations.
36. For detail, *see MacGillivray* and *Clarke*, *infra*.
37. *See infra* para. 140.

industry, with the IOB proving very successful and the model for later private sector bodies and the Financial Ombudsman Service (FOS) described below.

24. The statutory FOS is established under Part XVI of the Financial Services and Markets Act 2000. There is no doubt that this scheme has clear advantages over the IOB, not least because it is a compulsory scheme and if necessary its awards can be enforced through the courts. Further, the FOS has the statutory right to demand information under section 231 of the 2000 Act. The range of insurance consumers that can complain to the ombudsman includes small businesses, basically those with a turnover of less than Pound Sterling (GBP) 2 million per annum as well as individual consumers, and persons for whose benefit an insurance contract was taken out or a person on whom the legal right to benefit from a claim under a contract of insurance has been devolved by contract, statute or subrogation. The FOS' services are free to complainants. Further, it determines complaints by reference to what is 'fair and reasonable in all the circumstances of the case'.[38] This is amplified in the Dispute Resolution Rules issued under the Act, which state that in considering what is fair and reasonable in all the circumstances of the case, the Ombudsman will take into account the relevant law, regulations, regulators' codes and guidance and standards, relevant codes of practice and, where appropriate, what he considers to have been good industry practice at the relevant time.[39] In addition, the FOS can hear complaints about the selling of insurance by brokers and other intermediaries. The basic limit on awards is GBP 150,000, but the ombudsman can recommend that the respondent pay more if he considers that fair compensation requires this and can also award costs reasonably incurred by the complainant.

§5. Consumer Protection

25. The last half of the twentieth century witnessed an explosion in the volume of consumer protection legislation in the UK. This ranges from controls over contract terms by way of implying terms into certain types of contract and prohibiting or restricting the extent to which such terms can be excluded[40] to detailed legislation in some areas in effect prescribing in part the terms of certain contracts (especially hire purchase and other credit contracts).[41] In addition, there are criminal sanctions against persons who supply goods or services under false descriptions,[42] and in respect of product and food safety.[43]

---

38. Financial Services and Markets Act 2000, s. 228(2).
39. Insurers must also have and operate appropriate and effective internal complaint handling procedures, ensure that their literature refers to the FOS, and co-operate fully with the Ombudsman. A challenge to the Ombudsman's right to decide on the basis of what is fair and reasonable failed in *R. v. Financial Ombudsman Services Ltd,* ex parte *IFG Financial Services Ltd* [2005] EWHC 1153 (Admin).
40. For example, the Sale of Goods Act 1979, the Supply of Goods and Services Act 1982 and the Unfair Contract Terms Act 1977.
41. *See* especially, the Consumer Credit Act 1974.
42. Under the Trade Descriptions Act 1968.
43. *See* the Consumer Protection Act 1987 and the Food Safety Act 1990.

26. In sharp contrast, the legislature had rarely intervened to protect consumers of insurance.[44] This was not because of a lack of awareness that certain aspects of insurance contract law could operate unfairly so far as individual consumers were concerned. Official law reform bodies, the Law Reform Committee in 1957[45] and the Law Commission in 1980,[46] made recommendations for reform, particularly in respect of the duty of disclosure and associated aspects of the law, but legislative inaction was the result. More generally, it is clear that when the Law Commission recommended the introduction of what became the Unfair Contract Terms Act 1977, it intended the relevant part of that Act, giving the court jurisdiction to strike out certain terms on the ground of unreasonableness, to apply to insurance contracts. In this instance, the legislature chose to exempt contracts of insurance from the scope of the Act.[47] A report published in 1997 by the National Consumer Council – *Insurance Law Reform* – argued for widespread statutory reform of insurance contract law for the benefit of individual consumers. This was followed by a report prepared by the British Insurance Law Association (BILA) in 2002, as well as important lectures by senior members of the judiciary.[48] This has borne fruit in that the Law Commissions have engaged on a lengthy project examining insurance contract law. They issued their first Report – *Consumer Insurance Law: Pre-Contract Disclosure and Misrepresentation* – in December 2009[49] and the draft Bill therein was enacted in 2012. Most of the recommendations in their second Report[50] were implemented in the Insurance Act 2015, which came into force in August 2016, and the outstanding recommendation was added to the 2015 Act by the Enterprise Act 2016.

27. In place of legislation reforming insurance law, government was content generally and until recently to accept 'reform' by means of 'self-regulation'. This took the form of strictly unenforceable non-statutory *Statements of Practice*, which amounted to declarations by the large majority of the insurance industry that they would not in all respects rely upon their strict legal rights. These first appeared in 1977 as the quid pro quo for the exemption from the Unfair Contract Terms Act 1977.[51] They were revised in 1986 to reflect the recommendations of the Law Commission Report of 1982, when yet again the insurance lobby won the argument for no proper law reform.[52]

---

44. For general comments on this situation, *see* Birds, *The Reform of Insurance Law*, JBL 449 (1982) and *Self-Regulation and Insurance Contracts, New Foundations for Insurance Law* 1–18 (Rose ed., 1987). Note also that Australia passed a general reforming statute in 1984, the Insurance Contracts Act, which could usefully serve as a model for consumer protection in insurance under a common law system.
45. Fifth Report, *Conditions and exceptions in insurance policies*, *Cmnd* 62.
46. *Insurance Law: Non-Disclosure and Breach of Warranty*, Report No. 104, *Cmnd* 8064.
47. Schedule 1, para. 1(a).
48. Especially Longmore and Rix L.JJ., in lectures reproduced as appendices to the BILA report; *see* Longmore, *An Insurance Contracts Act for a new century*? LMCLQ 356 (2001).
49. Law Com. No. 319, Scot Law Com. No. 219, CM 7558.
50. Law Com. No. 353, Scot Law Com. No. 238, 2014.
51. *See* Birds (1977) 40 MLR 677.
52. *See* Birds, *supra* and Forte, *The revised Statements of Insurance Practice*, 49 MLR 754 (1986). The insurance industry operates with a relatively large number of agreements, outside the formal legal system; *see* Lewis, *Insurers' agreements not to enforce strict legal rights: bargaining with government and in the shadow of the law*, 48 MLR 275 (1985).

Although they did in practice mitigate some of the worst features of the law, they could not be regarded as a substitute for law reform since a minority of insurers operated outside their scope.[53] However, there can be no doubt that for the vast majority, the effect of the *Statements*, taken together with the existence and practices of the Ombudsman, led to a system where in many respects there was a different body of rules applying to personal insurances from those applying to commercial insurances.

28. The situation changed somewhat in 2005 when the former Financial Services Authority (FSA) introduced some parts of the former Statement of General Insurance Practice into its Insurance Conduct of Business Rules (ICOB), thus giving them statutory force. The Statement of General Insurance Practice was withdrawn, as subsequently was the Statement of Long-Term Insurance. ICOB was replaced in 2008 by the Insurance Conduct of Business Sourcebook (ICOBS). It has been adopted by the FCA, which took over this aspect of the work of the FSA. ICOBS applies to general insurance, which is essentially non-life insurance, and to what is called pure protection insurance, which is essentially life insurance contracts of a short-term duration and with no surrender value.[54] The particular impetus for this was the need to implement the Insurance Mediation Directive,[55] requiring the statutory regulation of insurance intermediaries, but the rules go further than that and apply generally to the conduct of general insurance business, on the ground that customers of insurers selling directly should receive the same level of protection, although some of the detailed provisions apply only to only to insurers and some only to intermediaries. Distinctions are also made in a number of the rules between the requirements in dealing with retail customers (i.e., mainly private individuals) and commercial customers. It was plausibly argued that ICOB represents a significant reform of insurance contract law,[56] and the same can be said of ICOBS, although the latter is more ‘principles based’ and less detailed than ICOB.

29. After its general application provision (ICOBS 1), ICOBS contains:

(1) general matters, including rules on communications with customers and prohibiting unfair inducements (ICOBS 2);

---

53. Technically, they were ‘binding’ on insurers who were members of the Association of British Insurers or Lloyd’s underwriters, which categories did not cover all British insurers, let alone insurers from other Member States or elsewhere selling insurance in the UK. The government expected all insurers to comply, but appeared to have no effective means of monitoring the situation. A further argument for actual law reform is that if an insurance company goes into liquidation, the liquidator would be bound to apply the law in dealing with unpaid claims.
54. ICOBS does not apply to the insurances of large risks, reinsurance and group policies. Most forms of life insurance are covered by the rules on investments generally and covered by the general Conduct of Business Sourcebook.
55. 2002/92/EC. There was also the need to implement the Directive on distance marketing of financial services (2002/65/EC).
56. *See* the excellent discussion by McMeel, *The FSA’s insurance conduct of business regime: a revolution in (consumer) insurance law*? LMCLQ 186 (2005). It is noteworthy that a breach of ICOB may be actionable under s.138D of the 2000 Act, which provides an action for breach of statutory duty for ‘private persons’ who suffer loss through breach by an authorized person. Time will tell whether s. 138D confers a significant weapon available against an insurer.

(2) rules regarding distance communications, implementing the relevant EC Directive[57] (ICOBS 3);
(3) general requirements for insurance intermediaries, including disclosure of their status and regarding the disclosure of fees and commission (ICOBS 4);
(4) rules on identifying client needs and advising (ICOBS 5);
(5) rules on product information to ensure that customers have the necessary information to make an informed choice about whether or not to buy a specific insurance contract and whether a contract continues to meet their needs (ICOBS 6);
(6) rules conferring cancellation rights on retail customers (ICOBS 7); and
(7) rules regarding the handling of claims, including rules restricting insurers' rights to repudiate a claim for non-disclosure, misrepresentation or breach of warranty (ICOBS 8).

30. Some of the more significant detailed provisions that are not referred to later are as follows. Firms must take reasonable steps to ensure that all communications with all customers are clear, fair and not misleading.[58] Firms must take reasonable steps to ensure that they do not offer, give, solicit or accept inducements which may conflict to a material extent with its duties to its customers; this is particularly directed at, for example, situations concerning insurers and intermediaries.[59] Exclusions of liability under the rules are prohibited.[60] There are specific provisions about distance contracts with retail customers, including ensuring that a paper copy of the terms and conditions must be provided at the customer's request.[61] Distance contracts are any where there is no face to face dealing, which will apply to all situations where negotiations are conducted on the telephone or over the Internet, something that is increasingly common these days. Intermediaries must not disclose their fees to their retail customers,[62] and commercial customers are entitled to know the amount of commission that an intermediary would receive.[63]

31. There are rules about what is called 'financial promotion', which means the advertising and marketing of insurance to ensure that it is fair, clear and not misleading.[64] The rules on advising and selling standards will apply especially to intermediaries who must, among other things, disclose the basis on which they recommend a particular insurance product on the basis of an analysis of the market, from a limited number of insurers or from a single insurer and who are under a duty to seek out information from a customer about their circumstances and objectives. These will clearly be relevant in assessing whether an intermediary can be liable for negligent advice.[65] The product disclosure requirements of ICOBS 6 and the cancellation rights conferred by ICOBS

57. *See* n. 64.
58. ICOBS 2.2.
59. ICOBS 2.3.
60. ICOBS 2.5.
61. ICOBS 3.1.16.
62. ICOBS 4.3.
63. ICOBS 4.4.
64. ICOBS 2.2. *See also* the general prohibition on financial promotion other than by authorized persons under s. 21 of the 2000 Act.
65. *See* Part VII, Ch. 2.

7 are considered later. The restrictions on the legal rights of insurers in ICOBS 8 are also considered elsewhere. More generally the rules provide detailed requirements on claims handling to ensure that they are handled fairly and settled promptly. Insurers must provide all customers with reasonable guidance to help them to make a claim and appropriate information on its progress.[66] Retail customers are given specific protection, which is also briefly considered later.

32. Another measure which has some impact on insurance contract law is Part 2 of the Consumer Rights Act 2015, replacing the Unfair Terms in Consumer Contracts Regulations 1999[67] and implementing the EC Unfair Contract Terms Directive.[68] This has a number of effects on insurance contracts effected with a consumer, that is a natural person not acting in the course of his business, that should be noted here.[69] There is a general requirement to use plain, intelligible and legible language. A very important point concerns the question of the application of the core part of the Regulations to the question of the cover provided by an insurance contract.[70] This strikes down any 'unfair term' which contrary to the requirement of good faith causes a 'significant imbalance in the parties' rights and obligations under the contract to the detriment of the consumer'. However, it does not apply to any term relating to 'the definition of the main subject matter of the contract' that is transparent and prominent. It is thought that the provisions concerning the risks covered and excepted under an insurance contract would normally fall within this exception,[71] as these define the main subject matter of the contract. There is some control of insurance policy conditions, as will be seen below.[72]

§6. Compulsory Insurances

33. A number of liability insurances are compulsory, whether by statute or by virtue of the rules of an association, although there is no real pattern in this respect. Without doubt, the most important class of compulsory insurance is motor vehicle insurance, which is considered in detail in Part IV below. Here, statute[73] does not just provide for compulsion but makes detailed provision regarding the protection of the road traffic accident victim. The system is backed up by the Motor Insurers' Bureau (MIB) in the event of a failure of insurance. Rather less detailed, although with some

66. ICOBS 8.1.1.
67. SI 1999/2083.
68. 93/29/EC.
69. *See also* para. 117.
70. Apart from the requirement of plainness and intelligibility of language which clearly applies.
71. Although the Act can quite properly go beyond what the EC Directive required, the provisions of the Directive must be an aid to construction. In the preamble to the Directive, it was stated that in insurance contracts, 'the terms which clearly define or circumstance the insured risk and the insurer's liability shall not be subject to (assessment of unfair character) since these restrictions are taken into account in calculating the premium paid by the consumer'. Assuming that the preamble qualifies the text of the Directive (*see* Duffy J.B.L. 67 at 71–72 (1993)), this seems effective to remove from its scope provisions defining the risk and exceptions to it.
72. *See* para. 117.
73. The Road Traffic Act 1988.

provisions protecting the injured third party, is the scheme for compulsory employer's liability insurance.[74]

34. The rules for other compulsory insurances tend to be lacking in any detail, merely requiring that liability insurance exists. By statute, such insurance is required of riding establishments,[75] the operator of nuclear establishments,[76] civil aviation[77] and oil pollution.[78] Professional indemnity insurance is required in respect of an increasing number of professions. So far the list includes solicitors,[79] financial services intermediaries including insurance brokers[80] and estate agents.[81]

§7. UK Insurance Law and 'Brexit'

As far as the law governing the contract of insurance is concerned, there appear unlikely to be any implications arising from the UK's decision to leave the EU ('Brexit'). However, there are potential implications for the law governing the regulation of insurance business, for motor insurance law and for the private international law rules applying to insurance disputes. As far as regulation is concerned, it seems unlikely that there will be substantial changes to the current requirements regarding the financial regulation of domestic insurers and information disclosure by insurers. Even though these currently are prescribed by EU law, they will almost certainly be retained as UK law. What is quite unclear at this stage is whether the provisions on 'passport' rights, regarding the freedom of insurers to establish and/or provide services throughout the EU, will remain, since this depends on whether or not the UK remains a member of the single market or in regulatory alignment with the EU single market; no agreement has yet been reached on this. Much of the UK motor insurance law is governed by EU law and Brexit could lead to changes, especially in terms of the protection given to victims of uninsured or unidentified drivers. However, this will certainly not be a necessary consequence. As far as private international law is concerned, jurisdictional issues within EU Member States are covered by EU law. It would seem sensible to mirror these following Brexit, but this outcome is as yet uncertain.

74. Under the Employer's Liability Insurance Act 1969 and regulations made thereunder; *see* Part III, Ch. 4.
75. Riding Establishments Act 1964, s. 1.
76. Nuclear Installations Act 1965–1969.
77. Regulation 785/04 of the European Parliament and Council, 21 Apr. 2004, O.J. L 138, as supplemented by the Civil Aviation (Insurance) Regulations 2005, SI 2005/1089.
78. Merchant Shipping Act 1995.
79. By virtue of the rules of the Law Society.
80. By virtue of requirements imposed under the Financial Services and Markets Act 2000.
81. By virtue of rules made under the Estate Agents Act 1979.

Part I. The Insurance Company

Chapter 1. Introduction

§1. Mutual and Premium Insurance

35. There is no formal distinction in UK law between mutual insurance and premium insurance. As seen below, with a limited number of exceptions, all insurers must be a company as defined in the Companies Acts,[82] an industrial and provident society or a body corporate established by charter or Act of Parliament; thus it is impossible for an individual or collection of individuals to act as an insurer, except in the case of Lloyd's underwriters considered below. However, beyond that the law neither imposes other formal requirements nor dictates how an insurer raises the necessary capital.[83] In practice, mutual insurance is well established in a number of fields. Many of the old-established life issurance companies are mutual organizations, reflecting their origins,[84] and this format is often adopted in the marine insurance market by the device of insurance clubs.[85] Virtually all large non-life insurers and composite insurers[86] have long adopted the ordinary registered company form.

There are no 'nationalized' insurers in the UK.[87] All insurers are privately owned. It is a matter for their choice as to whether, assuming they take the registered company form, they are public limited companies or private limited companies. In practice, many adopt a group structure, with a public limited company as the parent and a number of private companies as subsidiaries.

82. The Companies Act 2006 or one of its predecessors.
83. Except in respect of the solvency margin and minimum guarantee fund considered below. These do not impose any requirement as to, e.g., the amount of an insurance company's share capital, although it is a requirement that any share capital issued after 1 Jan. 1982 must be fully paid up.
84. Although a number of these have in recent years converted to the ordinary registered company form, with at least short-term financial benefits to their policyholders.
85. These are normally limited companies in form, owned by groups of shipowners.
86. That is, insurers offering both long-term and other insurance business.
87. There have been threats to nationalize insurance or some classes of it in the past. For example, motor insurance business was at risk immediately following the Second World War, but this was resisted. In the present political climate, it is most unlikely that there is any prospect of nationalization for whatever reason.

36. There are around 800 authorized insurers in the UK, although the number of active independent insurance companies or groups is probably nearer to 500, because many of the companies actually authorized either form part of larger groups or offer only very limited classes of insurance.[88]

37. An insurance company cannot carry on any commercial activities, whether in the UK or elsewhere, other than insurance business and activities directly arising from that business.[89]

§2. Lloyd's

38. As indicated earlier, Lloyd's is a unique organization and operates as such on a worldwide basis.[90] As far as organization is concerned, there is in fact no insurer called Lloyd's. The Corporation of Lloyd's, which is established under the Lloyd's Acts 1871–1982, neither does itself transact insurance business nor does it have any liability on policies issued by Lloyd's underwriters.[91] Its function is to control the membership of Lloyd's, to provide facilities for the conduct of members' business and, in part, to regulate the Lloyd's market under the Lloyd's Acts.[92]

Insurance at Lloyd's is effected with individual underwriters who for many years have been grouped into syndicates. Working members run the day-to-day business of the syndicates, the 'names' (who constitute the vast majority of the underwriters) being passive investors. Except for those who invest on a limited liability basis, each underwriter is potentially liable without limit on the contracts entered into on his/her behalf.

88. Detailed statistics are not produced by the current regulator, the Prudential Regulation Authority.
89. Rule 1.5.13 of the Prudential Sourcebook for Insurers. However, a breach is not an offence and does not make any transaction void or unenforceable: s. 138E of the Financial Services and Markets Act 2000.
90. It operates overseas of course through agency arrangements.
91. As to whether the Corporation of Lloyd's owes any duty of care to its 'names', *see Ashmore v. Corporation of Lloyd's* [1992] 2 Lloyd's Rep. 1; (*ibid., No. 2*) [1992] 2 Lloyd's Rep. 620.
92. Under Part XIX of the Financial Services and Markets Act 2000; *see* Ch. XII of the Financial Services and Markets Act 2000 (Regulated Activities) Order 2001. Following disastrous losses in the early 1990s, a complicated scheme was introduced in effect to save the whole institution. Legal challenges to the validity of the scheme were rejected in *Society of Lloyd's v. Leighs* [1997] C.L.C. 1398 and *Society of Lloyd's v. Fraser* [1999] 1 Lloyd's Rep. IR 156, and an action by dissentient names claiming that Lloyd's fraudulently induced them to become underwriters failed. Among the many other cases concerning the problems at Lloyd's and the attempts to resolve them, *see* especially the House of Lords' decision in *Society of Lloyd's v. Robinson* [1999] 1 W.L.R. 756, which, among other things, approved the judicial description of the Lloyd's market given in *Napier and Ettrick v. Kershaw* [1997] LRLR 1 at 7–8.

Chapter 2. Access to Business

§1. Authorization in the UK

39. Insurance business in the UK is regulated by the PRA under the Financial Services and Markets Act 2000, as amended by the Financial Services Act 2012, the regulations made under that Act and the rules of the PRA.[93] The 2000 Act brought the regulation of insurance business under the same umbrella as the regulation of other financial services,[94] although the system retained the features of the system that existed under the previous specific legislation, not least because most of the requirements stem from EU law.[95] An important feature of the 2000 legislation is that it brought Lloyd's of London fully within the regulatory umbrella. The 2000 Act itself provides only the broad structure under which the financial services industry is regulated. It has been augmented by a large volume of secondary legislation and by the regulators' Handbooks, made under Part X, Chapter 1 of the Act. The Handbooks are divided into a number of blocks. Those relevant to the regulation of insurance companies under the Act, and the individual components that are also relevant, are as follows:

- *High Level Standards*: This block includes the rules relating to Principles for Businesses; Senior Management Arrangements, Systems and Controls; Threshold Conditions; Statements of Principle and Code of Practice for Approved Persons; The Fit and Proper Test for Approved Persons; Financial Stability and Market Confidence Sourcebook; Training and General Provisions.
- *Prudential Standards*: This block includes the Prudential Sourcebook for Insurers.
- *Business Standards*: This block includes the Conduct of Business Sourcebook and the Insurance: Conduct of Business Sourcebook.
- *Regulatory Processes*: This block includes the rules relating to Supervision, Decision Procedure and Penalties.
- *Redress*: This block includes the rules relating to Dispute Resolution: Complaints and Compensation.

40. Insurers are authorized by reference to the classes of general insurance business and long-term insurance business defined in Schedule 1 of the Financial Services and Markets Act 2000 (Regulated Activities) Order 2001.[96] There is a general prohibition, in section 19, on carrying on a regulated activity in the UK unless the

93. The PRA, which is a division of the Bank of England, replaced the previous Financial Services Authority in this respect. The conduct of insurance business is regulated by the Financial Conduct Authority (FCA).
94. The regulation of the selling of most types of life insurance was already under the same umbrella.
95. As indicated above, it remains to be seen what in this respect is the result of the UK's departure from the EU.
96. SI 2001/544. There are eighteen classes of general business and nine classes of long-term business.

person in question is an authorized or exempt person.[97] By section 22, an activity is a regulated activity if it is an activity of a kind specified by the Treasury, which is carried on by way of business and relates to an investment of a specified kind. Schedule 2 of the Act includes 'rights under a contract of insurance' as an indicative regulated activity, and this is confirmed by Article 75 of the Regulated Activities Order. Article 10 of the Order amplifies this by separately specifying 'effecting a contract of insurance as principal' and 'carrying out a contract of insurance as principal' as regulated activities. The words 'carrying out' connote some element of continuity, as opposed to mere isolated transactions,[98] but it has been held on the construction of a similar statutory prohibition that a single transaction may afford sufficient evidence of 'carrying on business'.[99] Further, it was held that the equivalent prohibition in the former section 2 of the Insurance Companies Act 1982 was contravened by the negotiation of a prospective insurance contract without authorization.[100]

The separate specification, in Article 10 of the Regulated Activities Order, of 'effecting' and 'carrying out' contracts of insurance reflects the fact that insurance business contains two principal elements, first, the negotiation and conclusion of contracts and, second, the execution of those contracts by, in particular, paying claims. It also makes it clear that if either or both these activities take place in the UK, business is being carried on there. However, if neither activity takes place in the UK, business is not carried on there and the fact that insured property or insured persons may be located in the UK is irrelevant.[101] In this respect, UK law is sharply distinguished from that of most other countries, where its ambit is determined by the 'situs of the risk'. Activities in the UK that are customarily those undertaken by insurance brokers acting as such were held not to be evidence of the carrying on of insurance business in a decision under the former legislation.[102] The specific inclusion of the phrase 'as principal' in the current legislation reinforces this.[103]

A person is authorized under the 2000 Act if he has permission under Part IVA, is an EEA firm with passport rights or is otherwise authorized by or under the Act. There are two general exemptions. The first relates to trades unions and employers'

97. For the consequences of acting without permission, *see* ss 20 and 23; no transaction is void or unenforceable, but there is a limited right to compensation for anyone who suffers loss as a result of the contravention. Contravening the general prohibition is a criminal offence. For discussion, *see* *Re Whiteley Insurance Consultants* [2008] EWHC 1782 (Ch), [2009] Lloyd's Rep. IR 212.

98. Compare cf. *Smith v. Anderson* (1880) 15 Ch D 247, 277.

99. *Cornelius v. Phillips* [1918] A.C. 199.

100. *R v. Wilson* [1997] 1 All E.R. 119.

101. Compare *Re United General Commercial Ins Corp* [1927] 2 Ch 51.

102. *Re a company (No. 007816 of 1994)* [1995] 2 B.C.L.C. 539. It would clearly be otherwise if the brokers were authorized to take all effective decisions, including underwriting decisions: *see* *Re a company (No. 007923 of 1994) (No. 2)* [1995] 1 B.C.L.C. 594 and *Secretary of State for Trade and Industry v. Great Western Assurance Co SA* [1997] 2 B.C.L.C. 685, on appeal from the first-mentioned decision.

103. However, someone who ostensibly acts as agent for an insurer from which it had no authority or on behalf of unnamed and non-existent insurers is carrying on a regulated activity: *Re Whiteley Insurance Consultants* [2008] EWHC 1782 (Ch), [2009] Lloyd's Rep. IR 212.

organizations providing provident or strike benefits exclusively for their own members.[104] The second exempts a former Lloyd's underwriter who ceased to be an underwriting member of Lloyd's before 24 December 1996 from needing authorization to carry out contracts of insurance.[105] The Society of Lloyd's is an authorized person under the Act.[106] Insurers who were authorized under section 3 or 4 of the 1982 Act continue to be authorized under the 2000 Act.[107] Vehicle breakdown insurance does not require authorization.[108]

41. Application for permission to carry on insurance, under section 55A of the 2000 Act, must be made in accordance with the procedure laid down by the PRA. An application may not cover both long-term and general business unless the applicant's business will be restricted to reinsurance or the general business is restricted to accident and/or health insurance, and it must specify the classes of business to be carried on. Schedule 6 of the 2000 Act, as amended, specifies the threshold conditions that, under section 55B, the PRA must ensure that an applicant will satisfy. As they apply to insurance business, they are as follows:

(1) The applicant must be a body corporate (other than a limited liability partnership), a registered friendly society or a member of Lloyd's.
(2) The insurer's head office and registered office must be within the UK.
(3) The business of the applicant must be conducted in a prudent manner, which requires in particular that it has appropriate financial and non-financial resources as detailed in paragraph 4D of the Schedule.
(4) The applicant must be a fit and proper person, having regard to the PRA's objectives. This includes compliance with PRA requirements and requests and whether those managing its affairs have adequate skills and experience and may be expect to act with probity.
(5) The applicant must be capable of being effectively supervised by the PRA. The relevant matters in this respect include: (a) the nature and complexity of its regulated activities; (b) the complexity of its products; (c) the way its business is organized; (d) if it is a member of a group, whether that might prevent effective supervision; and (e) if it has close links with another person, being either a parent or subsidiary of another or where there is a 20% shareholding by one company in the other, whether that is likely to prevent effective supervision of the insurer.

§2. Freedom of Services Within the EU and the EEA

42. The rapid accomplishment within the European Community/Union of freedom of services, as well as freedom of establishment, in the areas of financial

104. The Financial Services and Markets Act 2000 (Exemption) Order 2001 SI 2001/1201, made under s. 38 of the 2000 Act, Sch., para. 43.
105. *Ibid.*, para. 46.
106. Section 315(1).
107. The Financial Services and Markets Act 2000 (Transitional Provisions) (Authorized Persons, etc.) Order 2001 SI/2636, Art. 14.
108. Regulated Activities Order, Art. 12.

services, including insurance, was reflected in substantial changes in British law.[109] The first directives were concerned to establish freedom of establishment within the Community, initially with regard to non-life insurance business and then with regard to life insurance. Later directives were concerned with freedom of services across Europe. The various directives are now implemented together by the 2000 Act[110] and the Financial Services and Markets Act 2000 (EEA Passport Rights) Regulations 2001.[111] Despite this, it seems that true freedom of services, in the sense that insurers from one state sell insurance to persons in another state, has not really happened, at least as far as consumers are concerned. This is probably at least partly attributable to the fact that the directives provide for the applicable law to be that of the consumer's habitual residence and it seems unlikely that insurers are willing to adjust their contracts to cover all the different laws applicable. This factor has led to the increased possibility of some degree of harmonization of insurance contract law or at least the possibility of an optional instrument establishing a regime of European insurance contract law.

The Non-life Insurance Services Directive[112] gave non-life insurers, licensed to write insurance business in any EC Member State, the right to offer 'large risks'[113] across national frontiers without the need for authorization. This was followed by the Second Life Directive.[114] These were quickly superseded, when in July 1992, the Council of Ministers adopted the Third Non-life Directive[115] and the Third Life Directive.[116] These took freedom of services to its logical conclusion by introducing the single European licence. An insurer authorized in any Member State is automatically allowed to sell most types of non-life insurance anywhere else in the Community, either through a branch or agency in the host State or via direct selling in the host State. The home State controls all its activities and its solvency.[117]

The UK implemented the Third Directives with effect from 1 July 1994. In consequence, as regards EC insurers, there is a distinction between the insurer who carries on business, which requires the company to have a UK branch, and the insurer who merely offers insurance in the UK, but who carries out the relevant paperwork

109. As far as UK law is concerned, this will probably be affected by the UK's departure from the EU.
110. Sections 31 and 37 and Schs 3 and 4.
111. SI 2001/2511.
112. 88/357.
113. There are three type of large risks, namely: (1) broadly, marine, aviation and transit business; (2) credit and suretyship insurance where the policy holder carries on business; and (3) property, pecuniary and liability insurances relating to a business carried on by the insured where the business meets two out of three criteria: (a) 250 employees; (b) an annual turnover of EUR 12 m ; (c) a balance sheet total of EUR 6.2 m .
114. 90/619.
115. 92/49.
116. 92/96. The three life insurance directives were consolidated by Directive 2002/83/EC.
117. Although there is provision for the host State to take action where the home State defaults in so doing. The Directive also requires that no new system of what is called 'material control', that is, any system for the prior approval of policy terms and premium rates, can be introduced. States that previously had such a system can retain it, but insurers authorized in a Member State that does not exercise such control will not be required to submit policy terms and premium rates to the authorities of any host State that does exercise such control.

elsewhere; the latter is merely a provider of insurance and not carrying on insurance business in the UK.

An EC insurance company wishing to carry on direct insurance business in the UK[118] must be authorized in its home State in accordance with the relevant provisions of the first Insurance Directives, and its supervisory authority must provide the PRA with a notice containing details of it and a certificate attesting to its margin of solvency and indicating the classes of business for which it is authorized. The details required are the name of the company and its authorized agent, the address of its UK branch, a scheme of operations prepared in accordance with any requirements of its supervisory authority and, in the case of a motor insurer, confirmation that it has become a member of the MIB.[119] In addition, either the PRA must have informed the supervisory authority of the conditions which, in the general good, must be complied with by the company in carrying on insurance business through the branch, or two months must have lapsed from the date of receipt of the notice and certificate.

EC insurers wishing to provide insurance in the UK must similarly be authorized to provide the relevant class or classes of business in their home State and are subject to generally similar conditions. So, their supervisory authority must provide a notice and a certificate, the only material difference being that in this case there will be no branch details or authorized agent.

In respect of any EC insurer operating in the UK market, the PRA has many of the general powers that it has in relation to UK companies. Specifically, it has the power to prevent the disposal of assets by the insurer, powers to obtain information, the general power to protect policyholders if requested to do so by the home State supervisor, a general power to intervene for the breach of any relevant legal provision and the power to withdraw recognition.

118. The requirements for insurers wishing to effect reinsurance business are similar.
119. As to the MIB, *see* para. 274.

Chapter 3. Supervision

43. British law contains a large number of provisions whereby the activities of insurers are closely supervised by the PRA.[120] Traditionally, supervision was limited to ensuring that insurers remain solvent and are properly run by competent persons. There is no state control of premium rates or policy conditions. The provisions do not apply to EC insurance companies carrying on business through a UK branch in respect of which the requirements described in paragraph 44 have been complied with, since they are subject to their home State supervisory regime.

Note, however, that there is control over the conduct of insurance business.[121]

§1. Solvency Control

44. The rules relating to solvency control are contained in the Prudential Sourcebook for Insurers issued by the PRA. Every insurer, whose head office is in the UK or whose business in the UK is restricted to reinsurance, must maintain a margin of solvency. If the insurer's head office is not within the EEA, it must maintain both a margin of solvency and a UK margin of solvency, although this does not apply where its UK business is restricted to reinsurance or it is a Swiss general insurer. If the insurer is authorized to carry on both general and long-term business, the required margins of solvency must be maintained independently. The formulae for calculating the margin of solvency are in the Prudential Sourcebook, as are the rules for valuing assets and liabilities. Separate rules relate to the calculation of the solvency margin of an insurer's parent company. A UK insurer must also secure that its liabilities under contracts of insurance are covered by assets of appropriate safety, yield and marketability, and that the assets are appropriately diversified. As regards long-term contracts that are linked to an index such as the retail price index, a UK insurer must also secure that its liabilities are covered by the assets on which the linking is based, and there must be reinsurance in place or other assets.

The margin of solvency must not fall below a minimum guarantee fund representing one-third of the solvency margin, and the minimum guarantee fund must itself not be less than the amount determined by calculations set out in the Sourcebook. For these purposes, special rules are laid down for valuation of the insurer's shares or, in the case of a mutual insurer, its rights to call on its members.

If an insurer fails to satisfy the necessary margin of insolvency, stops issuing new policies or is otherwise going through a period of uncertainty, the Supervision part of the Handbook requires the insurer to prepare and submit for the PRA's approval a scheme of operations. The scheme must describe the insurer's business strategy, and must include financial projections and a profit and loss account. If new policies are not issued, the insurer must submit a run-off plan, including a scheme of operations.

---

120. As far as UK law is concerned, aspects of this will probably be affected by the UK's departure from the EU.

121. *See* Introduction, s. 5.

Where an insurer has submitted a scheme of operations, it must notify PRA of its intention to enter into material transactions or to depart from the scheme.

Directive 2009/138/EC, which is generally known as 'Solvency II', as amended by Directive 2014/51/EU made substantial amendments to the previous Directives. They were implemented in the UK on 1 January 2016 under the Solvency 2 Regulations 2015.[122]

§2. Changes of Management and Control

45. Initial authorization will not be given by the PRA unless the insurer's controllers are fit and proper persons. If a person in the PRA's view ceases to be fit and proper, it may serve a warning notice on him, and this may be followed by a notice of objection, subject to the controller's right to appeal to the Financial Services and Markets Tribunal.[123]

Sections 178–192 of the Financial Services and Markets Act 2000, as amended, set out a procedure which enables the PRA to monitor changes in control.[124] The basic requirements are for a person who proposes steps to take or increase control of a regulated insurer to give notice of his intention to the PRA and then to notify the PRA when he has obtained or increased control, and for a person who has obtained control without taking such steps to notify the PRA within fourteen days. The notification obligation is imposed on both the controller and the insurer, although joint notification is possible, and the insurer itself is under a duty to keep itself informed as to identity of controllers, including monitoring its register of shareholders, public announcements and notifications to it under the Companies Act 2006. The insurer is also under a duty to notify the PRA of any changes in the circumstances of a controller such as legal action or investigation affecting him or his financial position.

On receipt, the PRA has three months to decide whether it wishes to approve the new controller conditionally or unconditionally: in the case of an unconditional approval, the controller must be notified, and in the case of a conditional approval he must be notified of the approval and given a warning notice of any conditions. There is an appeal to the Tribunal against the imposition of conditions. Alternatively, the PRA may oppose the change in control on the basis that the acquirer is not a fit and proper person or that the interests of consumers would be threatened. In the event of opposition, a decision notice must be issued, although the acquirer has the right to appeal to the Tribunal against an adverse decision imposing or refusing to vary a condition. A person whose control is reduced must also give notice to the PRA, although obviously in such a case the PRA has no available powers against the transferee: its powers are against the transferor.

---

122. SI 2015/575.

123. *See* Financial Services and Markets Act 2000, ss 187 and 188.

124. In essence, control is acquired where the acquirer (including his associates) holds 10% of the shares or voting rights in the insurer, can exercise significant influence over its management or has similar control over the insurer's parent undertaking. Control is increased where the controller acquires specified additional shareholding or voting rights in the insurer or its parent.

The PRA has a number of enforcement powers in the event of a breach of these provisions. If a person has acquired or continued to hold shares in breach of an order or conditions, the PRA may freeze voting rights and secure a court order requiring the shares to be sold. Further, breach of many provisions constitutes a criminal offence.

§3. General Powers of Intervention

46. The PRA has a general power to require an authorized person, including an insurer, to provide information or documents relevant to its regulatory functions, within a reasonable period.[125] In addition, the PRA may instigate investigations of the following types:

(1) It may commission an investigation and report from a person with the appropriate specialized skills into any matter falling within the regulatory functions of the PRA. Those under investigation must provide all necessary assistance.[126]
(2) It or the Secretary of State may appoint one or more inspectors to undertake an investigation into the affairs or business (whether or not regulated) of an authorized person, including a person in the same group.[127]
(3) The PRA or the Secretary of State may appoint one or more inspectors to undertake an investigation into one or more specified matters.[128] Those matters include, in relation to insurance: breach of the asset identification rules; failure to comply with an investigatory requirement; provision of false information to an auditor or actuary; misleading the PRA; failure to obtain authorization; false claims of authorization; false or misleading statements; the fit and proper status of any person; breach of a prohibition order; and misconduct by an approved person.

There are formal statutory requirements relating to the appointment of inspectors, relating to notice to be given to the firms under investigation,[129] and inspectors are given powers to obtain information from the person under investigation and any member of the same group.[130] Additional powers are conferred upon inspectors investigating specific matters under (3) above, as persons may be required to attend at specific times and places to answer questions and provide information.[131] Where there is a power vested in the PRA or an inspector to require the production of a document, it is also exercisable against a third person who is in possession of the relevant document.[132] Failure by a person to provide information or documents at the

125. Financial Services and Markets Act 2000, s. 165. The power may also be exercised at the request of an overseas regulator in relation to a firm operating within the UK: s. 169.
126. Financial Services and Markets Act 2000, s. 166.
127. Financial Services and Markets Act 2000, s. 167.
128. Financial Services and Markets Act 2000, s. 168. This power may also be exercised in support of an overseas regulator at the request of that regulator.
129. Financial Services and Markets Act 2000, s. 170.
130. Financial Services and Markets Act 2000, s. 171.
131. Financial Services and Markets Act 2000, ss 172 and 173.
132. Financial Services and Markets Act 2000, s. 175.

request of the PRA or an inspector can lead to the right of the PRA or the Secretary of State to secure a search warrant permitting entry and search.[133] There are criminal sanctions imposed upon any person who fails to comply with a requirement imposed by a person undertaking an investigation. Similarly, it is an offence for a person to falsify, conceal or destroy relevant documents or provide false information knowingly or recklessly, and to obstruct a person executing a search warrant.[134]

The PRA has a series of disciplinary powers which may be exercised against insurers who have contravened the requirements of the Act or the rules:

(1) It may withdraw or vary permission to carry on a regulated activity, in particular where the insurer is no longer meeting the threshold conditions for permission.[135] It may suspend permission or impose restrictions.[136]
(2) If the PRA considers that an authorized person has contravened a requirement imposed upon him by or under the Act, it may publish a public statement to that effect.[137] It must first publish a warning notice, to be followed by a decision notice, and there is an appeal to the Tribunal by a person adversely affected.[138]
(3) The PRA may impose a financial penalty upon an authorized person who has contravened a requirement imposed upon him by or under the Act, although it may not impose such a penalty if it has decided to withdraw the firm's authorization.[139] The PRA must first publish a warning notice, to be followed by a decision notice, and there is an appeal to the Tribunal by a person adversely affected.[140]
(4) The PRA or the Secretary of State may apply to the court for an injunction in a case where there is a reasonable likelihood that a person will contravene a requirement of the Act or has done so and the infringement is likely to continue.[141]
(5) A restitution order may be made by the court on the application of the PRA or the Secretary of State, if:[142] (1) the defendant has contravened a requirement of the Act (in the case of an application by the PRA) or has committed an offence which can be prosecuted by the Secretary of State (in the case of an application by the Secretary of State);[143] (2) profits have accrued to the defendant as a result of the contravention; and (3) one or more persons have suffered loss or have been otherwise adversely affected by reason of the contravention.
(6) The PRA may issue a prohibition order where it appears that an individual is not a fit and proper person to perform functions in relation to a regulated activity carried on by an authorized person.[144] The order may prohibit the individual from performing a specific function within the firm. The individual may apply to the

---

133. Financial Services and Markets Act 2000, s. 176.
134. Financial Services and Markets Act 2000, s. 177.
135. Financial Services and Markets Act 2000, ss 45–47.
136. Financial Services and Markets Act 2000, s. 206A.
137. Financial Services and Markets Act 2000, s. 205.
138. Financial Services and Markets Act 2000, ss 207–208.
139. Financial Services and Markets Act 2000, s. 206.
140. Financial Services and Markets Act 2000, ss 207–208.
141. Financial Services and Markets Act 2000, s. 380(1).
142. Financial Services and Markets Act 2000, s. 382(1).
143. Financial Services and Markets Act 2000, s. 382(9).
144. Financial Services and Markets Act 2000, s. 56(1)–(2).

PRA for variation or revocation of the order.[145] Breach of the order by the prohibited individual is a criminal offence subject to a reasonable care and due diligence defence,[146] and the firm itself must take reasonable care to ensure that a person does not carry out a prohibited function:[147] the firm is not guilty of any offence in this regard, but may face an action in damages by a private person who has suffered loss by reason of its breach.[148] A prohibited person has the right to appeal to the Tribunal against the making of an order or against the refusal of the PRA to vary or revoke the order.[149]

145. Financial Services and Markets Act 2000, s. 58.
146. Financial Services and Markets Act 2000, s. 56(4)–(5).
147. Financial Services and Markets Act 2000, s. 56(6).
148. Financial Services and Markets Act 2000, s. 71.
149. Financial Services and Markets Act 2000, ss 57(5) and 58(5).

Chapter 4. Technical Reserves and Investments

47. In addition to the general controls on an insurance company's solvency, as described in the previous chapter, there are special controls of relevance to companies carrying on long-term business.[150] These are briefly described in the following paragraphs.

48. An insurer carrying on long-term business must also appoint an actuary.[151] The firm must appoint an actuary, notify PRA without delay in case of a vacancy and fill a vacancy as soon as reasonably practicable. If it fails to do so within twenty-eight days, the PRA may do so. The actuary must inform the PRA if he is removed, resigns or is not reappointed, and must report any matter of concern relating to loss of office. The insurer must apply to the PRA for its approval of the actuary, and must first take reasonable steps to ensure that he has the required skill and experience and is a Fellow of the Institute of Actuaries or of the Faculty of Actuaries.

The basic duties of the actuary are: to identify and monitor risks run by the insurer so far as they have a material impact on the insurer's ability to meet liabilities to policyholders in respect of long-term contracts; and inform the insurer if he has doubts as to whether it is meeting liabilities or is effecting long-term contracts on inadequate terms or does not have assets to meet liabilities as they fall due. He must request information and explanations from the insurer. He must pay due regard to generally accepted actuarial best practice. The insurer must allow the actuary to perform his duties and must keep him informed of business and other plans and give him sufficient resources to do his job. He is also to be given access to books.[152] The provision of false information to an actuary is a criminal offence.[153] The firm is obliged to pay due regard to his advice. The actuary must be objective and must take reasonable steps to ensure that no conflict of interest.

In accordance with the demands of the EC's Insurance Directives, the Prudential Sourcebook requires a strict separation of long-term and general insurance business. The assets and liabilities attributable to long-term or industrial insurance business must be kept separate from general business assets. Long-term business assets are to be used only for long-term business, subject to a number of exceptions: excess assets may be used if determined by actuarial valuation; and the insurer may exchange assets for other assets, at fair market value. Dividends may not be paid out of the long-term fund if the assets are less than liabilities. It is permissible to allocate some of an established surplus to policyholders entitled to participate by way of bonus. There is a restriction on a company carrying on long-term business using more than a specified proportion of its long-term assets to enter into a contract which is for the benefit of a person connected with the company, for example, investment in the shares of, or loans to, subordinate companies. An insurer carrying on long-term business must secure that adequate arrangements are in force to secure that transactions affecting assets of the company do not operate unfairly as between long-term assets and other assets. A long-

150. As far as UK law is concerned, aspects of this will probably be affected by the UK's departure from the EU.
151. Financial Services and Markets Act 2000, s. 340.
152. Financial Services and Markets Act 2000, s. 341.
153. Financial Services and Markets Act 2000, s. 346.

term insurer must satisfy himself before entering into a long-term contract that the premiums plus income derived from them and other available resources will be sufficient to meet all commitments under the policy, although other resources may not be used to prejudice long-term solvency. As regards index-linked long-term contracts, benefits must not be provided only from specified property.

Chapter 5. Accountancy

49. Every insurer must appoint an auditor, fill any vacancy without delay and keep the PRA informed in the case of a vacancy: if no appointment is made within twenty-eight days, the PRA itself may make appointment. If the auditor is removed, resigns or is not reappointed, he must inform the PRA of any matter which may relate to his loss of office. An auditor, to qualify for appointment, must meet the eligibility requirements imposed by the Companies Act 2006 and must not have been disqualified to act by the PRA. The auditor must be independent of the firm, and must remain so, and it his duty to check for any conflicts of interest. It is the duty of a regulated firm to co-operate with the auditor in discharge of his functions, for example, by allowing access to books,[154] and it is a criminal offence to provide false information to the auditor.[155] If the auditor raises a matter with the firm, the firm must consider whether it should be referred to the PRA. The auditor is under a general duty to co-operate with the PRA, and under a specific duty to submit an annual report to the firm and then to the PRA on the firm's financial controls.

The rules regarding accounts are contained in the Prudential Sourcebook issued by the PRA. Every insurance company must prepare annual accounts and a balance sheet, the accounts and balance sheet are to be audited in the prescribed manner,[156] are to be deposited with the PRA and shareholders and policyholders are entitled to receive copies of the deposited documents. The auditor must prepare his own report: if the requirements of the audit have not been met, the report must say so, and the report must also state that accounts have been audited, that annual statements give a true and fair view of profit and loss account and, in the case of annual balance sheet, that it gives a true and fair view of the insurer's state of affairs.

154. Financial Services and Markets Act 2000, s. 341.
155. Financial Services and Markets Act 2000, s. 346.
156. IPRU (INS) para. 9.5.

Chapter 6. Transfers of Business

50. There are special provisions governing the situation where it is sought to transfer insurance business from one insurance company to another.[157,158]

51. Section 104 of the Financial Services and Markets Act 2000 prohibits the transfer of an insurance business unless a court order has been made sanctioning the transfer. A scheme is within the Act if the business transferred will be carried on from an establishment of the transferee in an EEA state, provided that any one of three conditions is met:[159] (a) the whole or part of the business to be transferred is carried on in one or more EC state by a UK-authorized person; (b) the whole or part of a reinsurance business to be transferred is carried on in the UK through a UK establishment by an EEA firm which has passport rights; or (c) the whole or part of the business to be transferred is carried on in the UK by a person with permission to carry out that business. The statutory controls do not apply: (1) to a friendly society; (2) where the business is reinsurance business carried on in the EEA but outside the UK by a UK-authorized insurer and the scheme has been approved other than by the UK or the host state regulator; (3) to a scheme where the business to be transferred is that of a UK-authorized insurer carried on outside the EEA, does not (other than in the case of reinsurance) include risks arising in an EEA state and has been approved outside the EEA; (4) the transfer of reinsurance business where all the policyholders have consented, or the transfer of a business where all policyholders are controllers of the transferor or within the same group as the transferor.

An application for court sanction has to be made by the transferor or the transferee, or both. The scheme must be advertised in all EEA Member States, but it has been held[160] that a failure to alert all policyholders to the scheme did not deprive the court of jurisdiction to approve the scheme. The application has to be accompanied by a scheme report prepared by a person approved by the PRA and in a form required by the PRA.[161] In the case of the transfer of life business, any scheme must be approved by an independent actuary. At the hearing itself, the PRA has a right to be represented, as does any person (including an employee) who alleges that he would be adversely affected by the carrying out of the scheme.[162]

Before a scheme can be sanctioned by the court, two important jurisdictional conditions have to be met: the transferee must have the necessary authorization to carry on the transferred business; and certificates conforming with the requirements

157. As far as UK law is concerned, aspects of this will probably be affected by the UK's departure from the EU.
158. These procedures do not apply where an insurance company is taken over by another, e.g., by reason of the purchase of a majority of the former's share capital, although the PRA would, if necessary, be able to intervene under the powers described earlier. In addition, in this and the situations described in the text, there might be control exercised by virtue of monopolies and competition legislation, whether UK or EC based.
159. Financial Services and Markets Act 2000, s. 105.
160. *Re Refuge Assurance,* 2001, unreported.
161. Financial Services and Markets Act 2000, s. 109.
162. Financial Services and Markets Act 2000, s. 110.

in Schedule 12 of the Financial Services and Markets Act 2000 must be obtained.[163] If the transfer is from a UK-authorized composite life and non-life insurer to an insurer authorized elsewhere in the EEA, there must be certificates by the host authority to the effect that the transferee possesses the necessary solvency margin before the transfer, and that the host authority has consented to the scheme or has not responded within three months. If the transfer is from a UK-authorized life insurer to an insurer authorized elsewhere in the EEA, there must be certificates by the host authority to the effect that the transferee possesses the necessary solvency margin before the transfer and that the host authority has consented to the scheme or has not responded within three months. If the transfer is from a UK-authorized general insurer to an insurer authorized elsewhere in the EEA, there must be certificates by the host authority to the effect that the transferee possesses the necessary solvency margin before the transfer and that the host authority has consented to the scheme or has failed to respond within three months.

If these conditions are met, the court must consider whether in all the circumstances the transfer should be approved,[164] and will do so only if it is shown that the interests of policyholders will not be prejudiced. An order sanctioning the transfer may deal with the following matters in such manner as the court thinks fit:[165] the transfer of the undertaking, property or liabilities; the allotment or appropriation of shares, debentures or policies; the continuation by or against the transferee of legal proceedings involving the transferor; and such incidental matters as are necessary to secure that the scheme is fully and effectively carried out. The court may subsequently make an order dissolving the transferor, dealing with the interests of any person objecting to the transfer, and, perhaps most significantly, reducing the benefits payable under the transferred policies. The last-mentioned order is designed to ensure that the policyholders of an insurer in financial difficulties all obtain some benefit from any transfer, even though this may mean reducing the benefits of one or more particular classes of policyholder entitled to disproportionate benefits, although such an order will not be made before the court has received an independent actuary's report on the request of the PRA.[166]

163. Financial Services and Markets Act 2000, s. 111.
164. Financial Services and Markets Act 2000, s. 111(3).
165. Financial Services and Markets Act 2000, s. 112.
166. Financial Services and Markets Act 2000, s. 113.

Chapter 7. Policyholder Protection

52. In the event that the regulatory structure established to ensure the solvency of insurance companies fails, there has for some years been a mechanism to ensure that policyholders are largely protected financially. Originally this was by virtue of the provisions of the Policyholders Protection Acts 1975 and 1997. This particular legislation, though, was replaced by the general scheme for compensating consumers of failed financial services providers under Part XV of the Financial Services and Markets Act 2000. Like the scheme under the 1975 and 1997 Acts, it does not apply to protect the policyholders of insurance companies that acted without authorization, nor does it apply to Lloyd's policyholders.

53. Section 212 of the 2000 Act requires the establishment of the scheme manager to exercise the functions under Part XV; this body is Financial Services Compensation Scheme Ltd (FSCS). Section 213 requires this where 'relevant persons', including authorized insurers, are unable, or are likely to be unable, to satisfy claims against them. Sections 214–217 indicate the rules that may be made to give effect to the scheme, and these are contained in the Compensation part of the Handbook. The scheme is funded by levies on authorized firms in accordance with the detailed rules in Chapter 13 of the Compensation Rules.

A person is entitled to compensation where an insurer has failed only where continuation of cover cannot be secured. With respect to long-term insurance, FSCS must make arrangements to secure continuity of such insurance where it is reasonably practicable to do so and one of the following has occurred:

(a) the insurer has passed a resolution for a creditors' voluntary winding up;
(b) the insurer's Home State regulator has determined that it appears unable to meet claims and has no early prospect of being able to do so;
(c) a liquidator or administrator, or provisional liquidator or interim manager has been appointed;
(d) the court has made an order for winding up or administration;
(e) a voluntary arrangement has been approved.

The arrangements contemplated may be securing or facilitating the transfer of the long-term business to another insurer or securing the issue of substitute policies by another insurer.

Different rules apply as regards any type of insurance issued by an insurer in financial difficulties. This is defined as where an insurer is in provisional liquidation, has been proved in winding up proceedings to be unable to pay its debts or is the subject of an application under Part 26 of the Companies Act 2006 for a compromise or arrangement to reduce or defer payment of the liabilities or benefits under its policies, or where the regulator determines that it is unlikely to be able to satisfy claims protected under the scheme. Here, FSCS must take such measures to safeguard policyholders on such terms (including terms reducing or deferring payment of any liabilities or benefits) as it considers appropriate if, in its opinion, the cost is likely to be less than the cost of paying compensation. These measures may amount to transferring the insurance business to another insurer or assisting the insurer in difficulties to enable it to continue to effect or carry out contracts of insurance. However, before taking these measures in respect of a long-term insurance contract, FSCS must reduce the insured's interest in the contract to 90% of what would otherwise have been payable and similarly reduce the amount of future premiums.

The persons who may benefit from compensation or continuity of cover under the scheme are called 'eligible claimants'. As far as long-term insurance is concerned, this category comprises any person other than directors or managers (and their close relatives) of the insurer in default, bodies corporate in the same group, 5% shareholders of the insurer or of any body corporate in the same group, the auditors of the insurer in default or of any body corporate in the same group or the appointed actuary of the insurer in default, persons who in the opinion of the FSCS are responsible or have contributed to the insurer's default, and persons whose claim arises from transactions in connection with which they have been convicted of an offence of money laundering.

As far as general insurance is concerned, claims under a reinsurance contract, a Lloyd's policy and an insurance contract relating to aircraft, ships, goods in transit, aircraft liability and liability of ships or credit are totally excluded. Subject to this, eligible claimants are essentially: (1) private persons; (2) any business qualifying as small at the date of commencement of the contract;[167] (3) a large partnership in respect of a relevant general insurance contract entered into before 1 December 2001; (4) a third party whose claim arises under the Third Parties (Rights Against Insurers) Act 1930;[168] and (5) any person in respect of a liability subject to compulsory insurance, that is under the Riding Establishments Act 1964, the Employers' Liability (Compulsory Insurance) Act 1969[169] and the Road Traffic Act 1988.[170]

A person is eligible for compensation or continuity of cover in respect of a protected claim, which is a claim under a protected contract of insurance. It is irrelevant that a policy evidencing the contract has not been issued, if the FSCS is satisfied that a person is insured under a contract with an insurance undertaking. The Compensation Rules distinguish between contracts issued after and before 1 December 2001.[171]

54. Contracts issued after this date must relate to a protected risk or commitment under one of the following three types of contract. The first is a contract issued by an insurer in default through an establishment in the UK where the risk or commitment is situated in an EEA State, the Channel Islands or the Isle of Man. The second is a contract issued by an authorized insurance company through an establishment in another EEA State where the risk or commitment is situated in the UK. The third is a contract issued through an establishment in the Channel Islands or the Isle of Man where the risk or commitment is situated in the UK, the Channel Islands or the Isle of Man.[172]

---

167. Basically any business with an annual turnover of less than GBP 1 million.
168. *See* para. 237.
169. *See* Part V, Ch. 1.
170. *See* Part IV.
171. The date when the 2000 Act was brought into force. This account does not deal with contracts issued before that date.
172. There are detailed rules determining where a risk or commitment is situated.

The FSCS is obliged to treat the following liabilities of an insurance undertaking as giving rise to claims under a protected contract of insurance:

(a) if the contract has not commenced, premiums paid to the insurance undertaking;
(b) proceeds of a long-term insurance contract that has matured or been surrendered but which have not yet been passed to the claimant;
(c) the unexpired portion of any premium in relation to relevant general insurance contracts;
(d) claims by persons entitled to the benefit of a judgment under section 151 of the Road Traffic Act 1988.[173]

As far as the amount of compensation is concerned, 100% of the whole claim must be paid in respect of a liability subject to compulsory insurance. As regards claims under the Third Parties (Rights Against Insurers) Act in respect of employer's liability insurance before it was compulsory, 90% of the claim must be paid. In all other cases of general insurance, 100% of the first GBP 2,000 and 90% of the remainder of the claim must be paid. In respect of long-term insurance, 100% of the first GBP 2,000 must be paid together with at least 90% of the remaining value of the policy, including future benefits declared before the date of the insurer's default. The same principle applies to cases where continuity of insurance cover is secured.

173. *See* para. 268.

Part II. The Insurance Contract: General

§1. Introduction

55. In this part of this work, the general principles of law applicable to contracts of insurance are examined. As already explained, the general law relating to non-marine insurance contracts was almost wholly based on case law; in respect of marine insurance contracts, the law as developed by the judges was codified in the Marine Insurance Act 1906. Apart from the peculiar principles applicable to marine insurance contracts, which are considered in detail in Part III, Chapter 3, the general principles are broadly the same for both types of contracts, and sections of the 1906 Act are often used as illustrative of the non-marine position. Where appropriate, therefore, reference is made in this Part to those sections. However, it should be noted that some of the case law and some provisions of the 1906 Act have been altered and amended by, respectively, the Consumer Insurance (Disclosure and Representations) Act 2012 and the Insurance Act 2015.

Chapter 1. Generalities

§1. Definition of Insurance

56. There is no statutory definition of what is a contract of insurance, except in respect of marine insurance,[174] but it is essential to attempt such a definition in order that the proper scope of the regulatory statutes can be ascertained[175] and so that we can be certain exactly which contracts are subject to the special attributes of insurance law. This matter has been explored in a number of cases,[176] and from these a standard definition is that the contract of insurance is a contract under which the insurer is legally bound to pay money or provide its equivalent on the occurrence of a future uncertain event[177] or a certain event, the date of which is uncertain,[178] provided that the insured has an interest in that event[179] and the event is outside the control of the insurer. The requirement of a lack of control has never been clearly identified in English cases, but it seems essential in order to distinguish a contract of insurance from such transactions as an ordinary manufacturer's guarantee.[180]

174. Marine Insurance Act 1906, s. 1; *see* para. 190.
175. As to these, *see* Part I. A further reason arising from statute is that the Unfair Contract Terms Act 1977 exempts 'contracts of insurance' from its scope (*see* para. 26), without defining these. In similar manner, neither the 2012 nor the 2015 Act contains a definition of 'contract of insurance'.
176. The leading modern cases, which adapted the definition given in *Prudential Insurance Co. v. Inland Revenue Commissioners* [1904] 2 KB 658, are *Department of Trade & Industry v. St Christopher's Association* [1974] 1 All ER 395(organization providing its members, in return for a subscription, with chauffeur services should they be disqualified for drink driving was carrying on insurance), *Medical Defence Union v. Department of Trade* [1979] 2 All ER 421, (body not legally obliged to indemnify members against their legal liability was not carrying on insurance) and *Re Digital Satellite Warranty Cover Ltd* [2011] EWHC 122 (Ch) (approved by the Supreme Court sub nom *Digital Satellite Warranty Cover Ltd v. Financial Services Authority* [2013] UKSC 7). *See also Re Sentinel Securities plc* [1996] 1 W.L.R. 316.
177. As in the case of non-life contracts, as described *infra* .
178. As in the case of life contracts, as described *infra* .
179. *See* Part II, Ch. 2.
180. *See Birds' Modern Insurance Law*, para. 1.6.4. Early cases (especially *Hampton v. Toxteth Co-operative Society* [1915] 1 Ch. 721 and *Hall D'Ath v. British Provident Association* (1932) 48 TLR 240) in which the courts took the view that, in addition to the contract having the features mentioned above, there must also be present what could be considered to be the standard indicia of insurance, viz., a policy and a premium, are too restrictive in the light of more recent cases and are distinguishable in any event on the basis of the then current statutory wording (*see* Birds, *supra*).

§2. Categories of Insurance

57. Subject to statutory modifications applying to various types of insurance, the general principles of insurance law apply basically to all kinds of insurance. One important distinction in insurance business, which is reflected in insurance law, is that between property and liability insurances on the one hand and life and related insurances on the other. In respect of the first type it is quite uncertain whether or not the risk covered by the contract will ever happen; in life insurance on the other hand, the event insured against will happen, what is uncertain is the date of its happening.[181] This distinction mentioned does have several important consequences in law. These follow from the fact that generally speaking, property and allied insurances are contracts of indemnity, in other words contracts to compensate only for a loss actually suffered and only in respect of the amount of that loss. Life insurance[182] and related insurances like personal accident insurance, however, are not contracts of indemnity, but simply contracts to pay an agreed sum on the happening of the event insured against, regardless of the amount of loss incurred by the insured. As a result, life contracts are often referred to as contingency insurances.

§3. Risk

58. As the definition given above indicates, the concept of risk is fundamental to insurance. Insurance is concerned with uncertainties and so, as a general rule, does neither cover losses deliberately caused[183] nor events that are not fortuitous, for example, losses that occur as a result of natural wear and tear or because of some inherent vice in the subject matter of the insurance. Life insurance constitutes a major qualification to this principle, both because it covers a natural event, i.e., death, and because it is possible for a life policy to cover suicide, i.e., the deliberate taking of a life.[184] It seems that the above points are inherent in the nature of a contract of insurance as a matter of its true construction.[185] However, they may well overlap with principles of 'public policy' as applied to contracts of insurance.[186]

In respect of non-life insurance, it does not matter prima facie that a loss results from the negligence of the insured or anyone else as opposed to being a pure accident. As was said in one case, 'an essential feature of insurance by fire is that it covers fire

---

181. Because of this it is said that the correct terminology for life business is assurance, and this description is still frequently used. Its usage is, however, by no means necessarily confined to the business of insuring lives – for example, Lloyd's underwriters, who never insure lives, use it generally. As there can therefore hardly be said to be a correct usage, in this book we shall use 'insurance', 'insurer' and 'insured' in all cases.

182. References to life insurance will generally include all kinds of life insurance, e.g., whole life, term and endowment.

183. *See* , e.g., *Britton v. Royal Insurance Company* (1866) 4 F & F 905 (arson not covered by a fire policy).

184. *Beresford v. Royal Insurance Company* [1938] AC 586.

185. *See ibid.*

186. *See infra* para. 68.

caused by accident as well as by negligence'.[187] However, insurers do sometimes seek to restrict cover by providing a term precluding recovery in the event of a failure by the insured to take reasonable care. It is well established that such a provision in a policy of liability insurance operates only if the insured is reckless, since otherwise the principal purpose of the insurance, that is indemnity against the insured against his liability in negligence to a third party, would be frustrated.[188] More recently, a similar interpretation has been given to such a provision in a policy of first party insurance on property. In *Sofi v. Prudential Assurance Company Ltd*,[189] conditions requiring the insured to take 'reasonable care to avoid loss' in a domestic all risks policy and a travel policy were interpreted in this way. Here, the plaintiff, who was travelling to France, arrived at the Dover ferry with time to spare. He left his car for fifteen minutes in the unattended car park at Dover Castle with GBP 50,000 worth of valuables locked in the glove compartment. During that time, the car was broken into and the valuables stolen. The Court of Appeal held that the plaintiff was entitled to recover, because, on the facts of the case, he had not acted recklessly. In the light of this decision, insurers who wish to limit their liability without having to prove recklessness have to insert more specific terms in their policies, for example, by excluding liability when goods are left unattended.

§4. Characteristics of Insurance Contract Law

59. Insurance contract law is in many ways merely a part of the general law of contract, but it is clear that it has its own peculiar attributes. The principal ones for present purposes are two, namely, the special position of the insurance contract as a contract *uberrimae fidei* and the special nature of the warranty in insurance law.

The principle of *uberrima fides* requires that both parties display the utmost good faith towards each other in their dealings. It is of long-standing[190] but has chiefly been developed in terms of imposing a duty of disclosure on the proposer for insurance and the actual insured. This issue is developed in detail later, but it should be noted at this stage that to some extent the duty of disclosure has been modified by statute.[191] The principle has been confirmed as being equally applicable to the insurer and to impose a duty of disclosure on him.[192] However, the remedy available to the injured

187. Kerr LJ in *Mark Rowlands Ltd. v. Berni Inns Ltd.* [1986] QB 211 at 232.
188. *See* especially, *Fraser v. Furman* [1967] 1 WLR 898.
189. [1993] 2 Lloyd's Rep. 559; *see* Birds (1991) 1 *Ins. L. & P.*18. *See also* the New Zealand case of *Roberts v. State General Insurance Manager* [1974] 2 NZLR 312 and *Port-Rose v. Phoenix Assurance Co. Ltd.* (1986) 136 NLJ 333. The latter case concerned a situation where the insured under an all risks policy took her eyes off her handbag containing her jewellery at an airport for a brief moment, while she helped a fellow elderly passenger, during which time it was stolen. Hodgson J. disallowed the insurer's reliance on a reasonable care provision, although it is arguable that on the facts there was no negligence involved. *See also Paine v. Catlins* [2004] EWHC 3043 (TCC), [2005] Lloyd's Rep. IR 665.
190. And is codified in s. 17 of the Marine Insurance Act 1906; *see* para. 176.
191. *See* Ch. 4, below.
192. *Banque Financière de la Cité v. Westgate Insurance Co. Ltd.* [1991] 2 AC 249. This confirmed dicta in earlier cases, especially in the founding case of *Carter v. Boehm* (1766) 3 Burr 1905.

party has been limited to avoidance or rescission of the contract and a return of the premium, and in particular damages are not available. As a result, practical application of the principle to impose any meaningful sort of duty on an insurer, at least in terms of a duty of disclosure, is most unlikely.[193]

The general principle of utmost good faith, as found in section 17 of the Marine Insurance Act 1906, was retained under the reforms introduced by the Insurance Act 2015, but the remedy for breach is no longer avoidance of the contract.[194] What is somewhat unclear at present is the extent to which a principle of good faith not confined to imposing duties of disclosure applies to the parties to an insurance contract. This is briefly discussed later.[195] The intention behind the retention of the principle is to allow the courts to develop it as and when they see fit.

In insurance law, the warranty is a fundamental term of the contract imposing duties on the insured in order to control the risk to which the insurer is subject. Traditionally a breach of warranty automatically discharged the insurer from liability, but this result no longer applies under the Insurance Act 2015. In contrast, in contract law generally,[196] a warranty is a minor term, breach of which can only ever give the injured party the right to claim damages. The detail on insurance warranties is given later.[197]

§5. Interpretation

60. The question of what risks are covered by an insurance contract is primarily a matter of construing the contract, although in a particular situation questions of causation and even of public policy may arise. These are considered below. As the insurance policy is a contract, the general principles of construction applicable to all commercial contracts apply. As indicated earlier, there has been no general legislative interference in the field of insurance, and in particular in the UK there is no control of contract terms and contracts of insurance are specifically exempted from the Unfair Contract Terms Act 1977. Therefore, there is neither rule that a policy be read as an ordinary insured would read it nor any requirement that the policy be intelligible to the average insured, nor that the size or colour of print be such that it is easily legible.[198] However, Part 2 of the Consumer Rights Act 2015 does impose a basic intelligibility requirement in respect of consumer insurance contracts, as explained in paragraph 32.

193. For discussion of the *Banque Financière* litigation and its consequences, *see* Birds, *Modern Insurance Law*, Ch. 8, and the sources cited therein.
194. *See* s. 14 of the 2015 Act.
195. *See* para. 105.
196. As codified in certain respects by the Sale of Goods Act 1979.
197. *See* Ch. 4, *infra* .
198. *See* *Koskas v. Standard Marine Insurance Co. Ltd.* (1927) 27 Ll LR 61. Note, though, that as a response to consumer pressure and the requirements of the Unfair Terms Regulations, insurance policies and proposal forms are increasingly drafted in 'plain English', with much less reliance on technical language. This does not always remove problems of interpretation.

This account will briefly review the rules of construction that have been shown to be of particular importance in the insurance field.[199]

61. The basic principle used to be that the intention of the parties, as discovered objectively from the whole of the contract, prevailed, but, as explained below, the modern approach is different in theory even if it will perhaps rarely produce a different result. The contract in general bore its literal meaning, and extraneous matters were irrelevant except where necessary to clarify the meaning.[200] The words used were to be read in their ordinary and popular sense. In *Thompson v. Equity Fire Insurance Company*,[201] a fire policy excepted the insurers from liability while gasoline was 'stored or kept' on the premises. The insured kept a small quantity of gasoline for cooking purposes. It was held that the insurers were liable when fire destroyed the premises, the exception being inapplicable. The words 'stored or kept' in their ordinary sense meant keeping a considerable quantity, for example, in a warehouse or shop. In *Young v. Sun Alliance & London Insurance Ltd*,[202] the plaintiff's household policy included cover for destruction or damage to his house from 'storm, tempest, or flood'. Water seeped into the downstairs toilet of the plaintiff's house and rose to a level of three inches above the floor, causing considerable damage. The plaintiff claimed that this was a 'flood', and therefore the insurers were liable to indemnify him for the cost of repairing the damage. It was held that they were not liable, 'flood' in its ordinary sense referring only to cases where the flow of water was violent and large.[203]

62. There are situations where the words used in a policy will not be read in their ordinary meaning. First is where words have a special business or commercial meaning, and particularly where they have a technical legal meaning. In this case the technical meaning prevails. A leading illustration is *London and Lancashire Fire Insurance Company v. Bolands Ltd.* [204] Bolands Ltd. held a policy of burglary insurance for their bakery in Dublin, which excepted any loss arising out of *inter alia*, 'riot'. The bakery was robbed in daylight by four armed men, there being no other disturbances within or outside the shop. It was held that the insurers were not liable. Although there might not have been a riot in the ordinary sense, the armed robbery did constitute a 'riot' in the criminal law sense, and riot being a technical legal term was to be read in that sense. A second situation is where the context in which a word appears dictates a departure from its ordinary meaning. This was an alternative reason for the decision

199. Further examples are given in Part III dealing with particular risks.

200. So in general oral evidence cannot vary what is written (a cardinal rule of English contract law). Further, the fact that a policy has a title such as 'comprehensive' or something else, possibly used for marketing purposes by the insurer, cannot affect its construction. The one qualification to this is the description 'all risks' which does have some legal significance as described in para. 157, *infra* .

201. [1910] AC 592.

202. [1977] 1 WLR 104. *See also* on flood, *Computer & Systems Engineering plc v. John Lelliot (Ilford) Ltd* [1990] 54 B.L.R. 1 and *The Board of Trustees of the Tate Gallery v. Duffy Construction Ltd* [2007] EWHC 361 (TCC), [2007] Lloyd's Rep. IR 758, but compare *Rohan Investments Ltd v. Cunningham* [1999] Lloyd's Rep. IR 190.

203. Cases construing when goods are left unattended are also examples of reading words in their ordinary sense: these are discussed in Birds, *supra* , para. 13.3.1.

204. [1924] AC 836. Compare *Canelhas Comercio Inportacao E Exportacao Ltd v. Wooldridge* [2004] EWCA Civ 984, [2004] Lloyd's Rep. IR 915.

in *Young v. Sun Alliance & London Insurance Ltd.*, described above, where some of the judges, recognizing that what happened might on one view ordinarily have been described as a flood, decided that anyway the word had to be read in the context as meaning some violent event, as it appeared in the same phrase as storm and tempest, which were both clearly abnormal events.

63. Where different provisions in a policy conflict, or words can be read in quite different ways, the courts will, unless they can reconcile the inconsistencies, construe the policy against the party who prepared it, normally the insurer. This is the application of the maxim of construction *contra proferentem*, which applies generally to contracts drafted by one party.[205] There must be a genuine ambiguity; it is not enough to apply the maxim simply that the insured may have read words more widely or more narrowly than the insurer, if on their true construction there is no doubt that they bear the meaning understood by the insurer. So in *Young v. Sun Alliance & London Insurance Ltd*, above, there was no ambiguity even though there was a difference of opinion as to the meaning to be ascribed to 'flood', once it was decided that its ordinary and/or contextual meanings were clear. The most often cited example of construction *contra proferentem* in the insurance context is *English v. Western*,[206] where a motor insurance policy taken out by a 17-year old agreed to indemnify the insured against liability to pay damages for injury caused to all persons except 'to any member of the insured's household who is being carried in the car'. The insured caused an accident and injured, among others, his sister who was a passenger and to whom he was liable to pay damages. The insurer claimed that the exception was applicable. It was held that 'any member of the insured's household' could mean either 'any member of the household of which the insured was the head', which was not the case, or 'any member of the same household of which the insured was a member', which was the case. Either construction being perfectly possible therefore, the phrase was ambiguous and to be construed against the insurer. In consequence the first meaning applied, and the insured was covered.

64. The modern approach to interpretation adopts a different starting point. It still has as its prime objective the ascertainment of the intention of the parties. In *Investors Compensation Scheme v. West Bromwich Building Society*,[207] the House of Lords set out several principles which judges ought to adhere to when interpreting contracts of any sort. The aim should be to find the meaning that the document would convey to a reasonable person having all the background knowledge that would reasonably be available to the parties in the situation in which they were at the time of the contract. Previous negotiations and declarations of subjective intent must be excluded, but included is the possibility of ambiguity and the realization of the possible misuse of words and syntax. The court is not obliged to ascribe to the parties an intention that plainly they could not have had and, in choosing between competing unnatural meanings, it was entitled to decide that the parties must have made mistakes as to meaning. One could add to these a further well-established principle of commercial contracts, which is that they ought to be construed in a way that makes 'good commercial

205. In respect of consumer insurance contracts, the Consumer Rights Act 2015 statutorily confirms the *contra proferentem* rule.

206. [1940] 2 KB 156.

207. [1998] 1 All E.R. 98. *See also Sirius General Insurance v. FAI General Insurance* [2004] UKHL 54, [2004] 1 W.L.R. 3251.

sense'.[208] This restatement of the principles of construction certainly has a bearing on the interpretation of insurance contracts,[209] but it is arguable that in reality the impact has been more limited than first appeared likely,[210] and it is arguable that recent Supreme Court decisions[211] have watered it down to some extent.

§6. Further Points on Coverage

65. Three further points surrounding the cover provided by an insurance policy are worth mentioning at this stage. The first is that it is essential in the ordinary case that the insured shows that an insured peril occurred during the period of the policy. This almost self-evident point was confirmed in *Kelly v. Norwich Union Fire Insurance Society Ltd.*[212] Here, leaks from water mains caused the clay under the plaintiff's property to expand and after a period this 'heave' caused damage to the property. The crucial leak occurred before the plaintiff effected the insurance with the defendant which provided that the latter would indemnify the insured 'in respect of events occurring during the period of the insurance'. The Court of Appeal held that the insurers were not liable. The most likely situation where in practice this principle will not apply is in the context of professional indemnity insurance, where the standard wording generally provides for retrospective cover.[213]

Second, insurances of property cover only the loss attributable to the value of the property and not consequential losses, unless the latter are separately insured.[214] Third, an insured will be able to recover where insured property itself has not been damaged or lost by an insured peril, but that peril has occurred and the insured property is lost or damaged by action that is necessary to save it from the insured peril.[215]

208. *See* Lord Diplock in *Antaios Cia Naviera SA v. Salen Raderierna AB* [1985] A.C. 191 at 221.
209. Recent insurance cases considering the principles include *Union Camp Chemicals Ltd v. ACE Insurance SA-NV* [2003] Lloyd's Rep. IR 487, *Canelhas Comercio Inportacao E Exportacao Ltd v. Wooldridge* [2004] EWCA Civ 984, [2004] Lloyd's Rep. IR 915, *McGeown v. Direct Travel Insurance* [2003] EWCA Civ 1606, [2004] Lloyd's Rep. IR 599, *Friends Provident Life and Pensions Ltd v. Sirius International Insurance Corp.* [2004] EWHC 1999 (Comm), [2005] Lloyd's Rep. IR 135 and *Royal & Sun Alliance Insurance plc v. Dornoch* [2005] EWCA Civ 544, [2005] Lloyd's Rep. IR 544.
210. *See* Clarke, *The Law of Insurance Contracts*, 5th ed., para. 15-3B1.
211. *See* , in particular, *Wood v. Capita Insurance Services Ltd* [2017] UKSC 24.
212. [1989] 2 Lloyd's Rep. 333.
213. That is, in respect of claims made against the insured during the policy period, whether or not the negligence occurred earlier.
214. *See Re Wright and Pole* (1834) 1 A & E 621; *Theobald v. Railway Passengers Assurance Co.* (1854) 10 Exch 45; *Maurice v. Goldsborough Mort* [1939] AC 452. Separate insurance is considered in Part III, Ch. 2.
215. *See* in particular *Symington v. Union Insurance Society of Canton* (1928) 97 LJKB 646. However, English law does not permit recovery in respect of the costs of preventing a loss: *Yorkshire Water Services Ltd. v. Sun Alliance & London Insurance plc* [1997] C.L.C. 213.

§7. Causation

66. In order for the insured to be able to recover, it is a fundamental rule that a loss under an insurance contract must have been proximately caused by a peril insured against. Proximate cause here does not necessarily mean the latest cause in time, but the real or the dominant cause. If the real cause of the loss is not covered by the policy the insured will not recover, even though a cause of the loss is covered. In a leading marine insurance case, *Leyland Shipping Company v. Norwich Union Fire Insurance Company Ltd*,[216] a ship was insured against loss due to the perils of the sea; losses arising as a consequence of hostilities were excepted. The ship was torpedoed during the 1914–1918 War. She reached port where she was moored but two days later, because of the action of the sea, she sank. It was held that the real and proximate cause of the loss was the fact that she had been torpedoed, a consequence of hostilities, and not the action of the sea. Hence the insured did not recover.

67. The determination of what is the proximate cause of any loss is a question of fact, to be decided on common-sense principles in the light of the particular case. In practice the question of causation becomes relevant only where there are two or more causes of a loss, one of which is covered by the policy and one of which is expressly excepted. Here it is obviously vital to determine which is the real cause.[217] The problem has arisen quite frequently in cases involving personal accident insurance where death or injury by accident is covered, but the insurer is generally declared not to be liable should death or injury result from natural disease or illness.[218] In practice, to guard against difficult arguments on the facts of any particular case, insurers offering personal accident policies modify the operation of the doctrine of proximate cause by providing that the accident must be the exclusive cause of loss independently of all other causes. Thus if there is any other cause, however minor, a claim will fail.[219] In a situation where one cause is covered by the policy and the other is excepted it may be genuinely impossible to determine which was the dominant cause. If this is so the insurer will not be liable; the excepted cause prevails.[220]

---

216. [1918] AC 350.

217. As, for example, in the *Leyland Shipping* case, *supra*, *J J Lloyd (Instruments) Ltd. v. Northern Star Insurance Co. Ltd.* [1987] 1 Lloyd's Rep. 32 supports this view that causation is relevant only where there are two or more causes, one of which is excepted. Here damage suffered by a cruiser was caused both by adverse weather conditions (an insured peril) and defective design. The latter was not an excepted peril, and it was held that the insurers were fully liable for the loss. *See also Global Process Systems v. Syarikat Takaful Malaysia Berhad, The Cendor MOPU* [2011] UKSC 5, [2011] Lloyd's Rep. IR 302.

218. *See Winspear v. Accident Insurance Association* (1880) 6 QBD 42 and *Lawrence v. Accidental Insurance Co.* (1881) 7 QBD 216.

219. *See* , e.g., *Jason v. Batten* [1969] 1 Lloyd's Rep. 281. Such an exclusion can also be found in other policies: *Oei v. Foster* [1982] 2 Lloyd's Rep. 170 (household insurance).

220. *See Wayne Tank & Pump Co. Ltd. v. Employers' Liability Assurance Corp. Ltd.* [1974] 1 QB 57.

§8. Public Policy

68. If an insured has suffered a loss caused by a peril insured against, his claim will still fail if it would be illegal or against public policy to enforce it. This principle in insurance law is merely an application of the general maxim *ex turpi causa oritur actio*. In part, this relates to the principle that an insured cannot recover an indemnity against the consequences of his own intentional act, described above. It also imports that he may not be able to recover an indemnity against the consequences of his criminal act. However, the cases are not entirely clear as to when recovery will be barred. Certainly it will be if a crime is deliberately committed. In *Beresford v. Royal Insurance Co*,[221] a claim under a life policy following intentional suicide failed, as at the time the case was decided suicide was a crime.[222] Public policy will debar someone who has murdered a life insured from claiming the proceeds of the policy as beneficiary under the life insured's will,[223] on the latter dying intestate or as co-insured or nominee under the policy.[224] It seems that, in general, the unintentional commission of a crime by the insured will also debar recovery, provided the offence is not merely technical. In *Haseldine v. Hosken*,[225] a solicitor was not entitled to be indemnified under his professional indemnity insurance policy against his tortious liability that had also involved the commission of a crime. In *Gray v. Barr*,[226] a man who shot his wife's ex-lover could not recover an indemnity from his liability insurers against his liability to pay damages to the widow, even though he was not regarded as guilty of deliberate murder. In *Geismar v. Sun Alliance and London Insurance*,[227] an insured who had smuggled jewellery into the country without paying excise duty on it could not recover for its subsequent theft. In contrast with the last case in particular, in *Euro-Diam Ltd v. Bathurst*,[228] insured diamonds were sent on a sale or return basis to a customer of the insured in Germany on an invoice understating the price. This was done to enable the customer to deceive the German tax authorities, of which the insured was probably aware. However, it was held that the insured was not prevented from recovering for the theft of the diamonds from the German warehouse as they were not relying on any illegality and the only person who stood to gain from it was the customer.[229] Although there have not been any recent decisions in this area concerning insurance claims, there have been important recent decisions on illegality as a defence on a civil claim, especially the Supreme Court decision in *Patel v. Mirza*.[230] This lays down a more

221. [1938] AC 586.
222. Since the Suicide Act 1961, which made suicide no longer a crime, a claim under a life insurance policy when the insured has committed suicide will succeed if the contract expressly covers this event.
223. *Cleaver v. Mutual Reserve Fund Life Association* [1892] 1 QB 147.
224. *Davitt v. Titcumb* [1989] 3 All ER 417.
225. [1933] 1 KB 822.
226. [1971] 2 QB 554.
227. [1977] 2 Lloyd's Rep. 62.
228. [1988] 2 All ER 23.
229. Public policy will not prevent a liability insured from being indemnified against liability to pay exemplary damages, at least where the insured did not act criminally: *Lancashire County Council v. Municipal Mutual Insurance Ltd.* [1996] 3 All E.R. 545.
230. [2016] UKSC 42.

flexible approach than earlier authorities, and it may be that some of the decisions mentioned above would not now be followed.

69. In any event, there are well-established situations, especially in respect of motor insurance, where the commission of a criminal act will not prevent a claim. When an insured motorist is liable to a third party in damages, the unintentional commission of a criminal act will not prevent the insured from recovering from his insurer an indemnity against the damages, even where the crime committed is the most serious unintentional crime of manslaughter.[231] This exception exists because the public policy that prevents indemnity for criminal acts is outweighed by the public policy that requires that the victims of road accidents receive any compensation awarded to them, and this is ensured only if negligent drivers can enforce their insurance policies. The same view is likely to be taken in other areas where insurance is compulsory, especially employers' liability insurance, although there have been no reported cases decided in these areas.

Further, in the same insurance situation but where the insured deliberately runs someone down with his motor vehicle, the latter will be able to recover from the insurers. In *Hardy v. Motor Insurers' Bureau*,[232] a security officer attempted to stop a car being driven by a thief. The latter drove on deliberately and injured the officer. The thief had no motor insurance policy, and the actual point for decision was whether the officer could recover from the defendant because he was the victim of an uninsured driver.[233] It was held that he could, although it was made clear that had the thief been insured and been seeking indemnity from his insurer against his liability to the officer, his claim would have been disallowed as being contrary to public policy, involving as it did the intentional commission of a criminal assault.

§9. Insurance as a Personal Contract

70. An important point is that most insurance contracts are regarded as contracts personal to the particular insured, the most significant consequence of which is that they cannot be assigned by the insured without the consent of the insurer.[234] In *Peters v. General Fire and Accident Insurance Company*,[235] a man sold his van and handed over his motor policy on it to the purchaser. It was held that this purported assignment was quite ineffective; the contract of insurance was personal to insured and insurer; the latter was not therefore liable to pay the damages awarded to a victim of the purchaser's negligent driving of the van.

---

231. *Tinline v. White Cross Insurance Association* [1921] 3 KB 327 and *James v. British General Insurance Company* [1927] 1 KB 311. In both cases, the insured killed people by the use of his car in circumstances such that he was convicted of manslaughter. In *Tinline* he drove too fast and in *James* he was drunk. Both insureds were held entitled to enforce their motor insurance policies to recover the damages for which they were liable.
232. [1964] 2 QB 745, followed and approved on very similar facts in *Gardner v. Moore* [1984] AC 548.
233. *See* Part IV.
234. Other consequences of this principle are seen later.
235. [1938] 2 All ER 267.

This general proposition is qualified in the following ways. First, a marine insurance policy is assignable.[236] Second, policies of life insurance also constitute an exception to the above rule.[237] Under the Policies of Assurance Act 1867, they can be assigned by endorsement on the policy or by a separate document using wording similar to that in the Schedule to the Act. Provided that notice in writing is given to the insurer, the assignee can sue on and enforce the policy in his own name. Furthermore, a policy of life insurance is a chose in action.[238] An assignment of a life policy that is not fully in accordance with the 1867 Act may operate as an equitable assignment of a chose in action in which case it is, at least as between the insured and his assignee, a perfectly effective assignment.[239]

71. Quite apart from the assignment of a policy itself, where this is permissible, the benefit of a contract of insurance, in other words the amount paid or payable in respect of a loss covered by the contract, as distinct from the contract itself is also in law a chose in action. It can be assigned under section 136 of the law of Property Act 1925 provided, among other things, that notice is given to the debtor, the insurer. An incomplete assignment will again operate as an equitable assignment and be enforceable at least as between the insured and the assignee.

Such an assignment can be of proceeds already recoverable, in respect of a loss that has already taken place, or of the proceeds of any future loss. The consent of the insurer is irrelevant unless the contract provides otherwise, since the assignor remains the insured, and it is only what he can recover that is the subject of the assignment. Thus this would not have availed the purchaser in the *Peters* case (above), as the vendor/insured having sold his van had no right to recover anything in respect of it. It may be different, however, if the vendor of property retains an insurable interest[240] in it.

236. *See* Marine Insurance Act 1906, ss 50 and 51.
237. Recognizing their different nature and their role as investment.
238. An item of intangible personal property. A chose in action is such as a share or a right under a contract.
239. A life policy can also be assigned under the provisions of s. 136 of the Law of Property Act 1925, described briefly below. It should be noted that neither in the case of statutory assignments nor equitable ones is it necessary that the assignee have an insurable interest (*see* Ch. 2, *infra*) in the life insured.
240. *See* Ch. 2, below.

Chapter 2. Insurable Risk

72. Quite apart from the general concept of what risks can be covered by insurance, it is essential that the insured in every contract of insurance possesses what is called an insurable interest in the event insured against, unless this requirement can be and is lawfully waived. This requirement differs somewhat in its nature, depending upon whether the insurance is life insurance or not; life insurance thus requires separate consideration. Further, in some cases insurable interest is required by statute, in some cases it is not so required but is required because of the nature of the contract. The most recent authority has cast some doubt on traditional interpretations of the requirement of interest, and this is considered separately.[241]

§1. Insurable Interest in Life Insurance

I. Requirement

73. The Common Law did not require an insured to have an interest in the person whose life he insured, and as a result the taking out of life policies that were no more than gambling, with no possible relationship between the insured and the life insured, became common. To remedy this Parliament passed the Life Assurance Act 1774, still in force today. Section 1 makes null and void[242] contracts of life insurance wherein the insured has no interest in the life insured at the time the policy is effected. Section 2 requires that the names of all persons interested, in other words all the insureds and their beneficiaries, if any, are inserted in the policy. If this is not done, again the policy is illegal, but this requirement has been relaxed in the case of group policies, that is, policies taken out for the benefit of a class of persons, for example, the employees of a particular employer, where it is sufficient that the group or class intended to benefit is clearly described.[243] Under section 3, no more can be recovered by the insured than the value of his interest in the life insured. The requirements of the Act have been developed by case law, so that there are two important issues as to insurable interest, first the time when interest is required and second the meaning of 'insurable interest'.

II. The Time When Interest Is Required

74. As the contract of life insurance is not a contract of indemnity, there is no requirement of insurable interest at the time of loss, the date of death of the life insured.

241. *See* para. 82.
242. Construed by case law to mean 'illegal', with the consequences described below: *Harse v. Pearl Life Assurance Company* [1904] 1 KB 558.
243. Section 50, Insurance Companies Amendment Act 1973.

In the leading case of *Dalby v. India & London Life Assurance Company*,[244] the plaintiff was a director of insurers who had issued policies on the life of the Duke of Cambridge. The insurers reinsured themselves against this risk with the defendant company. Later the original policies were cancelled, thus relieving the insurers of liability under them, but they kept up the reinsurance premiums until the Duke died, when they claimed from the defendant. It was held that the insurers were entitled to recover even though they had no insurable interest in the Duke's life at the date of death. The statutory requirements of sections 1 and 3 of the 1774 Act related only to the date of commencement of the policy, when the insurers clearly had an interest.

It follows from the principle established in *Dalby's* case that, as has already been seen,[245] a life insurance policy can be assigned or sold at any time during its existence and that the assignee or purchaser will be able to enforce it provided only that the original insured had an insurable interest at the date the policy was first effected.[246] However, it is clear that the requirements of section 1 cannot be evaded by the effecting of a policy by someone with interest who then immediately assigns the policy to another without interest.[247]

III. The Meaning of Insurable Interest in Life Insurance

75. As already mentioned, section 3 of the Life Assurance Act limits recovery by the insured to the value of his interest. This has had the effect that while the courts rejected the concept of indemnity as being relevant to life insurance at the date of loss, they were constrained by section 3 to apply a similar concept to define what is an insurable interest at the date of the policy. Generally an insured has an interest in the life insured only if and only to the extent that he has a pecuniary interest in that life; in other words only if he can prove that he would suffer financial loss on the death of the life insured. To this general rule, there are exceptions, recognized as being outside the mischief aimed at by the 1774 Act and hence outside its scope. These exceptions comprise insurance on the insured's own life[248] and on the life of a spouse[249] or a civil partner.[250] Here someone can validly insure for an unlimited amount.[251]

Otherwise, however, family relationships will not support life insurance in the absence of financial interest. A son does not automatically have an interest in the life of his mother or father,[252] although an infant child would have no difficulty in showing

244. (1854) 15 CB 365.
245. *See* para. 70.
246. The principle of *Dalby* has not been entirely free from criticism; *see* Birds, *Modern Insurance Law*, para. 3.3.1.
247. *See M'Farlane v. Royal London Friendly Society* (1886) 2 TLR 755, discussed in Birds, *supra* , para. 3.6. *See ibid.*, for discussions of the requirements of s. 2 of the 1774 Act.
248. *Wainewright v. Bland* (1835) 1 Moo & R 481.
249. *Griffiths v. Fleming* [1909] 1 KB 805.
250. Civil Partnerships Act 2004, s. 253.
251. The presumption of interest may well extend to situations of partners living together, and to fiancé and fiancée.
252. *Harse v. Pearl Life Assurance Company, supra* .

a pecuniary interest. A parent cannot insure the life of his or her child[253] unless, abnormally, he or she is financially dependent upon the child. Other moral obligations will not suffice; in *Anctil v. Manufacturers' Life Insurance Company*,[254] a legally appointed guardian had, it was held, no right to insure the life of the child as he could not show that he would suffer financially by the child's death.

There are cases outside family relationships where it is comparatively easy to show insurable interest, for example, where an employee insures the life of his employer[255] or a creditor insures the life of his debtor.[256] Even in these cases, though, the amount of interest is strictly limited in law; in the first case to the actual amount of agreed wages or salary that the insured would lose should his employer die, and in the second to the amount of the debt.

The categories of insurable interest in life insurance are therefore narrow. In practice, however, insurances are bona fide effected without satisfying the strict requirements; for example, employers insure the lives of 'key' employees for large sums where strictly they can insure only for what it would cost them to replace such employees in the event of death. Few people are truly irreplaceable. There is no doubt, though, that such insurances will be treated as perfectly valid by all parties concerned, and it is highly improbable that any legal difficulties surrounding them will be raised.[257]

§2. Insurable Interest in Indemnity Insurances

76. Problems of insurable interest in contracts of indemnity arise only really in the case of insurances on property of one sort or another. The other category of indemnity insurance, liability insurance, raises no real difficulties as one obviously always has an unlimited interest in insuring against one's potential liability to pay damages to a third party.

253. *Halford v. Kymer* (1830) 10 B & C 724.

254. [1899] AC 604. The decision to the contrary effect in *Barnes v. London, Edinburgh & Glasgow Life Assurance Co. Ltd.* [1892] 1 QB 864 is generally regarded as incorrect.

255. *Hebdon v. West* (1863) 3 B & S 579, or vice versa as in *Simcock v. Scottish Imperial Insurance Co* (1902) 10 SLT 286.

256. *Ibid.*

257. For this reason, it is clearly time that the law was reformed; *see* Birds, *supra* . In a modern case (*Fuji Finance Inc. v. Aetna Life Insurance Ltd.* [1996] 4 All E.R. 608), the sum insured on death was the same as the surrender value of the policy at any time, and the potential return on the policy was the same as the gross national product of the UK for 460,000 years. In fact the policy was surrendered for a 'mere' GBP 1,100,000. No question was raised as to the fact that this sum insured was almost certainly considerably in excess of the financial interest of the insured in the life insured. Reform may well result from the work of the Law Commissions, who issued an Issues Paper on Insurable Interest in 2008 and a Consultation Paper in 2011 (LCCP 201/SLCDP 152. They propose to produce a Report covering this in 2015 or 2016. *See* briefly Birds, *supra* , para. 3.8.

I. The Nature of Insurable Interest in Property Insurance

77. As with life insurance, the meaning of insurable interest in property insurance is fairly narrow as a matter of strict law. To be able to insure property, the insured must have a recognized right in it or contractual right over it – 'a right in the property, or a right derivable out of some contract about the property',[258] or the existence of a legal obligation to bear any loss arising from destruction of, or damage to, the insured property.[259] A mere expectation of loss from the destruction of or damage to property is not enough. An example illustrates the distinction. The owner of a hotel has an insurable interest in it; he has a clear proprietary right and can insure it against damage or destruction from any cause up to its full value. But the owner of a petrol filling station next door, whose trade largely depends upon the hotel's guests, does not have an insurable interest in the hotel, even though his business would suffer considerably should the hotel be destroyed or damaged.

The trustee and beneficiary of property have insurable interests in it, as do a landlord and tenant, mortgagor and mortgagee, and vendor and purchaser under a contract of sale.[260] The mere possession of property, however, does not found insurable interest unless the possessor bears some legal responsibility for it, for example, because he is in law a bailee of the property. A creditor has no insurable interest in his debtor's property unless he has a proprietary interest such as a mortgage in it, even though he may be largely dependent for the repayment of his debt upon the continued safety of that property. In the leading case of *Macaura v. Northern Assurance Company Ltd.*,[261] Macaura sold his timber-estates to a company in which he was the sole shareholder. He was a creditor of the company. He effected with the insurers a policy of fire insurance on all the timber, the policy being in his own name. Fire destroyed the greater part of the timber, but Macaura's claim on his insurance was denied. It was held that he was not entitled to recover as he himself had no insurable interest in the timber. Neither as shareholder nor as creditor did he have any proprietary right to the property owned in law by the company.[262] It should be noted that the strictness of the rule, clearly illustrated by the decision in *Macaura*, can be mitigated if insurances other than straightforward insurances on property are effected. For example, a creditor can insure against the insolvency of his debtor that might be caused by the loss of property, and a shareholder

258. Per Lord Eldon in the leading case of *Lucena v. Craufurd* (1806) 2 B & P N R 269 at 321.
259. *Glengate-KG Properties Ltd. v. Norwich Union Fire Insurance Society* [1996] 1 Lloyd's Rep. 613.
260. The extent of their interest may be limited, however; *see infra*.
261. [1925] AC 619.
262. The strictness of the law, as exemplified particularly by this decision, has been criticized and, indeed, not followed in other common law jurisdictions: *see*, e.g., the decision of the Canadian Supreme Court in *Kosmopoulos v. Constitution Insurance Co. of Canada* (1987) 34 DLR (4th) 208, which reviews the law in a highly persuasive manner. However, it may be that a wider definition of insurable interest would not make much difference in practice. For detailed discussion, *see* Birds, 'Recent common law developments regarding insurable interest and subrogation' (1988) 1 *Insurance Law Journal* 171 and 'Insurable Interests' in *Interests in Goods*, eds. Palmer and McEndrick, 2nd ed., 1998.

may insure his shares against any loss in value by the failure of an enterprise undertaken by the company or the loss of property owned by the company.[263]

II. Extent of Insurable Interest in Property Insurance

78. As indicated, anyone with an interest in property can insure it, and quite lawfully insure it for the full value of the property. However, if there is a loss, the value of the interest becomes crucial and the insured can prima facie recover only sufficient to indemnify him.[264] In certain circumstances, as explained below, the insured can recover more than this, although he will never be able to retain for himself more than the value of his interest. If insured separately, the insured has an interest to insure an expectancy based upon his proprietary interest, for example, in the profits he would expect to make from his ownership or occupation of the property.[265]

III. When Insurable Interest in Property Must Be Shown

79. It is inherent in the nature of a contract of indemnity that interest must exist at the date of loss,[266] and in the absence of this, the insured's claim will fail.[267] Although it can still be argued that the Life Assurance Act 1774 applies to insurances of land and buildings,[268] modern authority treats that Act as inapplicable to such cases,[269] and in practice it seems that the application of the Act to land and buildings is ignored. However, there is common law authority that supports the requirement of interest at the time of policy.[270]

80. Whatever the strict legal position as regards land and buildings, it has long been clear that, in respect of insurance on goods, an insurable interest in the strict sense is not required at the date of the policy because of the clear exemption from the 1774 Act.[271] This exemption is convenient in several respects. For example, it allows the insurance of goods not yet the insured's property but which will become so, for

263. *Wilson v. Jones* (1867) LR 2 Ex 139.
264. *See* , e.g., *Westminster Fire Office v. Glasgow Provident Investment Society* (1888) 13 App Cas 699 (a mortgagee who had insured the property which was mortgaged to him could recover only the value of his outstanding debt).
265. *City Tailors Ltd. v. Evans* (1922) 91 LJKB 379.
266. Unless this requirement is waived; *see infra* .
267. The policy is not itself void or illegal, as was made clear in the *Macaura case*, *supra* , so that, among other things, the insurers will be able to rely on its terms to enforce an arbitration clause and the insured will not be able to claim a return of premium.
268. *See* Birds, *supra* , para. 3.9.1.
269. *Siu Yin Kwan v. Eastern Insurance Co. Ltd.* [1994] 1 All ER 213. For the earlier cases, *see Re King* [1963] Ch 459 at 485 as compared with *Mark Rowlands Ltd. v. Berni Inns Ltd.* [1986] QB 211 at 227.
270. *Sadler's Co. v. Badcock* (1743) 2 Atk 554. This does not import the full requirements of the 1774 Act, e.g., as to naming under s. 2.
271. Previously a policy without any conceivable sort of interest would have been void under anti-gaming legislation, but this general provision has been repealed.

example, under a contract for the sale of goods where the property has not yet passed to the purchaser or under a contract of hire purchase, and it allows bailees of goods and others in a similar position to insure them for their full value, regardless of their legal responsibility.

IV. Waiver of Interest in Property Insurance

81. Because the requirement of interest at the time of loss is only a contractual requirement, rather than required by an overriding rule of law, it can be waived if the parties wish.[272] In *Thomas v. National Farmers' Union Mutual Insurance Society Ltd*,[273] Thomas had been the tenant of a farm that he left, leaving behind a quantity of hay and straw. This was insured against damage by fire with the defendant, the policy providing that it did not cover anything that ceased to be the property of the insured unless this happened 'by operation of law'. When Thomas left the farm, the property in the hay and straw passed under an Act of Parliament, and hence by operation of law, to his landlord. Later the hay and the straw were destroyed by fire. It was held that Thomas was entitled to recover under the insurance policy, even though he no longer had an insurable interest in the property, because the policy expressly waived the need for this by providing by implication that it did continue to cover property that passed from Thomas by operation of law.[274]

§3. Insurable Interest in Miscellaneous Cases

82. While recognizing the traditional strict view of insurable interest in straightforward life and property insurances, recent Court of Appeal authority has stated that there exists a category of cases that recognize interests that are not pecuniary.[275] The case itself involved a strange arrangement so that what was in reality liability insurance taken out by a shipowner was in the form of accident insurance, and clearly the court was not prepared to let a technical defence stand in the way of a just result. However, the reasoning is somewhat difficult, and it is difficult to be sure exactly how much the approach involves any real change in the law.[276]

---

272. Further consequences of this will be seen in Ch. 6, *infra* .
273. [1961] 1 WLR 386; *see also Prudential Staff Union v. Hall* [1947] KB 685.
274. It is clear that Thomas would hold the money received for the benefit of his landlord, by analogy with cases discussed in Ch. 6, below.
275. *Feasey v. Sun Life Assurance Corporation of Canada* [2003] EWCA Civ 885, [2003] Lloyd's Rep. IR 637.
276. For further details and comments, *see* Birds, *supra* para. 3.5.

Chapter 3. Formation of the Insurance Contract

§1. Pre-contractual Phase

83. There are no overriding rules of law as to how an insurance contract is negotiated, but long-established practice dictates that there are two standard ways when an insurance contract is first entered into.[277] In practice, both of these involve an offer made by the prospective insured or proposer. The first way involves the completion of a proposal form, which is a standard form produced by the insurer.[278] The second involves the proposer (or an intermediary on his behalf) using some other document. Normally this is termed a slip and is used when proposals are made to Lloyd's underwriters or in some other parts of the London market. The proposal form is used for most situations of consumer insurances and commercial insurances offered by insurance companies. The significance of these documents in legal terms concerns issues of misrepresentation and non-disclosure, which are considered later.[279]

§2. Formalities

84. As a general rule, there is no particular form required for non-marine insurance contracts, although marine insurance contracts must be embodied in a formal policy.[280] A totally oral contract of insurance is quite legally binding, provided that agreement on the material terms can be proved if necessary.[281] The only formalities relate to life insurance and these do not qualify the above basic proposition. They are considered later.[282] In practice, the vast majority of, if not all, insurance contracts will be embodied either in a policy (into which the proposal form, if any, is usually incorporated)[283] or in a cover note; the latter is dealt with separately below.

85. There are significant disclosure requirements imposed by the ICOBS,[284] some of which were required by the Third EC Insurance Directives and some by the Directive on the distance marketing of financial products.[285] This account, which deals with the requirements for general insurance,[286] deals first with the requirements imposed

277. The position on renewal is considered in para. 90.
278. Increasingly this is done online or on the telephone, at least as far as consumers are concerned.
279. *See* Ch. 4, *infra* .
280. Section 22, Marine Insurance Act 1906. Guarantee policies must also be evidenced in writing: s. 4, Statute of Frauds 1677.
281. *Murfitt v. Royal Insurance Co.* (1922) 38 TLR 334.
282. *See* Part V, Ch. 4.
283. *See* para. 109.
284. As to ICOBS generally, *see* para. 28 *supra* .
285. 2002/65/EC.
286. The requirements in respect of life insurance are briefly described in para. 312.

under the distance marketing Directive and then describes the product disclosure requirements including those imposed under the Insurance Directives.

86. A distance contract is essentially one concluded over the Internet, by telephone or by post. It will therefore be found in a great number of consumer insurance situations. Distance marketing disclosure is governed by ICOBS 3. The information required, which must be produced by the insurer and provided by it if there is no intermediary involved, must be provided in good time before conclusion of the contract and in a clear and comprehensible manner. Customers must be provided with all the contractual terms and conditions and the information listed below in writing or in another durable medium available and accessible to them in good time before the conclusion of any distance contract, unless the contract has been concluded at the customer's request using a means of communication that does not enable the provision of the information in that form in good time before the conclusion of the contract. In the latter case, the information must be provided immediately after the conclusion of the contract. Where a contract is concluded by telephone, only abbreviated information (*see* Annex 3 to ICOBS 3) has to be provided during the telephone conversation, but the basic obligation to provide the full information still applies before the conclusion of the contract unless the exception described above applies.

87. The following is the key information required (Annex 2 to ICOBS 3): (1) the name and the main business of the firm, the geographical address at which it is established and any other geographical address relevant for the consumer's relations with the firm; (2) where the firm has a representative established in the consumer's EEA State of residence, the name of that representative and the geographical address relevant for the consumer's relations with the representative; (3) an appropriate statutory status disclosure statement, namely a statement that the firm is on the Financial Services Register and its registration number; (4) a description of the main characteristics of the service the firm will provide (5) the total price to be paid by the consumer to the firm for the financial service, including all related fees, charges and expenses, and all taxes paid through the firm or, when an exact price cannot be indicated, the basis for the calculation of the price enabling the consumer to verify it; (6) notice of the possibility that other taxes or costs may exist that are not paid through the firm or imposed by it; (7) any limitations on the period for which the information provided is valid, including a clear explanation as to how long a firm's offer applies as it stands; (8) the arrangements for payment and for performance; (9) details of any specific additional cost for the consumer for using a means of distance communication; (10) the existence or absence of a right to cancel under the cancellation rules and, where there is such a right, its duration and the conditions for exercising it, including information on the amount which the consumer may be required to pay (or which may not be returned to the consumer) in accordance with those rules, as well as the consequences of not exercising the right to cancel; (11) the minimum duration of the contract; (12) information on any rights the parties may have to terminate the contract early or unilaterally under its terms, including any penalties imposed by the contract in such cases; (13) practical instructions for exercising any right to cancel, including the address to which any cancellation notice should be sent; (14) the EEA State or States whose laws are taken by the firm as a basis for the establishment of relations with the consumer prior to the conclusion of the contract; (15) any contractual clause on law applicable to the contract or on the competent court, or both; (16) in which language, or languages, the contractual terms and conditions and the other information in this Annex will be supplied, and in which language, or languages, the firm, with the agreement of the consumer, undertakes to communicate during the duration of the contract; (17) how to complain to the firm, whether complaints may subsequently be referred to the FOS and, if so, the methods for having access to it, together with equivalent information about any other applicable named complaints scheme; and (18) whether compensation may be available from the compensation scheme, or any other named compensation scheme, if the firm is unable to meet its liabilities, and information about any other applicable named compensation scheme.

88. Product information requirements are covered by ICOBS 6. There are disclosure requirements related to general insurance contracts (accident and sickness policies and all forms of indemnity insurance), and more detailed requirements relating to protection policies (pure protection contracts (primarily life insurance with no surrender value or where benefits are only payable on death)) and payment protection policies (non-investment insurance contracts with elements of a general insurance contract and the benefits of which are described as enabling a policyholder to protect his ability to continue to make payments due to third parties, or can reasonably be expected to be used in this way). There is a general requirement that a firm takes reasonable steps to ensure that a customer is given appropriate information about a policy in good time and in a comprehensible form so that they can make an informed decision about the arrangements proposed. This may be provided to consumers in a policy summary (as described in ICOBS 6, Annex 2) but this is not a requirement except for protection policies.

89. The non-life Directive requirements are in ICOBS 6.2.2, 6.2.3 and 6.2.4. Before a contract is concluded, the customer who is a natural person must be told: (1) the law applicable to the contract where the parties do not have a free choice or, where they do, the law the insurer proposes to choose; and (2) the arrangements for handling complaints including, where appropriate, the existence of the FOS, without prejudice to the right to take legal proceedings. If the insurer is an EEA firm, it must inform any customer, before any commitment is entered into, of the EEA State in which the head office or branch with which the contract is to be concluded is situated. The contract, or any other document grating cover, together with the insurance proposal where it is binding on the customer, must state the address of the head office or branch. Consumers must be told of the right to cancel a policy, which is described below, in good time before the conclusion of the contract.

§3. Formation of the Contract

90. Usual contractual requirements apply to the formation of the insurance contract. An offer made by one party on all the material points must be accepted by the other. As already indicated, in insurance, the offer will generally be made by the proposer when he submits a completed proposal form. Once that is accepted by the insurer, there is normally a binding contract, even though a formal policy may not yet have been issued, provided that all material terms (*see below*) are agreed.[287] If the insurer does not unequivocally accept the insured's proposal, but its acceptance is qualified by being subject to the payment of a premium or the issue of a policy, this in law will constitute a fresh offer by the insurer[288] which must be accepted by the insured before a binding contract comes into existence (*see infra*).

Occasionally the offer may be made by the insurer. This will normally happen upon the renewal of cover[289] when the insurer offers renewal and, possibly, to provide temporary cover upon expiry of the old contract and pending completion of the new one. To rely upon such an offer the insured must show clear acceptance of it, by words or conduct.[290]

§4. Agreement on Material Terms

91. As mentioned above, the offer and acceptance must include agreement on the material terms of the contract. Thus the amount and subject matter of the insurance and the commencement and duration of the risk must be agreed upon. In most cases these matters will be evident from the proposal form and the surrounding circumstances. For example, if necessary the duration of the risk will be easily implied, as most indemnity contracts run for a year and most life contracts are entire. Finally the amount of the premium must be quantified.[291]

92. It has been said that there must be express agreement on all the other terms and conditions of the insurance contract before such a contract comes into existence.[292] However, the decision in *General Accident Insurance Corporation v. Cronk* [293] does not support such a requirement. There the policy delivered to the insured contained conditions of which there had been no intimation on the proposal form. It was held that the contract was effective and the insured was liable to pay the agreed premium, as 'he must be taken to have applied for the ordinary form of policy issued by the Company'. This seems to be the guiding principle so that express agreement on the material terms mentioned above only is required. In practice the problem will not usually arise as proposal forms invariably stipulate that what the insured is applying for is subject to the insurer's usual terms and conditions.

---

287. *Adie v. The Insurances Corporation* (1898) 14 TLR 544.
288. It may even be only an invitation to treat, so that the proposer must make a new offer on this basis: *Locker v. Law Union and Rock Insurance Co. Ltd.* [1928] 1 KB 554.
289. As explained below, in non-life contracts the practice is for policies to be of limited duration and renewal of the policy will constitute a new contract.
290. *See Taylor v. Allon* [1966] 1 QB 304, a motor insurance case, where the practice of temporarily extending cover, to satisfy the compulsory insurance requirements of the Road Traffic Act 1988, is common.
291. *Alliss-Chalmers Company v. Fidelity and Deposit Company of Maryland* (1916) 114 LT 433.
292. *Ibid.*, at 434.
293. (1901) 17 TLR 233. *See also Rust v. Abbey Life Assurance Co. Ltd.* [1979] 2 Lloyd's Rep. 334.

§5. Payment of Premium and Issue of Policy

93. It is clear that in general it is not essential either that the premium is paid or that a formal policy is issued before a binding insurance contract comes into existence. However, either or both may be expressed to be a condition precedent to the existence of the contract. This frequently happens in certain insurances, particularly life insurance.[294] If so, an insurer's acceptance of the insured's offer subject to either requirement constitutes in law a counter-offer which must be accepted by the insured and can only be accepted in the absence of a change of circumstances. In *Canning v. Farquhar*,[295] the proposal form for a policy of life insurance stated that no insurance should take effect until the premium was paid. After completing the form, the proposer suffered a serious fall, as a consequence of which he later died. It was held that the insurer was not bound to issue a policy and accept the premium tendered, and hence was not liable. The 'acceptance' was a counter-offer of insurance upon the terms existing at the time. As there had been a dramatic alteration in these terms, because of the fall, the insurer could properly revoke its offer.[296]

§6. The Insurance Contract at Lloyd's

94. Where the insurer concerned is a Lloyd's underwriter, the position as to the formation of the contract is rather different. The proposed never deals directly with an underwriter, but always through the medium of a Lloyd's broker. A proposal for insurance is made on a slip, which is taken by the broker to a number of underwriters, normally within the same syndicate or group. Those willing to accept the risk initial the slip and signify the proportion of the risk they are willing to underwrite. As soon as any one underwriter has initialled the slip, that constitutes on his part a complete acceptance of the insured's offer, and hence he is contractually bound.[297]

§7. Cover Notes

95. It is common practice when a proposer desires immediate cover, particularly for motor insurance, for an insurer to issue a cover note, providing such temporary cover pending full consideration of the proposal form and issue of a policy proper. A

294. Compliance with such a condition precedent can be waived by the insurer, as in *Roberts v. Security Co. Ltd.* [1897] 1 QB 111.
295. (1886) 16 QBD 727; *see also Harrington v. Pearl Life Assurance Co.* (1914) 30 TLR 613.
296. It was stated by two of the judges that if there had been no alteration in the risk, the insurer would have been bound to the contract. It does seem therefore that acceptance by an insurer subject to the payment of a premium or the issue of a policy is not a completely true counter-offer, which normally can be revoked at any time before acceptance by the other party. This type of counter-offer is revocable only in the limited circumstances described.
297. *General Reinsurance Corporation v. Forsakringsaktiebolaget Fennia Patria* [1983] QB 856. In reaching this decision, the court applied the well-established customs of the London insurance market, even though oddities may arise, e.g., if a later underwriter refuses to accept the proposer's offer and the proposer cannot withdraw from the partially completed contract.

properly issued cover note is a valid contract of insurance. All that is required is agreement as to the duration and nature of the risk and the premium payable.[298] The normal incidents of the insurance relationship apply so that, for example, it is the duty of the insured applying for a cover note to disclose all material facts.[299] It will usually be the case that an agent of the insurer, who would not normally have authority to issue a full policy, will have authority to issue a cover note.[300]

298. In theory difficult questions can arise as to the other terms incorporated in a cover note, although in practice this will not normally arise since cover notes are stated to be subject to the insurer's usual policy terms. For discussion, *see* Birds, *Modern Insurance Law*, para. 5.6.3.

299. *Marene Knitting Mills Pty. Ltd. v. Greater Pacific General Insurance Ltd.* [1976] 2 Lloyd's Rep. 631. As to disclosure generally, *see* para. 97, *infra* .

300. *Mackie v. European Assurance Society* (1869) 21 LT 102. Even a broker, who is normally in law the agent of the insured (*see* Part VII, Ch. 2), will have authority to issue cover notes binding on the insurer: *Stockton v. Mason* [1978] 2 Lloyd's Rep. 430.

Chapter 4. Obligations of the Insured

96. The obligations of the insured arise:

(1) before the contract is concluded, as regards the description of the risk under a duty to disclose material facts and not to misrepresent material facts and by virtue of standard contract terms;
(2) when the contract is concluded, in terms of paying the premium;
(3) during the contract itself, by virtue of standard terms as to disclosing increases in risk and concerning when a claim is made; and
(4) on renewal when a new contract comes into effect and the original obligations as to disclosure, etc. arise again. These various obligations are examined in this chapter, although not necessarily in the above order.

§1. Description of the Risk

97. The law concerning non-disclosure and misrepresentation provides the principal circumstances when an insurance contract will be voidable at the option of the insurer, in other words when the insurer is entitled to treat the policy as never having existed in law. However, the law has been substantially reformed so far as consumer insurance contracts are concerned by the Consumer Insurance (Disclosure and Representations) Act 2012 and has been modified in respect of business insurance contracts by the Insurance Act 2015. The account in §§2 and 3, below, is therefore now only applicable to consumer insurances effected before 6 April 2013, and the modified law for business insurances came into effect as regards contracts effected on or after 12 August 2016. The new laws are described in §§4 and 5, below, but an account of the traditional law is retained in §§2 and 3 as they will be relevant for some time to come, for example, to consumer life insurance contracts taken out before 6 April 2013 and to business contracts taken out before 12 August 2016 or those effected after that date when the provisions of the 2015 Act are excluded by the terms of the contract. In addition, it is necessary to consider warranties and conditions in insurance law, since these can operate to impose obligations as to the description of the risk on the insured.

§2. Misrepresentation under the Common Law and the Marine Insurance Act 1906

98. Misrepresentation has in general the same meaning and application as for all contracts, and an insurer can avoid the contract if it was induced to enter into it by a material misstatement of fact made by the insured.[301] Materiality has the same meaning

301. Although the codification in marine insurance law in s. 20 of the Marine Insurance Act 1906 does not include the requirement of inducement, the House of Lords confirmed that it is to be implied: *Pan Atlantic Insurance Co. Ltd. v. Pine Top Insurance Co. Ltd.* [1994] 3 All ER 581.

as it bears for non-disclosure and is considered below. In practice, misrepresentation by itself is rarely used by insurers as a defence because the wide scope of the duty of disclosure of material facts incorporates misrepresentations, and an incorrect statement made by an insured has generally been regarded as a non-disclosure rather than, or at least as well as, a misrepresentation.

If a statement by the insured is made to the best of his knowledge and belief, which is commonly the case in respect of the statements on modern proposal forms, then the only obligation of the insured is to give an honest answer and it does not matter whether or not he had reasonable grounds for his belief. Such a misstatement is therefore actionable as a misrepresentation only if made fraudulently.[302]

§3. Non-disclosure under the Common Law and the Marine Insurance Act 1906

99. The general nature of the insurance contract as a contract *uberrimae fidei* has been explained earlier.[303] Its most important consequence in practice is a duty of disclosure, which can be expressed in the following basic way. A proposer for insurance is under a duty to disclose, prior to the conclusion of the contract,[304] all material facts within his knowledge; failure to do so, whether innocent or negligent, renders the contract voidable at the option of the insurer.[305] The right to avoid must be exercised within a reasonable time of discovery of the facts; failure to do so will bar the right to avoid. If the insurer does avoid the contract, it is treated as avoided *ab initio*, that is, it is deemed never to have existed.[306]

100. The duty to disclose applies only to questions of fact and not matters of opinion. The distinction between facts and opinions is not always an easy one as is revealed particularly in life insurance cases where a proposer may very well not know the significance of matters affecting his health. Thus in *Joel v. Law Union & Crown Insurance Co*,[307] a statement by the proposer as to her state of health was regarded as a matter of opinion not fact and not actionable. In contrast, in *Godfrey v. Britannic Assurance Co. Ltd.*,[308] a proposer who failed to disclose a visit to a specialist was held to have been guilty of a material non-disclosure even though he did not know that there was anything seriously wrong with him. The visit by itself was material. The

302. *Economides v. Commercial Union Assurance plc* [1997] 3 All E.R. 636.
303. *See* para. 65.
304. The same duty arises upon renewal of non-life insurance contracts, which typically run for one year only. *See* especially *Lambert v. Co-operative Insurance Society* [1975] 2 Lloyd's Rep. 485.
305. The duty of disclosure arises quite independently of the proposal form and any questions or statements thereon, although, as will be seen, the proposal form may have an effect on the scope of the duty.
306. Section 18 of the Marine Insurance Act 1906 codified the law for marine insurance, but is also regarded as setting out the basic position as regards all contracts of insurance.
307. [1908] 2 KB 863.
308. [1963] 2 Lloyd's Rep. 515.

insured is bound to disclose only material facts that he knows or is deemed to know.[309] In *Joel v. Law Union & Crown Insurance Co.*, another issue was whether the proposer was bound to disclose the fact that she had suffered from acute depression, it being accepted that she was unaware of the fact. It was held that she was not bound to disclose this. However, it is long-established that it is quite irrelevant that the proposer does not know that he is under a duty to disclose material facts or that he honestly does not believe a fact to be material; innocent non-disclosure will entitle the insurer to avoid the policy.

101. The insurer cannot complain of the non-disclosure:

(1) of facts which he knows or is deemed to know, for example, matters of public knowledge or general business usage;
(2) of facts which diminish the risk; or
(3) of facts of which he waives knowledge.

Deemed knowledge is most likely where an agent of the insurer, acting within his authority, knows of a fact but fails to pass on his knowledge.[310] The partial disclosure of facts relating to a particular matter by the insured will put the insurer on enquiry so that the latter cannot complain of the non-disclosure of the full facts relating to that matter if he fails to enquire further. Although as a general rule the completion of a proposal form does not relieve the proposer of his duty of disclosure,[311] waiver will arise if questions expressly asked of a proposer limit the scope of the relevant information,[312] if the insurers' statements on a proposal form can be read as dispensing with the disclosure of information outside the questions expressly asked[313] or if the insured leaves blanks on the proposal form which the insurer does not challenge.[314]

102. The onus of proving that non-disclosed facts are material lies on the insurer. Of crucial importance is the matter of the test to be applied to determine whether or not a fact is material.[315] A fact is material if it would influence the judgment of a prudent or reasonable insurer in deciding whether or not to accept the risk or what premium

309. The disclosure of what an insured is deemed to know (constructive knowledge) is limited to commercial insurances, in which an insured is bound to disclose what he ought to know in the ordinary course of his business: *Simner v. New India Assurance Co* [1995] LRLR 240, *PCW Syndicates v. PCW Reinsurers* [1996] 1 Lloyd's Rep. 241.

310. As for example in *Woolcott v. Excess Insurance Co. Ltd.* [1979] 2 Lloyd's Rep. 210 where the agent's knowledge of the proposer's criminal history was imputed to the insurer.

311. *Glicksman v. Lancashire & General Assurance Society* [1927] AC 139; *Schoolman v. Hall* [1951] 1 Lloyd's Rep. 139.

312. For example, by asking only of facts within a limited time. *See Doheny v. New India Assurance Co. Ltd* [2004] EWCA Civ 1705, [2005] Lloyd's Rep. IR 251, especially at [14] to [20] and [37].

313. As in *Hair v. Prudential Assurance Co. Ltd.* [1983] 2 Lloyd's Rep. 667.

314. This will not be so, however, if the leaving of the blank raises the obvious inference of an incorrect negative answer (*Roberts v. Avon Insurance Company* [1956] 2 Lloyd's Rep. 240.

315. This is a matter of law, although its application to any particular circumstance is a question of fact. The courts will generally listen to evidence of insurers as to materiality, although this does not bind them.

to charge.[316] In *Container Transport International Inc. v. Oceanus Mutual Underwriting Association (Bermuda) Ltd.*,[317] it was held that the proper interpretation of this test did not require that it had to be shown that such an insurer would have acted differently if he had known the fact, for example, by charging a higher premium or refusing the risk, but merely that he would have wanted to know of the fact when making his decision; the word 'judgment' was construed as meaning 'the formation of an opinion' not as 'the final decision'. Subsequently, the House of Lords, in *Pan Atlantic Insurance Co. Ltd. v. Pine Top Insurance Co. Ltd.,* [318] approved this interpretation.

At the same time, recognizing that this test of materiality places a very heavy burden on the insured, the House of Lords held that there is an additional requirement that the insurer, in order to avoid the contract, must prove that he was induced by the non-disclosure to enter into it. This is perhaps better expressed as the requirement that the non-disclosure was an effective cause of the insurer entering into the contract, although it does not need to have been the sole cause.[319] The insurer must show that had he known the non-disclosed fact, he would not have concluded the contract on the same terms or at all, because if he would have made the same contract, the non-disclosure cannot have made any difference.[320] One way of doing this is to show that disclosure of the relevant fact would have led the insurer to ask further questions, which, if answered correctly, would have led him to impose different terms.[321] If a fact is obviously material,[322] the court may be justified in inferring that the insurers were induced even where they do not give evidence and thus to this extent they can benefit from a presumption of inducement.[323] This will normally be the situation when other insurers' evidence as to materiality has been accepted.[324]

103. It is appropriate to give examples of what are material facts even though, strictly speaking, what is material is a question of fact to be decided in every case. It

---

316. *Lambert v. Co-operative Insurance Society, supra*, holding that s. 18(2) of the Marine Insurance Act 1906, which lays down this test, was generally applicable. *See also Highlands Insurance Co. v. Continental Insurance Co.* [1987] 1 Lloyd's Rep. 109.
317. [1984] 1 Lloyd's Rep. 476.
318. [1994] 3 All ER 581.
319. *St Paul Fire & Marine Insurance Co (UK) Ltd v. McDonnell Dowell Constructors Ltd* [1995] 2 Lloyd's Rep. 116; *Assicurazioni Generali SpA v. Arab Insurance Group* [2002] EWCA Civ 1642, [2003] 1 W.L.R. 577 at [59], [87].
320. *See* especially *Assicurazioni Generali SpA v. Arab Insurance Group, supra* ; *Drake Insurance plc v. Provident Insurance plc* [2003] EWCA Civ 1834, [2004] Lloyd's Rep. IR 277.
321. *International Management Group v. Simmonds* [2004] 2 Lloyd's Rep. IR 247. In another case it was held that a liability insurer had been induced by the non-disclosure of a claim for USD $5 million that had been made against the insured because the premium would have been raised, even if the precise amount of the increase could not be shown: *New Hampshire Insurance Co. v. Oil Refineries Ltd* [2003] Lloyd's Rep. IR 386.
322. *See* below for examples of facts that have normally been regarded as material.
323. *See St Paul Fire & Marine Insurance Co (UK) Ltd v. McDonnell Dowell Constructors Ltd, Assicurazioni Generali SpA v. Arab Insurance Group, supra* and *Bate v. Aviva Insurance UK Ltd* [2013] EWHC 1687 (Comm), upheld [2014] EWCA Civ 334.
324. *See* , e.g., *Marc Rich & Co AG v. Portman* [1996] 1 Lloyd's Rep. 430, *Aneco Reinsurance Underwriting Ltd v. Johnson & Higgins* [1998] 1 Lloyd's Rep. 565, *Insurance Corporation of the Channel Islands v. Royal Hotel Ltd* [1998] Lloyd's Rep. IR 151, *International Management Group v. Simmonds, supra* and *Toomey v. Banco Vitalicio Espana* [2004] Lloyd's Rep. IR 354.

is conventional to describe material facts as affecting either the 'physical hazard', for example, the character of insured property, or the 'moral hazard'. Because most of the former have long been the subject to questions expressly asked of a proposer, and are thereby presumed to be material, most of the recent case law has been concerned with moral hazard issues and it is logical to concentrate on these. It is clearly a material fact that the proposer has been refused similar insurance by another insurer. This was even so in a case where two partners made the proposal for burglary insurance and the previous refusal, made for unknown reasons, was only of a proposal by one of them when he traded on his own.[325] It may be a material fact that the proposer has been declined insurance of a different kind,[326] although it is likely that such a refusal will be regarded as material only if it relates in some way to the insured's honesty.[327]

A line of case law reveals that outstanding examples of facts relating to the moral hazard are many types of criminal conviction and allegations of criminality. In *Schoolman v. Hall*,[328] it was held that convictions relating to offences of dishonesty fifteen years before a proposal for jewellery insurance were material.[329] In *Regina Fur Company v. Bossom*,[330] a conviction more than twenty years previously was held material to a proposal for all risks insurance on furs. It has been decided more recently that a conviction for robbery was material to a proposal for a standard fire insurance policy on a house.[331] Although judicial opinion has been divided as to whether a proposer must disclose the fact of arrest where he was innocent, the prevailing view is that allegations of serious criminal conduct and serious criminal charges should be disclosed, even if they prove to be baseless.[332] However, it must be noted that the duty of disclosure in respect of criminal convictions may be affected by the provisions of the Rehabilitation of Offenders Act 1974. Under this Act, some convictions are, after certain periods, treated as spent and deemed never to have existed. By section 4(3), a contract of insurance cannot be avoided for failure to disclose a spent conviction.[333]

Proven dishonesty, even in the absence of a criminal conviction, may be a material fact. In *Insurance Corporation of the Channel Islands v. Royal Hotel Ltd*,[334] a director of the insured, who was also its company secretary, had prepared false invoices in

325. *Glicksman v. Lancashire & General Assurance Company Ltd.* [1927] AC 139.
326. In *Locker & Wolf Ltd. v. Western Australian Insurance Company* [1936] 1 KB 408, a previous refusal of motor insurance was held to be a material fact requiring to be disclosed to a fire insurer.
327. *Ewer v. National Employers' Mutual & General Insurance Association* [1937] 2 All ER 193.
328. [1951] 1 Lloyd's Rep. 139.
329. It was irrelevant the information expressly solicited by the insurer on the proposal form did not cover such matters and also referred only to events within the previous five years.
330. [1957] 2 Lloyd's Rep. 466. *See also Roselodge Ltd. v. Castle* [1966] 2 Lloyd's Rep. 113.
331. *Woolcott v. Sun Alliance & London Insurance Ltd.* [1978] 1 All ER 1253.
332. *See* especially *Brotherton v. Aseguradora Colseguros SA* [2003] EWCA Civ 705, [2003] Lloyd's Rep. IR 758; *North Star Shipping Ltd v. Sphere Drake Insurance plc* [2006] EWCA Civ 378, [2006] Lloyd's Rep. IR 519.
333. For more detail on the Act, *see* Birds, *Modern Insurance Law*, para. 7.11.3.
334. [1998] Lloyd's Rep. IR 151. *See also Gate v. Sun Alliance Insurance Ltd* [1995] LRLR 385, *Markel International Insurance Co. v. La Republica Cia Argentina de Seguros* [2004] EWHC 1826 (Comm), [2005] Lloyd's Rep. IR 90 and *Sharon's Bakery (Europe) Ltd v. Axa Insurance plc* [2011] EWHC 210 (Comm), [2012] Lloyd's Rep. IR 164.

order to give the insured's bankers a more favourable impression of its profitability. Although these had not been used by the time of the insurance proposal, and no criminal offence had actually been committed, it was held that this kind of dishonesty was material.

104. The law, except in cases of fraud, will uphold clauses that exclude the remedies for misrepresentation or exclude or limit the duty of disclosure or the remedies for breach.[335] Insurers will waive the right to avoid for non-disclosure or misrepresentation if they elect to continue with the contract and so affirm it.[336] They must have actual, not constructive, knowledge of the non-disclosed fact and know that they have the right to avoid. They have a reasonable time for decision, and there must be an unequivocal communication to the insured by words or conduct that they have made an informed choice to affirm. An unequivocal communication depends on how a reasonable person in the position of the insured would interpret the insurer's word or conduct. Delay by itself is not sufficient but will count if the insured is prejudiced by it or it is explicable only on the basis that the insurers are affirming the contract. Otherwise any kind of conduct by the insurers that leads the insured reasonably to believe that the insurers intend to continue to insure him is sufficient. This can include failing to avoid and return the premium while refusing to pay a claim, making an interim payment, accepting a premium and giving instructions to the insured concerning the subject matter of the insurance.

§4. Restrictions on Insurer's Rights and Reform for Consumers

105. The duty of disclosure was developed in the early days of insurance,[337] when communications were poor, the insured was obviously in a far superior position to know of the risks involved than the insurer, and it was clearly just to place the onus on him. The justice of the doctrine's broad application in modern times to all classes of insurance has been questioned by many commentators, judges and others and recommendations for reform were made by official law reform agencies.[338] As a result the majority of insurers agreed in respect of consumer insurances, in the *Statements of Insurance Practice*, to rely upon a non-disclosure only when a policyholder could reasonably be expected to have disclosed the fact in question. This was in effect a non-legislative implementation of the 1980 proposals of the Law Commission.

In 2005, the *Statement of General Insurance Practice* was withdrawn when the FSA promulgated the ICOB, now replaced by the ICOBS.[339] ICOBS 8.1.1 provides that an insurer must not unreasonably reject a claim made by a customer; and 8.1.2

335. *HIH Casualty & General Insurance Ltd v. Chase Manhattan Bank* [2003] UKHL 6, [2003] Lloyd's Rep. IR 230.
336. *Insurance Corporation of the Channel Islands v. Royal Hotel Ltd* [1998] 1 Lloyd's Rep. IR 151; *Spriggs v. Wessington Court School Ltd* [2004] EWHC 1432 (QB), [2005] Lloyd's Rep. IR 474.
337. Notably in the case of *Carter v. Boehm* (1776) 3 Burr 1905.
338. *See* especially the Fifth Report of the Law Reform Committee, 1957, Cmnd 62 and the Law Commission's Report No. 104, 1980, Cmnd 8064.
339. *See* para. 28.

states that rejection is unreasonable, except where there is evidence of fraud, if, as regards contracts entered into or varied on or before 5 April 2013, it is for non-disclosure of a fact material to the risk which the policyholder could not reasonably be expected to have disclosed or non-negligent misrepresentation of a fact material to the risk. This applies to non-life insurance and a limited range of life insurance.[340] In effect insurers were no longer allowed, as regards consumers, to rely on an innocent non-disclosure or misrepresentation to avoid a claim on pain of being subject to action taken by the FSA for breach of the rules and potentially to an action for breach of statutory duty under section 138D of the Financial Services and Markets Act 2000. It should be noted that this rule does not remove the insurer's right to avoid the contract. As far as contracts entered into or varied after 5 April 2013 are concerned, ICOBS 8.1.1 now reflects the statutory reforms in the 2012 Act discussed below.

A further qualification of the law in practice arose from decisions made by the Insurance Ombudsman, now followed by the FOS. In appropriate cases, the Ombudsman applied a principle of proportionality rather than allowing the insurer to repudiate all liability. By this, the insurer has to pay the proportion of a claim that the premium actually paid bears to the premium that would have been charged if the insurer had known the truth.

Another development was the suggestion, in one or two cases, that an insurer's right to avoid for non-disclosure might be restricted when the insurer failed to act in good faith. This reflects more general developments regarding the doctrine of good faith in insurance law, in respect of which the law is clearly not yet settled, and it has to be admitted that it is as yet not at all clear that there does exist such a restriction.[341]

The Law Commissions' project on insurance contract law[342] resulted in actual law reform so far as consumer insureds are concerned.[343] In December 2009, they produced a Report on *Consumer Insurance Law: Pre-Contract Disclosure and Misrepresentation*.[344] In substance this recommended legislative enactment of the rules in ICOBS together with the practice of the Ombudsman. The draft Bill in the Report was enacted more or less unchanged as the Consumer Insurance (Disclosure and Representations) Act 2012.

106. This Act only applies to contracts entered into or renewed after the date of commencement, which was 6 April 2013, so this new law did not apply until April 2014 to some contracts, that is ordinary indemnity contracts of house or motor insurance and the like taken out or renewed before the date of commencement, and will never apply to most life insurance contracts entered into before that date.

340. *See* para. 28, *supra* .

341. Compare in particular two conflicting Court of Appeal decisions. In the first, *Brotherton v. Aseguradora Colseguros SA (No. 2)* [2003] EWCA Civ 705, [2003] Lloyd's Rep. IR 758, the court expressly refused to allow such a restriction. In contrast, in *Drake Insurance plc v. Provident Insurance plc* [2003] EWCA Civ 1834, [2004] Lloyd's Rep. IR 277, a differently constituted court took the view, although strictly *obiter*, that an insurer's right could be disallowed in such circumstances.

342. *See* para. 26.

343. There is more modest reform for commercial insurances in the Insurance Act 2015.

344. Law Com. No. 319, Scot Law Com. No. 219, CM. 7758.

The Act effectively enacts the approach that the FSA and the FOS took. A 'consumer' for this purpose means an individual contracting 'wholly or mainly for purposes unrelated to the individual's trade, business or profession'. There may be borderline cases, for example, someone taking out a motor policy that covers business as well as private use or a household policy taken out by someone who runs their business from home.

Section 2 contains the first key point of the Act. It abolishes the pure duty of disclosure and the application of sections 18–20 of the Marine Insurance Act 1906 as far as consumer contracts are concerned. In this context there is longer a concept of a 'material circumstance' or a 'material fact'. Instead, the Act imposes a duty on a consumer to take reasonable care not to make a misrepresentation to the insurer, which includes a failure to comply with the insurer's request to confirm or amend previously given information. So in essence, it is only misstatements on a proposal form or in answer to questions posed on the telephone or electronically that are actionable in the situation of an original proposal for insurance. The 'failure to comply' is aimed particularly at the situation on renewal, for example, if the insurer chooses to resend a proposal form to the insured and ask if any of the information thereon has changed. It remains to be seen whether this leads to lengthier proposal forms than have been common in some situations.

Under section 3, reasonable care is judged by the standard of a reasonable consumer in the light of all the relevant circumstances, namely an objective test not whatever might be the opinion of the actual consumer proposer, the actual insurer or a reasonable insurer. The section gives examples of what the 'relevant circumstances' might be: (a) the type of policy in question and its target market; (b) any relevant explanatory material or publicity produced or authorized by the insurer; (c) how clear and how specific the insurer's questions were; (d) on renewal or variation, how clearly the insurer communicated the importance of answering questions or the possible consequences of failure to answer; and (e) whether or not an agent was acting for the consumer. In addition, account must be taken of any particular characteristics or circumstances of the actual consumer that the insurer knows or ought to know. A dishonest misrepresentation will always be regarded as made without reasonable care.

107. Remedies are covered by sections 4 and 5 and Schedule 1, and there is a remedy for breach of the duty to take reasonable care only if a misrepresentation was a 'qualifying misrepresentation'. The definition of this does not encompass innocent misrepresentation so that, even if such a misrepresentation could be regarded as breaching the duty, the insurer has no remedy for breach. This is another of the most notable differences from the law described earlier.

To be a 'qualifying misrepresentation', the insurer must have been induced to enter into the contract or a variation of the contract or do so on different terms and be either (a) deliberate or reckless or (b) careless. A deliberate or reckless misrepresentation is where the consumer both knew that or did not care whether the misrepresentation was untrue or misleading and knew that or did not care whether the subject matter relevant to the insurer. In such a case, the insurer can avoid the contract, refuse any claim and retain the premium unless that would be unfair to the consumer.

As regards a careless misrepresentation, the insurer can avoid the contract and reject any claims if it would not have entered into contract at all. Otherwise, if the insurer would have entered into the contract on different terms (except as regards the amount of premium), the contract is to be treated as if entered into on those terms. So, if, for example, the insurer would have imposed a particular term, say regarding security precautions had the insured not misrepresented that the current precautions were not working properly, a claim for loss which would not have been covered had that term been included can be rejected. If a higher premium would have been charged, then the insurer pays the proportion of claim that premium actually paid bears to the higher premium that would have been charged. In both these instances, other than in respect of a life insurance contract, the insurer may terminate the contract.

108. Section 7 of the Act contains a fairly complex provision concerning group insurance to ensure that where a group policy effected for benefit of one or more consumers, and a consumer provides information to the insurer (directly or indirectly), the scheme of the Act applies and a breach by one consumer does not affect the contract so far as other consumer beneficiaries are concerned. The insurer here may a have remedy against the policyholder.

There is a second special provision, section 8, concerning insurance on life of another. It assumes that the life insured not a party to insurance contract. Here, information provided by the life insured is treated as if provided by the person who is the party to the contract and it will be the life insured's knowledge, etc. that is relevant for determining whether there is a breach of duty and the type of breach.

109. Many consumer insurance contracts are effected through an intermediary, whether that be a traditional agent or broker or through an online agent. As explained in Part VII, it is not always easy to know whether an agent is in law agent of the insured or of the insurer, something that has caused particular problems over the years. Rather than laying down binding rules, the Act provides, in section 9 and Schedule 1, rules for the purposes of the Act only.

An agent is taken to be the insurer's agent in three situations: (a) when they do something in their capacity as an appointed representative of the insurer; (b) when they collect information from the consumer having been expressly authorized to do so by the insurer; and (c) when they enter into the contract as the insurer's agent having been given express authority to do so.

Otherwise it is presumed that an intermediary is acting as the insured's agent unless, in the light of all the relevant circumstances, the contrary appears. The Act then lists factors that may be relevant to determine this. Those tending to confirm that an intermediary is acting for the consumer are where: (a) the agent undertakes to give impartial advice to the consumer; (b) the agent undertakes to conduct a fair analysis of the market; and (c) the consumer pays the agent a fee. Those tending to confirm the contrary are where: (a) the agent places insurance with only a small proportion of the insurers who provide the relevant type of insurance; (b) the insurer provides the relevant insurance through only a limited number of agents; (c) the insurer permits agent to use the insurer's name in providing the agent's services; (d) the insurance in question is marketed under the name of the agent; and (e) the insurer asks the agent to solicit the customer's custom.

§5. Modification of the Law for Business Insurance Contracts

110. As indicated earlier, the Insurance Act 2015 modifies the law as far as business insurance contracts are concerned. These are defined in section 1 by reference to a 'non-consumer insurance contract'. Thus anything that does not fall within the definition in the 2012 Act is governed by the 2015 Act. The result is that there is no distinction in the law that depends on the size of a business and that insurance effected by bodies such as charities is classed as business insurance. A business insurance contract will be able to exclude the reforms, as described below, but in practice this seems only a relevant possibility in this context so far as the modification of the traditional remedy of avoidance is concerned.

111. Part 2 rewrites, rather than makes a general reform of, the duty of disclosure of and the duty not to misrepresent material facts as encapsulated in the Marine Insurance Act 1906, sections 18–20; these provisions were repealed when the 2015 Act came into in force. It replaces the previous law by a duty of fair presentation (section 3). The duty of fair presentation is effectively a modern rewriting of the previous law, reflecting the way in which it has been described in recent case law. Section 3(1) requires the insured to make a fair presentation of the risk to the insurer before the contract is entered into (or before it is varied – *see* section 2(2)). First, this imposes a duty to disclose every material circumstance which the insured knows or ought to know or disclosure that gives the insurer sufficient information to put a prudent insurer on notice of the need to make further enquiries (section 2(3)(a) and (4), subject to the exceptions in subsection (5), which mirror the previous law and include situations where the insurer knows or ought to know or is presumed to know a circumstance). The disclosure must be in a manner that would be reasonably clear and accessible to a prudent insurer (section 2(3)(b)). Section 7(3) defines what is a material circumstance in words that are effectively the same as those in the previous law, as contained in sections 18(2) and 20(2) of the 1906 Act. There are examples in section 7(4). Second, a fair presentation is one in which every material representation of fact is substantially correct and every material representation as to a matter of expectation or belief is made in good faith (section 2(3)(c)). It is clear that much of the previous case law, as summarized in §3 above, will continue to be relevant.

112. However, most importantly, the remedy for a failure to disclose or a misrepresentation is amended in a similar way to that found in the 2012 Act (section 8 and Schedule 1), so that an insurer can only avoid the contract in the case of a deliberate or reckless breach or where it can show that it would not have entered into the contract at all had it known the truth. In all other cases, where the breach of the duty is negligent or innocent, the insured will have the right to a proportion of a claim in the same way as described in paragraph 107, except that for business insurance there will remain a remedy for an innocent non-disclosure or misrepresentation.

113. It is possible for an insurer to exclude the application of Part 2 of the 2015 Act. Exclusion of the duty of fair presentation is highly unlikely, given that it simply rewrites the previous law. More likely is exclusion of the consequences of a breach of the duty, effectively retaining the right of avoidance. Any such exclusion will have to satisfy the requirements of sections 16 and 17 of the 2015 Act, which are described in more detail below.[345]

114. What either party knows or ought to know or is presumed to know has long been an important aspect of this part of insurance law that has not always perhaps been entirely clear. Rather than leaving this to the general law, especially the law of agency, sections 4 and 5, dealing respectively with the knowledge of the insured and the knowledge of the insurer, make detailed provision for what is sometimes a difficult issue.

An individual insured knows only what he actually knows or what any individuals responsible for the insured's insurance know. An insured who is not an individual, such as a company, knows only what is known to any individuals who are part of the insured's senior management or responsible for the insured's insurance. Individuals responsible for the insured's insurance may be employees of the insured or their agent, for example, a broker. In the latter case, knowledge does not extend to confidential information acquired through a business relationship with a person who is not connected with the contract of insurance; a person connected is the insured and any other persons covered by the contract.

An insurer knows something only it is known to one or more of the individuals who participate on behalf of the insurer in the decision whether to take the risk and if so on what terms. Thus the fact that, for example, an insured's claims record is known to the claims department of the insurer does not mean that it is known to the underwriting department. The latter may be deemed to know as it is further provided that an insurer ought to know something if an employee or agents knows it and ought reasonably to have passed it on to someone deciding on the risk or the insurer hold the information and it is readily available to someone deciding on the risk. An insurer is presumed to know things that are common knowledge and things which an insurer offering insurance of the class in question to insureds in the field of activity in question would reasonably be expected to know in the ordinary course of business.

§6. Disclosure During Contract

115. While a proposer for business insurance is under a duty to disclose material facts or make a fair presentation of the risk before an insurance contract is concluded, and this includes before every renewal,[346] neither he nor a consumer insured is in contrast, under the general law, bound to disclose at the time material facts that happen during the period of the insurance contract.[347] Commonly, however, certain insurance policies, particularly on property, contain a clause requiring such disclosures, and providing that if any fact increasing the risk is not notified to the insurer, the policy will be voidable. They may also contain clauses governing specific facts that may

345. *See* para. 131.
346. *See* Ch. 7, below as regards renewal of policies.
347. *Pim v. Reid* (1843) 6 M & G 1; *Kausar v. Eagle Star Insurance Co. Ltd.* [1997] C.L.C. 129.

materially increase the risk.[348] In law such clauses will be warranties, the legal nature of which is examined below. Under an 'increase of risk' clause, the insured must disclose all matters, but only those matters, which permanently affect the risk run by the insurer. For example, a change to the use of more dangerous machinery in a factory should be disclosed, but not the fact that workmen use blowlamps for a short period while effecting plumbing repairs.[349]

§7. Warranties and Conditions

I. General Remarks

116. The obligations of the insured, in terms of both aspects of description of the risk and obligations arising on the occurrence of an insured event, will arise by virtue of terms in the policy that will be either warranties or conditions. Terms may arise from the questions and answers or the declarations on a proposal form, as invariably this is expressly incorporated into the subsequently issued policy, or they may simply be contained in the policy document itself. Due to the peculiar history of the insurance contract, insurance law has developed its own principles in the area of warranties and conditions, quite different in many respects from those applying in general contract law. In particular, a warranty is traditionally a more fundamental term in insurance than a condition, whereas in all other contracts the converse is the case, although, as will be explained below, there has been reform of the law of warranties under the Insurance Act 2015. Another important point to note is that often these terms are not actually described as being what in law they in fact are. It may therefore not be easy to spot at first sight what is a warranty or a condition and quite difficult questions of construction may be involved.

348. Though these will be strictly construed. For example, in *Exchange Theatre Ltd. v. Iron Trades Mutual Insurance Co. Ltd.* [1984] 1 Lloyd's Rep. 149, a clause in a fire policy requiring disclosure of alterations in the building was not held applicable to any alteration of the contents even though the latter increased the risk. Compare *Ansari v. New India Assurance Ltd.* [2009] EWCA Civ 93, [2009] Lloyd's Rep. IR 562, where the insurer was not liable because a clause required 'material changes' to be notified, and this was held applicable to a situation where an automatic sprinkler system in the insured premises has been turned off. An important analogous provision requires notification of unoccupancy of a building for more than a specified period.

349. *See* , e.g., *Shaw v. Robberds* (1837) 6 Ad & l 75, where the insured, who had a fire policy on his granary in which there was a kiln which he used to dry corn, allowed a third party on one occasion to dry bark in the kiln, something much more hazardous and which in fact caused a fire. It was held that the policy could not be avoided for this merely temporary unnotified alteration in business. In *Kausar v. Eagle Star Insurance Co. Ltd., supra* , the insured was not obliged to tell the insurers that threats had been made to damage the insured property. On the other hand, in *Farnham v. Royal Insurance Co.* [1976] 2 Lloyd's Rep. 437, the insured farmer stored metal containers in his barns, a fact known to the insurer, and then allowed welding repair work to be done therein, a fact not told to the insurer. It was held that the insurer could avoid liability for this unnotified increase in risk.

117. Obligations of the insured imposed by warranties and conditions are, where the insured is an individual consumer, potentially subject to control under Part 2 of the Consumer Rights Act 2015.[350] The extent of control depends on what is meant by terms that specify 'the main subject-matter of the contract', as these are not at risk of being unfair provided that they are transparent and prominent. These require that a term is expressed in plain and intelligible language, is legible and is brought to the consumer's attention in such a way that the average consumer would be aware of it. It seems possible that a warranty whose purpose is to control the risk (*see infra*) is within this exception. However, conditions imposing other obligations are subject to being held to be unfair; this is when 'contrary to the requirement of good faith, the term causes a significant imbalance in the parties' rights and obligations arising under the contract, to the detriment of the consumer'.[351] Assessment must take account of the nature of the services and refer, as at the time of the conclusion of the contract, to all circumstances attending the conclusion of the contract and to all the other terms of the contract.[352] Schedule 2 contains an indicative and illustrative list of terms which may be regarded as unfair. Even if the Act does apply to obligations affecting the risk, it does not follow that they can be struck down as unfair. For example, a common requirement on an insured to take reasonable care of insured property[353] may well be quite fair in the circumstances of the contract. What would clearly not survive the Act are conditions which impose unreasonable deadlines on the insured, for example, in giving notice of a loss,[354] and, possibly, terms which give the insurer complete control over the actions of an insured following an insured loss, for example, some of the standard terms in liability insurance policies.[355]

II. Warranties

118. As indicated above, the law of warranties has been reformed by the Insurance Act 2015. However, as this Act did not come into force until 12 August 2016 there will no doubt be situations arising under contracts entered into before that date for some time to come. In addition in a non-consumer contract it will be possible to exclude the relevant provision, as described in paragraph 131 below, and contractually provide for a warranty to have the effect of the general law. For these reasons an explanation of that law remains necessary and continues in the immediately following paragraphs.

Traditionally, a warranty is a term made by or imposed upon the insured describing that a particular state of affairs exists or will exist and thus controlling the risk run by the insurer, such that if it is broken, the insurer will be relieved from liability, regardless of whether or not the breach of warranty by the insured contributed to or caused a loss. In *Bank of Nova Scotia v. Hellenic Mutual War Risks Associates Ltd., The Good Luck*,[356]

350. *See* para. 32.
351. Section 62(4).
352. Regulation 6(1).
353. *See* para. 65.
354. *See* para. 134.
355. *See* para. 241.
356. [1991] 3 All ER 1.

the House of Lords held that on a breach of warranty in a marine policy, the insurer was automatically discharged from liability,[357] applying the literal meaning of the words in section 33(3) of the Marine Insurance Act 1906. The same result has been held to apply to warranties in non-marine policies.[358] The result is that the contract itself may survive the breach, for example, for purposes of the insurer's right to rely upon an arbitration clause, although in practice it does not have to. It is clear that the insurer can waive the breach, that is, ignore it completely, if it chooses.[359] As will be seen below, the decision in *The Good Luck* has been statutorily overturned, although it will be possible in a non-consumer contract to provide for the same result by contract terms.

119. A warranty may be one or both of two kinds. The first is a warranty as to past or present facts, that is that particular facts are true at the date the warranty is made; this type usually arose from a completed proposal form, although that will no longer be possible as described below. In the event of a breach, the insurer was never under any liability. The second is a warranty as to the future: that a stated fact or state of affairs will be true or will continue to be true or complied with. The latter, which is frequently termed a 'promissory warranty', might have arisen as the result of answers to questions on the proposal form (but again that will no longer be possible) or from provisions in the policy itself. If a promissory warranty is broken, the insurer will be discharged from any liability, unless he waives this right, but only from the date of breach; he remains liable for prior losses, if any.

120. The most straightforward way in which warranties were created was by the operation of the proposal form, wherein the questions and answers thereon were made the basis of the contract.[360] However, this device was abolished in consumer insurance contract with effect from 6 April 2013 under section 6 of the Consumer Insurance (Disclosure and Representations) Act 2012 and was abolished in other insurances with effect from 12 August 2016 under section 9 of the Insurance Act 2015. As this latter provision is not one whose operation can be excluded, it is no longer necessary to give any further detail.

---

357. The reason why the point arose was because of an undertaking the insurers had given to the banks who were mortgagees of the insured ships. Under this the insurers had promised to notify the banks if the ships ceased to be insured. They should have done so as soon as they were aware of the insured's breach, because the insurance ceased automatically and was not dependent upon a later decision of the insurers. In the intervening period the banks advanced further loans to the insured, which they would not have done if they had been advised by the insurers, and for this loss the insurers were held liable to compensate the banks.
358. *Hussain v. Brown* [1996] 1 Lloyd's Rep. 627; *Kumar v. AGF Insurance* [1999] Lloyd's Rep. IR 147.
359. *Compare* s. 34(3) of the Marine Insurance Act 1906. Waiver here means waiver arising by estoppel rather than by election: *HIH Casualty & General Insurance v. Axa Corporate Solutions* [2002] EWCA Civ 1253, [2003] Lloyd's Rep. IR 1; *Argo Systems FZE v. Liberty Insurance (Pte)* [2011] EWHC 301 (Comm), [2011] 2 Lloyd's Rep. 61, reversed on the facts ([2011] EWCA Civ 1572).
360. The leading authorities were *Thomson v. Weems* (1884) 9 App Cas 671 (a life insurance case) and *Dawsons Ltd. v. Bonnin* [1922] 2 AC 413. *See* , for a recent example, *Genesis Housing Association Ltd v. Liberty Syndicate Management Ltd* [2013] EWCA Civ 1173.

121. Warranties may be created by the express use of the word 'warranty' or expressions like 'the insured warrants that ... '.[361] Or a particular term in a policy may provide that the insurance will be void or voidable[362] if something does or does not happen or if the insured does or fails to do some specified thing.[363] It may also be the case that an obligation described as a condition precedent to the insurer's liability under the policy creates a warranty.[364]

122. While a warranty must be strictly complied with, in the sense that traditionally any breach enabled the insurer to avoid liability, it may not be immediately clear what is its scope, although there will rarely be problems of interpretation in relation to straightforward questions and answers on the proposal form as to facts existing at the time it was completed. However, promissory warranties can raise difficult questions of construction. The courts operate on the principle that they must be construed reasonably and, if there is any ambiguity, in favour of the insured and against the insurer who drafted them. A useful illustration is the decision in *Provincial Insurance Company Ltd. v. Morgan.*[365] Coal merchants insured a lorry under a standard motor policy. The completed proposal form, containing a basis clause which was effective at the time, included the following: 'State (a) the purpose in full for which the vehicle will be used; and (b) the nature of the goods to be carried. (a) Delivery of coal; (b) Coal.' One day the lorry carried timber as well as coal. The timber and some of the coal had been delivered when the lorry was involved in an accident. The insurers were held liable for the loss. The House of Lords regarded the quoted question and answer as constituting a promissory warranty, there being a clear reference to the future. However, on a reasonable construction, the insured was only warranting that the lorry would carry coal, which was true, not that it would carry exclusively coal.[366]

123. Many policies contain a number of different types of cover and warranties relating to one type may not be in any sense applicable to another or indeed any others. Such a multi-section policy will be regarded, as far as warranties are concerned as in effect consisting of several different insurance contracts, so that a breach wholly unrelated to the type of cover that is the subject of a loss will not discharge the insurer from liability.[367]

124. In certain cases, statements on proposal forms and even terms in a policy purporting to be warranties have been construed not as warranties in the strict sense but rather as clauses or terms descriptive of or delimiting the risk. The effect is that the policy is in force so long as the statement remains true, but is suspended if and for so long as the statement becomes untrue, so that the clause operates rather like an exception to the risk contained in the main body of the policy. In *Farr v. Motor Traders'*

---

361. Even this form of words may not be conclusive; *see* , e.g., cases discussed in para. 124, below.
362. Strictly this usage is inaccurate. The insurer is discharged from liability, as explained *supra* .
363. A common example of a warranty, of a promissory character, created in this manner is the standard clause requiring notification of increases in risk (*see supra*).
364. The matter is not clear from the case law; *see* Birds, *Modern Insurance Law*, 9.4.
365. [1933] AC 240.
366. If the question had referred to 'the only purposes ...', there would have been a breach of warranty once timber was carried and the insurers could have avoided liability. *See also Pratt v. Aigaion Insurance Co. SA* [2008] EWCA Civ 1314, [2009] Lloyd's Rep. IR 225.
367. *Printpak v. AGF Insurance Ltd* [1999] Lloyd's Rep. IR 542.

Mutual Insurance Society Ltd.,[368] on the proposal form containing the usual basis clause for insurance of his taxi cabs, the insured stated that the vehicles would be driven in just one shift per twenty-four hours. In fact one of the cabs was later used twice on one day. It was held that the clause operated to suspend the risk on that day, but as the accident in respect of which the plaintiff was claiming occurred subsequently, he was entitled to recover. This appears to be a benevolent construction, to protect the insured from an unjust result, when the term in question could not be read as a clear promissory warranty. However, similar results have been reached even in cases where the term 'warranted' was used, and most notably in *CTN Cash & Carry Ltd. v. General Accident Fire & Life Assurance Group plc.*,[369] where the device was used to the benefit of the insurers. Following previous losses, on renewal of the insured's general commercial policy, the insurers inserted a term under which the insured 'warranted' that the cash kiosk would be manned at all times when their warehouse was open. This was held to be descriptive of the risk allowing the insurers to repudiate a claim for a robbery that occurred when the term was broken without having to repudiate the whole policy (which the insurers had not done). The only conclusion to be drawn is that it is difficult to predict with certainty exactly which description a court will attach to such a term.[370] However, the reforms of the law of warranties discussed below mean that it will probably no longer be necessary to make the distinction between warranties and these other terms.

125. The harshness of the law of warranties has often been pointed out and previous proposals have been made to reform the law. As well as the abolition of basis clauses in consumer contracts, the ICOBS[371] required a causal connection between the breach and a loss in such contracts before the insurer could refuse to meet a claim. The Law Commissions' recommendations to reform the law of warranties[372] to put this on a proper statutory footing have been enacted in the Insurance Act 2015.

126. As already indicated, the provisions of this Act came into force on 12 August 2016 and apply to contracts entered into or varied after this date. Section 10 abolishes the rule that a breach of warranty automatically discharges the insurer from liability, providing instead that an insurer is not liable in respect of any loss occurring, or attributable to something happening, after a warranty has been breached but before the breach has been remedied, but that it is liable for a loss before the breach or a loss

368. [1920] 3 KB 669.

369. [1989] 1 Lloyd's Rep. 229. *See also De Maurier (Jewels) Ltd v. Bastion Insurance Co.* [1967] 2 Lloyd's Rep. 550.

370. The insured's policy had a large number of sections of which the 'warranty' could be applicable to only two. Therefore to hold that the insurers could have repudiated the whole contract would have been ridiculous. In effect the court reached the same result as in the *Printpak* case (para. 123), but for quite different reasons. A more recent decision in line with the *CTN* case is *Kler Knitwear Ltd v. Lombard General Insurance Co Ltd* [2000] Lloyd's Rep. IR 47, which seems to indicate further a judicial trend to mitigate the harshness of the law of warranties. *See also HIH Casualty & General Insurance Ltd v. New Hampshire Insurance Co* [2001] Lloyd's Rep. IR 596, *GE Frankona Reinsurance Ltd v. CMM Trust No. 1440* [2006] EWHC 429 (Admlty), [2006] Lloyd's Rep. IR 704 and *Sugar Hut Group Ltd v. Great Lakes Reinsurance (UK) plc* [2011] EWHC 2636 (Comm), [2011] Lloyd's Rep. IR 198.

371. Rule 8.1.3.

372. Law Com. No. 353, Scot Law Com. No. 238, CM 8898.

after remedy of the breach. In addition, the insurer will be liable for a loss if, because of a change of circumstances, the warranty ceases to be applicable to the circumstances of the contract, if compliance is rendered unlawful by any subsequent law and if the insurer waives the breach of warranty. A breach is regarded as remedied in two situations. The first is where a warranty requires something to be done or not done, or a condition is to be fulfilled, or something is or is not to be the case and that requirement is not complied with, but the risk to which the warranty relates later becomes essentially the same as that originally contemplated by the parties. The second is in any other case if the insured ceases to be in breach of the warranty.

127. A second reform, in section 11, may also apply to a warranty in the strict sense but applies particularly to other terms, including terms describing or delimiting the risk and certain conditions of the sort described in the following paragraphs. It applies to a term other than a term describing the risk as a whole if compliance with it would tend to reduce the risk of loss or a particular kind, loss at a particular location and/or loss at a particular time. If a loss occurs and the term has not been complied with, the insurer cannot rely on the non-compliance if the insured can show that non-compliance could not have increased the risk of the loss that actually occurred in the circumstances in which it occurred. So if, for example, a warranty or condition in an insurance of a building requires the maintenance of a security system and is not complied with, but the loss is caused by fire and the breach had no connection with the fire, the insurer will be liable.

III. Conditions

128. The description 'condition' in insurance law has conventionally been regarded as covering matters which are not fundamental to the risks covered by a policy, in the way that historically the warranty has been regarded. On this basis, it is clear that to rely upon a breach of condition to repudiate liability for a loss, the insurer must show a causal connection between the breach and the loss[373] and there is authority that compliance with a condition can be dispensed with if it is unnecessary, for example, because the insurer has obtained the relevant information from another source.[374] Conditions in this sense are collateral promises given by the insured,[375] and they are generally found in a list in an insurance policy under the heading 'conditions'. However, this general description may be misleading; some such 'conditions' may on their proper construction be warranties if they provide that on breach the insurer will be discharged from all liability. The essential point about conditions is that at the most a failure by the insured to comply with a condition will entitle the insurer to avoid only a particular liability for a particular causally related loss; the insurer will continue to be liable

373. *W. J. Lane v. Spratt* [1970] 2 QB 480.

374. *Lickiss v. Milestone Motor Policies at Lloyd's* [1966] 2 All ER 972.

375. Policies will also contain 'conditions' of a quite different sort, namely ones which confer rights upon the insurer either confirming or adding to rights given by the general law. Common examples of this sort of condition are rights of cancellation and rights relating to subrogation and contribution.

under the policy for losses where the conditions are complied with.[376] Note also the effect of section 11 of the Insurance Act 2015, discussed above.

129. The effect of a breach of condition depends upon whether or not the policy provides that compliance with it is precedent to the liability of the insurer. If there is no such provision, breach of condition merely confers on the insurer the right to claim such damages as he has suffered by virtue of the breach.[377] If an individual condition provides that it is precedent to the right of the insured to recover or to the liability of the insurer, a failure to comply, however inadvertent, will entitle the insurer to avoid liability. It is more usual, however, to find a general declaration in a policy that all its conditions, so far as the nature of them permits, will be conditions precedent to the liability of the insurer. Such a declaration is effective in respect of those conditions that can be precedent, that is ones that involve promises by the insured.[378] If, however, included within the one condition are several provisions, some of which can and some of which cannot by their nature be conditions precedent, none of the provisions will be regarded as conditions precedent, but merely conditions a breach of which gives the insurer the right to claim damages.[379] Insurers are likely to draft carefully today to avoid this result. Breach of a condition precedent can only be waived by estoppel and not by election.[380]

IV. Onus of Proof

130. In respect of any of the terms reviewed, whether warranties, conditions or anything else, the onus is always on the insurer to prove a breach that would relieve him of liability.[381]

V. Exclusion of the Insurance Act in Non-consumer Contracts

131. As was indicated earlier, certain provisions of the Insurance Act 2015 can be excluded in a non-consumer insurance contract.[382] It seems that it was necessary to provide for this in order that the reforms were not regarded as too controversial and

376. Yet again, the law is not clear as to the categorization of insurance terms.
377. *Friends Provident Life & Pensions Ltd v. Sirius International Insurance* [2005] EWCA Civ 601, [2006] Lloyd's Rep. IR 45. It may not be easy for the insurer to prove the necessary causal link between breach of a mere condition and loss for it to be able to recover more than merely nominal damages: *see Porter v. Zurich Insurance Company* [2009] EWHC 376 (HC). Note, however, that in *Milton Keynes BC v. Nulty* [2011] EWHC 2847 (TCC), a failure to give notice in time in breach of a mere condition in a liability policy was held to have lost the insurers the chance to prove that the insured had not been negligent. They were entitled to deduct 15% from the sum due to the insured.
378. *London Guarantee Company v. Fearnley* (1880) 5 App Cas 911.
379. *Re Bradley and Essex and Suffolk Accident Indemnity Society* [1912] 1 KB 415.
380. *Kosmar Villa Holidays plc v. Trustees of Syndicate 1243* [2008] EWCA Civ 147, [2008] Lloyd's Rep. IR 489.
381. *Bond Air Services Ltd. v. Hill* [1955] 2 QB 417.
382. Special provision is made for exclusions in group insurance in s. 18.

the justification is said to be freedom of contract. Whether this is entirely apposite as regards all non-consumer contracts, particularly where the insured is a small business, may perhaps be open to question, although the transparency requirements described below ought to work to the advantage of such an insured, and only time will tell how far insurers seek to take advantage of this facility. Contracting out is possible with regard to the provisions on non-disclosure and misrepresentation, those on warranties and similar terms, both of which have been examined already, and those concerning fraudulent claims, to be discussed later. As already indicated, as regards non-disclosure and misrepresentation contracting out is likely to be confined to the provisions regarding remedies.

132. An appropriate exclusion clause must satisfy the requirements of section 17. What the Act describes as a 'disadvantageous term' must be clear and unambiguous as to its effect. In addition, the insurer must take sufficient steps to draw it to the insured's attention before the contract is entered into or before any variation of the contract, except where the insured or his agent had actual knowledge of it at that time. In deciding on whether these requirements have been met, a court must take into account the characteristics of insured persons of the kind in question and the circumstances of the transaction.

§8. Payment of Premium

133. The premium, which is the consideration given by the insured in return for the insurer's undertaking to cover the risks insured against,[383] will normally involve the payment of money, although this is not essential and in some cases may involve, for example, a liability to contribute to the funds of the insurer.[384] In the UK, there is no system for prior approval of premium rates. A tax is levied on premiums paid for most types of insurance.[385]

134. There is no general rule that the premium must be paid before the insurer is at risk, although in certain classes of business, especially, life insurance, this is likely to be the result of standard policy terms.[386] As well as payment in cash or by cheque, in practice the insurer is likely to offer the insured some or all of the other modern means of satisfying a contractual payment obligation, such as the bank giro system and the use of a credit card.[387]

383. *Lewis v. Norwich Union Fire Insurance Co.* [1916] AC 509.
384. This will probably be the case where insurance takes a mutual form, e.g., membership of a shipowners' club.
385. *See* Part IX.
386. *See* para. 93.
387. Payments by individuals or partnerships on credit are likely to be subject to the requirements of the Consumer Credit Act 1974 and regulations made thereunder.

§9. Obligations in the Case of Insured Event

135. Assuming that an insured has suffered a loss properly covered under his insurance policy, in order to make a valid claim under the policy he will be required to comply with various stipulations. Very few of these, however, arise as a matter of general law, rather they are imposed by several of the conditions to be found in any standard insurance policy. They will almost invariably be conditions precedent to the insurer's liability to pay for a particular loss, as discussed above.

136. It is likely that every insurance policy contains a condition requiring the insured to give the insurer formal notice of a loss; in the absence of such a condition a court would probably hold that notice was required within a reasonable time. The wording of conditions requiring notice of loss varies, but it can be stated that a basic principle that they will be construed strictly against the insurer who drafts them. For example, a condition requiring notice 'as soon as possible after the loss or accident has come to the knowledge of the insured's representative' was construed as meaning that all the circumstances, including the representative's knowledge of the existence of the policy, should be taken into account.[388] A similar construction would probably be adopted in all insurances which require only that the insured will report a claim and subsequent developments 'as soon as reasonably possible'.[389]

Often in commercial insurances, however, conditions are clearly drafted in a much stricter way, requiring notice within a stated number of days. Here impossibility of compliance will be no excuse. For example, in *Adamson v. Liverpool, London & Globe Insurance Co.*,[390] the insured had a cash-in-transit policy which required notice of any loss 'within fourteen days of its occurrence'. Over a period of two years an employee entrusted with money to buy National Insurance stamps embezzled it. The insured notified his insurer immediately the fraud was discovered, but it was held that they were liable only for the loss that had occurred within the fourteen days of notification.[391]

137. The question whether an insured is under a duty to furnish particulars and provide documentary proof of loss will depend entirely on the terms of the contract. If there is no relevant condition, the insured will simply have to prove his loss in the normal way. The usual condition will place a heavier burden on the insured. The condition may require the insured to give 'full particulars'. This means the best particulars the insured can reasonably give, which must be sufficient to enable the insurer to ascertain the nature, extent and character of the loss.[392] Alternatively or in

388. *Verelst's Administratrix v. Motor Union Insurance Co.* [1925] 2 KB 137.
389. This used to be 'required' in consumer insurances by virtue of the *Statement of General Practice*, but as we have seen (para. 28), this was withdrawn when the Insurance Conduct of Business Rules (now the Insurance Conduct of Business Sourcebook) were made. The Sourcebook does not contain this requirement but it does require that an insurer must not unreasonably reject a claim.
390. [1953] 2 Lloyd's Rep. 355.
391. It may be that the relevant condition requires notice to be given to the insurer's head office; if so, notice given elsewhere, for example to a local agent, will not suffice: *Brook v. Trafalgar Insurance Co.* (1946) 79 LlLR 365.
392. *Mason v. Harvey* (1853) 8 Ex 819.

addition, it may require all such proofs and information with respect to the claim as may reasonably be required by the insurer. What is reasonable will depend upon the circumstances, but would almost certainly include such matters as the details of bank accounts used for the insured's business.[393] A condition as to particulars may be satisfied if the insurer receives the full details from a third party though not from the insured within the specified time.[394] A condition may require the insured, if the insurer denies liability for a loss, to contest this denial by legal proceedings within a stated period.[395]

138. The matters discussed so far will be purely contractual requirements, in other words they apply only in so far as the policy provides. Satisfaction of them will not affect the principle that should a loss be disputed, the burden of proof that a loss falling within the cover provided by the policy occurred remains on the insured.[396]

§10. Fraudulent Claims

139. There is no doubt that basic principles of public policy preclude an insured from recovering in respect of a fraudulent claim, something that an express policy term often reinforces. What was somewhat unclear was whether in general fraud, which also is regarded as a breach of the principle of utmost good faith, gave the insurer the right to avoid the contract from the beginning. Case law had eventually made it clear that they might have the right to repudiate the whole policy for the future, and not just liability for the particular fraudulent claim, but there would be no right to avoid from the beginning.[397] Repudiation for the future would only be allowed if the fraud would have an effect on the insurer's ultimate liability and the gravity of it or its consequences would entitled the insurers to repudiate the contract for breach.[398] With effect from 12 August 2016, the Insurance Act 2015, sections 12 and 13, has put the matter into clear statutory form, although these provisions may be excluded in a non-consumer insurance contract.[399] By section 12, if an insured makes a fraudulent claim, the insurer is not liable to pay the claim, may recover from the insured any sums paid by it in respect of the claim and may by notice to the insured treat the contract as having been terminated with effect from the time of the fraudulent act. If the contract is terminated, the insurer may refuse all liability in respect of a relevant event occurring

393. *Welch v. Royal Exchange Assurance* [1939] 1 KB 294.

394. *Lickiss v. Milestone Motor Policies at Lloyds* [1966] 2 All ER 972. However, the authority of this case is somewhat doubtful; *see Birds' Modern Insurance Law*, 14.7.1.

395. *See Walker v. Pennine Insurance Co.* [1980] 2 Lloyd's Rep. 156.

396. *Watts v. Simmons* (1924) 18 Ll LR 177.

397. *See* in particular *Galloway v. Guardian Royal Exchange (UK) Ltd* [2000] Lloyd's Rep. IR 209, *Manifest Shipping Co Ltd v. Uni-Polaris Co Ltd, The Star Sea* [2001] UKHL 1, [2003] AC 469, *Agapitos v. Agnew, The Aegeon* [2002] EWCA Civ 247, [2003] QB 556, *Axa General Insurance Ltd v. Gottlieb* [2005] EWCA Civ 112, [2005] Lloyd's Rep. IR 369, *Direct Line Insurance plc v. Fox* [2009] EWHC 386 (QB), [2009] 1 All E.R. (Comm) 1017.

398. *K/S Merc-Scandia v. Certain Lloyd's Underwriters, The Mercandian Continent* [2001] EWCA Civ 1275, [2001] 2 Lloyd's Rep. 563. *See also The Aegeon, supra*, which drew a distinction between a fraudulent claim per se and 'fraudulent devices' used in furtherance of a claim. Use of the latter would not entitle the insurer to repudiate the whole contract as opposed to the claim.

399. *See* s. V, above.

after the time of the fraudulent act and need not return any premiums paid under the contract, but the termination does not have retrospective effect and will not invalidate a prior claim. 'Relevant event' is defined as whatever gives rise to the insurer's liability and includes, for example, the occurrence of a loss, the making of a claim or the notification of a potential claim, depending on how the contract is written. Section 13 makes equivalent provision for group insurance contracts, so that an innocent co-insured or beneficiary is not affected by the fraud of another.

The 2015 Act does not define fraud, so the case law meaning will be applicable. A claim is fraudulent if the insured has not in fact suffered a loss or has deliberately caused the loss, puts forward an exaggerated claim with the intention of recovering more than he is entitled to, or uses fraudulent devices to support an otherwise honest claim.[400] If, however, an insured innocently exaggerates a claim or puts forward an exaggerated figure in the belief that insurers always pay less than the amount claimed, this may not constitute a fraudulent claim.[401]

§11. Arbitration Clauses

140. It is usual in insurance policies to find conditions that provide for the settlement of disputes between insurer and insured by arbitration. Such conditions are valid and enforceable so long as they do not attempt ultimately to oust the jurisdiction of the courts.[402] Generally arbitration clauses cover only disputes over the quantum of the insurer's liability, rather than over liability itself.[403] When a dispute supposedly subject to an arbitration clause comes before the court, it will generally stay the proceedings and enforce the clause, but it does have, under section 86 of the Arbitration Act 1996, a discretion to allow the case to proceed in court. The onus is on the party who wants to keep the dispute out of arbitration and in general the only reason that will justify a stay of arbitration is that there are difficult questions of law involved.[404]

---

400. *Central Bank of India v. Guardian Assurance Co. Ltd.* (1936) 54 Ll LR 247; *Orakpo v. Barclays Insurance Services Co. Ltd.* [1994] C.L.C. 373; *Galloway v. Guardian Royal Exchange (UK) Ltd, supra* ; *The Aegeon, supra* ; *Stimson v. AMP General Insurance (NZ) Ltd* [2006] UKPC 30.

401. *Ewer v. National Employers Mutual General Insurance Ass Ltd.* [1937] 2 All ER 193. This authority may be somewhat doubtful, but the idea that mere exaggeration is not fraudulent was accepted in *Danepoint Ltd v. Underwriting Insurance Ltd* [2005] EWHC 2318 (TCC), [2005] Lloyd's Rep. IR 429.

402. *Scott v. Avery* (1856) 5 HLC 810.

403. Because of concern about the use of arbitration in insurance disputes, chiefly because of the lack of publicity involved and the fact that legal aid is not available to insureds appearing before an arbitrator, the majority of insurers have undertaken not to enforce their right to go to arbitration in most cases (*see* Fifth Report of Law Reform Committee, 1957). In some categories of insurance, particularly marine and aviation, arbitration is still widely used as the undertaking did not extend to these.

404. *Clough v. County Livestock Insurance Ass. Ltd.* (1916) 85 LJKB 1185; *Smith v. Pearl Assurance Co.* [1939] 1 All ER 95.

§12. Waiver and Estoppel

141. It is in the context of the claims process that allegations are often likely to be made by insureds that an insurer has lost the right to rely upon a breach of condition by reason of the doctrines of waiver or estoppel; the latter is sometimes called waiver by estoppels as opposed to waiver by election. Waiver and estoppel are in theory distinct pleas,[405] although both may arise on the same facts. Waiver arises where one party to a contract, with knowledge of his rights, that is a breach by the other party, elects by words or by conduct not to rely upon them. Estoppel is where the party in breach relies upon the acts to his detriment in consequence of a representation by the other party, by words or by conduct, that the latter will not act upon the breach.

142. Waiver may be easier to show than estoppel. The insured does not have to show that he relied upon any representation by the insurer. If the latter knows of a breach of condition, but gives some indication that he still regards himself as liable under the policy, he will be deemed to have waived the breach. However, it has been decided that waiver by election does not apply to the breach of a condition that is made precedent to the liability of the insurer.[406] In such situations the insured will have to show reliance on the insurer's representation, but where a condition is not made precedent, waiver by election might still be available. In *Lickiss v. Milestone Motor Policies at Lloyds*,[407] a condition precedent in the insured's motor policy required that notice of any intended prosecution relating to any accident be forwarded to the insurer immediately on receipt. The insured received a notice of prosecution, which he never sent on. However, before the date of the prosecution the insurer received full details from the police and wrote to the insured referring to this and indicating that they wished to arrange his defence. It was held that they could not rely upon the insured's breach of condition, as their letter clearly implied that they were not going to do so and they had thus waived their rights. Similarly, in *Yorkshire Insurance Company v. Craine*,[408] the insured failed to comply with a condition in his fire policy requiring delivery of particulars of the loss. Knowing this, the insurer continued to exercise their right under another condition to remain in possession of the insured property. It was held that they were thereby precluded from relying upon the breach. An insurer must consciously elect not to rely upon a breach of condition. Mere delay in deciding will not amount to waiver. In *Allen v. Robles*,[409] the insured informed his motor insurer of a claim against him two months after an accident whereas the condition in his policy required notification within five days. The insurer did not deny liability for several months but

405. *See* the judgment of Lord Goff in the non-insurance case of *Motor Oil Hellas (Corinth) Refineries SA v. Shipping Corporation of India, The Kanchenjunga* [1990] 1 Lloyd's Rep. 391.
406. *Kosmar Villa Holidays plc v. Trustees of Syndicate 1243* [2008] EWCA Civ 489, [2008] Lloyd's Rep. IR 489. As to the distinction between mere conditions and conditions precedent, *see* para. 129, *supra* .
407. [1966] 2 All ER 972.
408. [1922] 2 AC 541.
409. [1969] 1 WLR 1193.

did nothing to indicate that they accepted liability. It was held that they could rely upon the breach of condition.[410]

410. The court did accept that a lapse of time could constitute waiver provided that there were other factors involved, e.g., if the rights of third parties were involved, or if the delay was so long that it could not reasonably be said that the insurer had declined to accept liability.

Chapter 5. Obligations of the Insurer

143. As described earlier,[411] insurance contracts other than life insurance are contracts of indemnity.[412] The most important obligation of the insurer under such a contract is to indemnify the insured when a loss is suffered. This may be by the payment of money or by some form of reinstatement. In addition, an insurer who pays a claim unjustifiably late will be liable to pay damages to the insured under section 13A of the Insurance Act 2016, which imposes a statutory duty to satisfy a claim within a reasonable time.[413] Section 13A was inserted into the Insurance Act by the Enterprise Act 2016 and came into force on 4 May 2017. The duty to pay within a reasonable time can be excluded in a non-consumer insurance contract, but only in respect of a breach that is not reckless or deliberate (*see* section 16A). The other important consequences of the principle of indemnity, namely subrogation and contribution, are also examined in this chapter, although strictly they are not obligations cast on the insurer.

§1. The Measurement of Loss

144. An overriding point is that the insurer can never be liable to pay more than the maximum, if any, expressly stated in the policy (the sum insured).[414] In practice, all property insurances and virtually all liability insurances will have such a maximum.[415] In practice, the only problems in determining the amount of the insurer's liability will arise in respect of insurances on property. Liability insurance causes no real difficulties, the amount of loss being the amount of the insured's liability, subject to any excess[416]

411. *See* para. 55.
412. For this purpose, personal accident contracts are treated like life contracts as non-indemnity, even though they may have significant 'indemnity' elements: *Theobald v. Railway Passengers' Assurance Co.* (1854) 10 Exch 45. There is no decided case law on health insurance policies, but these would almost certainly be characterized as contracts of indemnity.
413. At common law, a claim under an insurance contract is categorized as a claim for damages for breach of contract, even if the insurer does not dispute liability or quantum (*see Edmunds v. Lloyds Italico & L'Ancora Compagnia di Assicurazioni & Riassicuriazione SpA* [1986] 1 Lloyd's Rep. 326) but the promise of indemnity in an insurance contract is simply 'a promise to hold the indemnified person harmless against a specified loss or expenses' (per Lord Goff in *The Fanti* [1991] 2 A.C. at 35), and this means that the insured is not entitled to damages beyond the basic measure of indemnity: *The Italia Express* (No. 2) [1992] 2 Lloyd's Rep. 281; *Sprung v. Royal Insurance (U.K.) Ltd.* [1997] C.L.C. 70.
414. It is on this that the amount of premium will prima facie be calculated. The sum insured also has important consequences when there is double insurance; *see infra* .
415. The notable exception is motor insurance, where, in respect of third party liability for personal injury or death, statute forbids any limit: Road Traffic Act 1988, s. 145(3)(a). It is conventional also for motor liability insurance for property damage to be unlimited, although the Act allows a sum insured of not less than GBP 1.2 million (s. 145(4)(b)).
416. *See* para. 148.

and to the sum insured.[417] As far as property insurances are concerned, there may be differences depending upon whether or not insured property is totally lost or destroyed or simply partially lost or damaged.

145. If insured goods are totally lost, the insured is entitled to recover their value at the time and place of loss.[418] This value is determined by asking what the property would have fetched in a sale between a willing buyer and a willing seller, in other words its second-hand value at the time of loss.[419] There is no compensation for sentimental value nor strictly under an indemnity policy should the measure recoverable necessarily reflect the cost of replacing lost property. The same principles apply to a loss which is treated as a total loss. In marine insurance, the insured may sometimes abandon partially lost property and recover for a constructive total loss.[420] There is no such right in non-marine insurance law, but in practice an insurer may in certain cases agree to take partially damaged insured property as salvage, for example, a badly damaged car which is not quite a 'write-off', and pay the insured as for a total loss.[421]

146. Because the principle of indemnity is only an implied term of the normal contract of insurance, it can be excluded. Thus as respects goods, which tend to depreciate in value, it is possible to insure to cover the cost of replacement under what are commonly called 'new for old' policies. This sort of insurance, which has become increasingly common in recent years although naturally it costs more than indemnity insurance, is without doubt a substantial deviation from the traditional principle of indemnity.

147. As far as insurances of land and buildings are concerned, it is clear that in the normal case of the insured who intends to reoccupy the building when restored, his loss is to be assessed by reference to the cost of rebuilding.[422] It will be otherwise if there is no intention to reoccupy, when indemnity based on the market value of the property before loss, less any value left in the site, will sufficiently compensate.[423] In the case of a partial loss, that is when property is damaged as opposed to being completely destroyed or otherwise ceases to exist, the cost of repair, subject to the

---

417. This can include exemplary damages: *Lancashire County Council v. Municipal Mutual Insurance Ltd.* [1996] 3 All E.R. 545.
418. *Re Wilson and Scottish Insurance Corporation Ltd.* [1920] 2 Ch. 28.
419. *Richard Aubrey Film Productions Ltd. v. Graham* [1960] 2 Lloyd's Rep. 101.
420. *See* para. 222.
421. A number of issues surrounding the true measure of indemnity, particularly as concerns cars, are not wholly clear as a matter of law. One common situation, a variant of that in the text, concerns the vehicle which is 'written off' as a total loss because the cost of repair exceeds its pre-loss market value, even though it is not a true total loss and the sum insured is sufficient to cover the cost of repair. In practice it is thought that insurers would pay only market value, but whether this is strictly in accordance with the law is not certain.
422. *Leppard v. Excess Insurance Company* [1979] 1 WLR 512.
423. This is actually what happened in the *Leppard* case, but the statements of principle in the judgments support the general principle. The result was not entirely fair given that the insured was obliged to insure for full rebuilding cost under a warranty in the policy and the insurer would have been able to repudiate liability if he had failed to do so. *See* Birds (1980) 43 MLR 456.

sum insured, is treated as the amount recoverable.[424] If the repaired property is worth more than it was worth before the loss, then an allowance in respect of this should properly be made, otherwise the insured will be more than fully indemnified.[425]

148. The measure of recovery under a contract of indemnity insurance may be affected by the presence in the policy of a franchise clause or an excess clause. Under the former the insured agrees to bear the whole of any loss that amounts to less than a specified percentage of the value of the insured property, the insurer bearing the whole of any loss above that figure. An excess clause on the other hand provides that the insured will always bear the first part of any loss, expressed as either a sum of money or a percentage of the loss. Excess clauses are widespread across a large number of insurances.

149. It is possible, although rare outside marine insurance, for a policy on property to be a valued policy, although this is so only if the policy is actually described in this way. Under a valued policy the insured, in the event of a total loss, will be entitled to the stated value, regardless of its relationship to market value or cost of replacement (the usual bases as described below). This is because the parties have expressly contracted out of the principle of indemnity. In the case of a partial loss, the percentage of depreciation in the value of the property resulting from the loss is applied to the valued sum insured to produce the amount recoverable. If the property with a market value of GBP 50,000 is insured under a valued policy for GBP 100,000 and partially damaged, reducing its value to GBP 40,000, the insured will recover GBP 20,000; in other words the amount of depreciation (GBP 10,000) over market value (GBP 50,000) applied to the sum insured.[426] It will not matter, it seems, whether the cost of repair is above or below the resulting figure.

§2. Under-Insurance

150. As has been seen, an insured can recover only up to the maximum 'sum insured' in the policy. Thus, if this does not represent the actual value of the insured property, he is under-insured and in the case of a total loss will recover only the sum insured. What the insured will be entitled to in respect of a partial loss depends upon whether or not the principle of average applies. If the principle of average applies, the insured is deemed to be his own insurer for the difference between the actual value and the insured value of the property, and he will recover only the proportion of the loss that the insured value bears to the actual value. If the policy is not subject to average then generally the insured will recover the full value of his loss provided that it is within the sum insured. The only case where he will not recover is if he gave an

424. *Reynolds v. Phoenix Assurance Co. Ltd.* [1978] 2 Lloyd's Rep. 440, where the cost of repair awarded of a building worth less than GBP 30,000 was over GBP 200,000.

425. This is known as 'betterment' and was upheld in the *Reynolds* case, *supra* .

426. *Elcock v. Thomson* [1949] 2 KB 755.

express warranty as to value which has been broken.[427] In this situation, the insurer will, if it chooses, be completely discharged from all liability.[428]

All marine insurance policies are by statute made subject to average[429] and non-marine insurance policies often contain an express average condition. It is sufficient that the policy provides simply that it is 'subject to average'. Whether the principle of average would be implied where it has not been expressed has never been firmly decided. It probably would be in commercial policies,[430] but it is unlikely that it would be in domestic property insurances.

§3. Reinstatement

151. In some situations, there may a right to insist upon reinstatement or repair rather than the payment of money. Reinstatement in this context means restore, in the case of goods, and rebuild, in the case of buildings. The right to insist upon reinstatement may be vested in the insurer under the policy or in the insurer or others by statute. Many different types of insurances of property commonly grant the insurer the right to repair or reinstate lost or damaged property at his option, alternatively to the payment of money. Insurers reserve this right to protect themselves against fraud and excessive demands.[431] Once an insurer elects to reinstate he is bound by that election and as a general rule the reinstatement must be exact. If it is not, for example, if rebuilt property is smaller than before, he will be liable to compensate the insured for any loss of value, even if the reason for the failure to reinstate properly is solely the action of third party, for example, a planning requirement imposed by a local authority.[432] However, in practice insurers avoid the strictness of this principle by providing in the policy that reinstatement will be 'as circumstances permit and in reasonably sufficient manner'.

There is authority that if an insurer elects to reinstate, he is bound to that even if it becomes impossible, for example, because the property must be completely demolished; he must therefore pay the insured full compensation for the totally lost property, even if originally the loss was only partial.[433] Now it would probably be held that such a contract to reinstate could be discharged by frustration, provided it has really become impossible and neither party is at fault. If so, it seems that the original liability of the insurers will revive so that once again they will be able to elect whether to pay money or to reinstate; obviously there is no real choice, reinstatement already having become impossible.[434]

427. These are quite common. Alternatively, the policy may be voidable for non-disclosure of a material fact. It is clear that excessive under-insurance would be regarded as material.
428. *See* para. 118.
429. Section 81 Marine Insurance Act 1906.
430. *Carreras Ltd. v. Cunard Steamship Co.* [1918] 1 KB 118.
431. An insurer in the process of reinstating is regarded as being under the obligations of a building contractor and hence will be liable for any loss or damage which occurs while he is in possession, e.g., from a second fire: *Smith v. Colonial Mutual Fire Insurance Co.* (1880) 6 VLR 200.
432. *Alchorne v. Favill* (1825) 4 LJ (OS) 47.
433. *Brown v. Royal Insurance Co.* (1859) 1 El & El 853.
434. *Anderson v. Commercial Union Assurance Co.* (1885) 55 LJQB 146.

152. The most important statutory provision regarding reinstatement is, it seems, little used, but is potentially of quite broad application. Section 83 of the Fires Prevention (Metropolis) Act 1774 applies only to fire policies on houses and other buildings. Under the section, following a loss by fire, an insurance company[435] may be required to apply the relevant insurance monies, so far as they will go, towards reinstatement upon the request of any person interested in the building; and it may choose to do so if it suspects that the insured is guilty of fraud or arson. The request needed to bring the section into operation must be a clear and unequivocal request for reinstatement and not, for example, merely for the payment of money, and it must be made before the insurers have paid out any money under the policy.[436] The most notable point about section 83 is that it confers a statutory right on 'any person interested' in the damaged or destroyed building. The latter need have no interest in the insurance contract nor even a full insurable interest in the property. Thus where the relevant policy was taken out by the mortgagor of a building, it was held that the mortgagees could require reinstatement under section 83, even though the debt owing to them, and thus the amount of insurable interest they would have had, was much less than the loss under the policy.[437] So, for example, a tenant of property can insist upon reinstatement by his landlord's insurer, or vice versa, and the same would apply as between the vendor and purchaser of land. Where a landlord had covenanted to insure for the benefit of the tenant, the latter was held entitled to insist upon the insurance monies being used for reinstatement under section 83, notwithstanding that by the time of the relevant fire, the landlord had contracted to sell its interest in the property and hence its own insurable interest was virtually reduced to nil.[438]

§4. The Doctrine of Subrogation

I. Definition

153. The doctrine of subrogation[439] applies to every contract of insurance that is a contract of indemnity.[440] The doctrine has its origins in both equity and the common law, but subrogation rights can be and frequently are modified or extended by an express term in the insurance policy. The fundamental point is that the insured 'shall

435. But not a Lloyd's underwriter.
436. *Simpson v. Scottish Union Insurance Co.* (1863) 1 H & M 618.
437. *Sinnott v. Bowden* [1912] 2 Ch 414.
438. *Lonsdale & Thompson Ltd. v. Black Arrow Group plc.* [1993] 3 All ER 648.
439. The leading common law monograph, although now very dated, is Derham, *Subrogation in Insurance Law*, Law Book Company, 1985.
440. Thus it does not apply to life insurance (*Solicitors & General Life Assurance Society v. Lamb* (1864) 2 De GJ & S 251) and personal accident insurance (*Theobald v. Railway Passengers' Assurance Company* (1954) 10 Exch 45), although if the latter pays on a true indemnity basis, there is no reason why in principle subrogation should not be applicable. The same would be true of health insurances, although the position has never been considered in cases in the UK; *see Birds' Modern Insurance Law*, para. 17.1.

be fully indemnified, but shall never be more than fully indemnified'.[441] Thus the insurer is first entitled to recoup any profit the insured makes from his loss and second to pursue, in the name of the insured, any right or remedy which the insured possesses which may diminish the loss insured against. These two aspects of subrogation must be considered separately.

II. The No-Profit Rule

154. The classic illustration of this aspect of subrogation, which exists to prevent unjust enrichment, is the case of *Castellain v. Preston.*[442] Here the insured vendor of a house recovered the insurance monies when it was burnt down after he had contracted to sell it but before completion of the sale. He also recovered the full purchase price upon completion of the purchaser who, it had been decided earlier,[443] was not entitled to the benefit of the insurance monies. It was held therefore that the insured must account to his insurer for the profit. Because of the partly equitable origins of the doctrine, the money that the insured receives is held in equity for the benefit of the insurer who has a lien or charge over it.[444]

It is clear that the insured must have been properly indemnified under the policy before his duty to account arises. In *Scottish Union and National Insurance Co. v. Davis,*[445] the defendant's car, damaged in an accident and insured with the plaintiff, was repaired quite unsatisfactorily by one garage which nonetheless was paid by the insurer. The defendant recovered damages from the third party responsible, which he used to have the car properly repaired. It was held that the insurers could not claim these damages, as they had not properly indemnified the defendant by reason of the unsatisfactory nature of the repairs. However, it is not necessary that the insured has been fully compensated for his loss. If, as is common, he must bear the first part of any loss by virtue of an excess clause, or by virtue of the fact that he is under-insured, the insurer is entitled to any surplus beyond the sum he has actually paid out.[446]

If the insured receives a gift from a third party as a result of the loss, he will have to account for it if it was intended to mitigate the effects of the loss.[447] If, however, he can show that the gift was intended to benefit him in addition to the insurance monies, he will be entitled to keep it.[448] The insurer is entitled to recover only the sum

441. Per Brett LJ in *Castellain v. Preston* (1883) 11 QBD 380.
442. *Supra. See also Darrell v. Tibbits* (1880) 5 QBD 560.
443. *Rayner v. Preston* (1881) 18 Ch D 1. *See* further, para. 179.
444. *Napier v. Hunter* [1993] 2 WLR 42.
445. [1970] 1 Lloyd's Rep. 1.
446. *Napier v. Hunter, supra* .
447. *Stearns v. Village Main Reef Gold Mining Company* (1905) 10 Com Cas 89, where the 'gift' was money from the Government to keep the insured mine open.
448. *Burnand v. Rodocanachi* (1882) 7 App Cas 333, where the gift was money paid by the United States government following the loss of the insured ship under a statute which made it clear that the money was intended to benefit the insured over and above any insurance moneysmonies.

paid out by him under the policy. If any payment by a third party produces a surplus, the insured will be allowed to retain that.[449]

III. The Insurer's Right to Take Action

155. The insurer's right to use the insured's name in litigation against a third party alleged to be responsible for the loss is long-established[450] and if necessary the court will order the insured to allow his name to be used.[451] However, the insurer's right is subject to several limitations as described in the following paragraphs.[452]

156. As with the first aspect of the doctrine, subrogation does not arise at common law until the insured has been indemnified in respect of all claims arising out of the particular event,[453] and until this time the insured himself retains the right to use the third party, although he must act in a way that does not prejudice the insurer.[454] In practice, however, this principle may be modified by an express condition in the policy under which the insured can be required to take action by the insurer before or after indemnification.[455] An insurer will not possess subrogation rights if the insured cannot in fact sue the third party. In *Simpson v. Thomson,*[456] for example, the tortfeasor was in fact the insured, one of whose other ships had negligently collided with the insured ship. It was held that the insurer had no right to use the insured's name to sue the insured himself.[457]

If, following a loss, the insured does anything that prejudices the insurer's potential subrogation rights, he will be liable in damages. If, for example, an insured landlord agrees not to sue his tenant for breach of a repairing covenant which would

---

449. *Yorkshire Insurance Company v. Nisbet Shipping Company* [1962] 2 QB 330 (another fairly unusual situation where the surplus resulted because of a devaluation of currency).

450. *See* the *dictum* of Lord Mansfield in *Mason v. Sainsbury* (1782) 3 Doug KB 61 at 64: 'Every day the insurer is put into the shoes of the assured.'

451. There has been criticism of the uncontrolled use of subrogation; *see* , e.g., Parsons, 'Individual responsibility *versus* enterprise liability' (1956) 29 ALJ 714, commenting on the notorious case of *Lister v. Romford Ice and Cold Storage Ltd.* [1957] AC 555, where insurers used the name of the insured employer to sue an employee in negligence, and Hasson, 'Subrogation in insurance law – a critical evaluation' (1985) 5 Oxford J Legal Stud 416.

452. Instead of exercising subrogation rights, an insurer can take an assignment of its insured's right of action against a third party (*Compania Columbiana de Seguros v. Pacific Steam Navigation Co.* [1965] 1 QB 101). If so, the cause of action will be entirely the insurer's, and thus in its name, and, *inter alia,* there will be no requirement that the insured necessarily be indemnified and the insurer will be entitled to retain all it recovers, even if this amounts to more than it paid the insured. In practice assignment is rarely used because of the adverse publicity it might attract for insurers.

453. *Page v. Scottish Insurance Corporation* (1929) 98 LJKB 308.

454. *Commercial Union Assurance Company v. Lister* (1874) LR 9 Ch 483.

455. As to standard express terms covering subrogation, *see* Birds, 'Contractual subrogation in insurance' [1979] JBL 124.

456. (1877) 3 App Cas 279.

457. This principle often applies where the insured has taken action against and recovered from a third party, for example, following a motor accident: *see* , e.g., *Buckland v. Palmer* [1984] 1 WLR 1109.

cover the loss,[458] or if an insured compromises his claim against a tortfeasor liable for the loss,[459] he will be liable in damages for the amount paid out by his insurer, in other words the amount which the latter has lost the right to claim by subrogation. The defendant third party cannot, in a subrogation action, plead that the plaintiff is in reality an insurer nor that the nominal plaintiff has in fact been indemnified for the loss caused by him. Nor is it a defence that the insurer exercising subrogation rights was not actually legally bound to indemnify the insured.[460]

157. There are a number of situations where subrogation will not apply because of some form of agreement which, properly construed, denies its applicability. First, insurers may expressly agree, whether in the policy[461] or more generally, to forgo their rights. For example, following the case of *Lister v. Romford Ice and Cold Storage Co. Ltd.*,[462] it was felt not to be good for industrial relations that employers should be appearing, albeit in name only, to be suing their employees in such circumstances, and employers' liability insurers have agreed amongst themselves that they will not exercise subrogation rights in that situation.[463] Further, it used to be common for motor insurers to enter into 'knock-for-knock' agreements, under which they agreed to pay the amount of their own insured's losses in respect of car damage following a motor accident, regardless of questions of legal liability, and not to pursue subrogation claims in their insureds' names against drivers whom the law would deem accountable. These agreements, however, are much less common than previously.[464]

Second, subrogation may be inapplicable in situations where two or more persons, for example, landlord and tenant or mortgagor and mortgagee, are interested in the same property insured. If both are separately insured, any loss will fall on the party legally liable for it as between them, and hence on that party's insurer.[465] However, if only one is insured, it may be that the insurance ensures to the benefit of the other so that the insurer can have no recourse by way of subrogation against the latter. This depends on the true construction of the agreement between the two persons. In *Mark Rowlands Ltd. v. Berni Inns Ltd.*,[466] property leased by the plaintiffs to the defendants was damaged by the negligence of the defendants. Under the terms of the lease the plaintiffs covenanted to insure and the defendants covenanted to pay a sum (an 'insurance rent') equal to one-quarter of the premium. Further, the defendants were

458. *West of England Fire Insurance Company v. Isaacs* [1897] 1 QB 226. *See also Phoenix Assurance Company v. Spooner* [1905] 2 KB 753.
459. *Law Fire Assurance Company v. Oakley* (1888) 4 TLR 309.
460. *King v. Victoria Insurance Company Ltd.* [1896] AC 250.
461. Professional indemnity and certain other liability policies, which may be instances of co-insurance, usually contain a waiver of subrogation rights against the insured's employees.
462. *Supra.*
463. *See* Gardiner (1959) 22 MLR 652.
464. These agreements did not prohibit an insured from himself taking action for his full damages, if, for example, the indemnity from his insurer was less than he would recover from the tortfeasor, although he would generally recover only those costs appropriate to an action for the difference between indemnity and full damages (*Hobbs v. Marlowe* [1977] 2 All ER 241) and would obviously have to account to his insurer for the surplus recovered. *See* further, Birds (1978) 41 MLR 201.
465. *See* further below.
466. [1986] QB 211.

relieved from their covenant to repair in respect of 'damage by or in consequence of any of the insured risks'. It was held that the plaintiff's insurers could not exercise subrogation rights against the defendants, the intention of the agreement contained in the lease being that in the event of damage by fire, whether accidentally or negligently caused, the plaintiffs' loss was to be recouped from the insurance monies and they were to have no further claim against the defendants.[467] The principle will only be applicable if the lease in any particular case can be similarly construed.[468]

A different situation is where both parties are insured under the same policy. In *Petrofina Ltd. v. Magnaload Ltd.*,[469] it was held that insurers under a contractors' all risks insurance policy could not use the name of the principal insureds, the owners of the property, to sue the negligent subcontractors responsible for the loss. The latter were within the contract definition of 'the insured', so that the case was one of co-insurance and the principle applied was merely an extension of that which forbids the insurer from exercising subrogation rights to sue its own insured. The 'Petrofina' principle, as it is known, has been approved in a number of recent authorities,[470] although the basis for it has changed. In situations such as this, where a commercial contract makes detailed provision regarding the insurance obligations of the parties, whether or not subrogation will apply against a co-insured is now more likely to be viewed as a matter of construction of that contract rather than the insurance contract.[471]

158. In addition to situations of agreement restricting subrogation rights, it has been decided in one case that the court can restrain someone in a position of an insurer from exercising subrogation rights where it would be unjust and inequitable to allow

467. It may be relevant to other situations of two persons interested in the same property, e.g., vendor and purchaser of land, owner and hirer of goods or the parties to a repair contract (*Talbot Underwriting Ltd v. Nausch, Hogan & Murray Inc* [2006] EWCA Civ 889, [2006] Lloyd's Rep. IR 531). *See* further discussion in Birds (1986) 6 Oxford J Legal Stud 304. Compare *Woolwich Building Society v. Brown* [1996] C.L.C. 625, where the principle was held not to apply to mortgage indemnity insurance. The principle of *Mark Rowlands* was applied, obiter, in *Quirkco Investments Ltd v. Aspray Transport Ltd* [2011] EWHC 3060 (Ch), where there was also a waiver of subrogation clause. It was also applied in *Frasca-Judd v. Golovina* [2016] EWHC 497 (QB).

468. *Lambert v. Keymood Ltd* [1999] Lloyd's Rep. IR 80

469. [1983] 2 Lloyd's Rep. 91.

470. *See* , especially *Co-operative Retail Services Ltd v. Taylor Young* Partnership [2000] 2 All ER 865 (decision upheld by the House of Lords at [2002] UKHL 17, [2002] 1 WLR 1419 on other grounds) and *Talbot Underwriting Ltd v. Nausch, Hogan & Murray Inc, supra* . There are likely to be analogous situations where this principle might apply, for example, an insurance effected in the name of both the owner and the hirer of goods under a hire purchase contract and construction arrangements under a shipbuilding contract: *Stone Vickers Ltd. V. Appledore Ferguson Shipbuilders Ltd.* [1991] 2 Lloyd's Rep. 288; *National Oilwell (UK) Ltd. V. Davy Offshore Ltd.* [1993] 2 Lloyd's Rep. 583. The one case where it would not is where the party causing the loss did so deliberately.

471. *Tyco Fire & Integrated Solutions (UK) Ltd v. Rolls-Royce Motor Cars Ltd* [2008] EWCA Civ 286, [2008] Lloyd's Rep. IR 617, *Rathbone Brothers plc v. Novae Corporate Underwriting Ltd* [2014] EWCA Civ 1464. *See also Cape Distribution Ltd v. Cape Intermediate Holdings plc* [2016] EWHC 1119 (QB) and the Supreme Court decision in *Gard Marine & Energy Ltd v. China National Chartering Co Ltd (The Ocean Victory)* [2017] UKSC 35.

them to proceed. In *Morris v. Ford Motor Company Ltd.*,[472] M, an employee of C, a cleaning firm, was injured while working at Fords by the negligence of R, an employee of Fords. Under the cleaning contract between C and Ford, C agreed to indemnity Ford against any liability Ford incurred to an employee of C, so putting C in the position of an insurer. Ford were held vicariously liable to M and pursuant to the indemnity agreement C paid the damages awarded. C then sought to be subrogated to Ford's right to sue R for failing to take reasonable care and skill. Influenced by the agreement entered into by insurers following *Lister's* case,[473] the court refused to allow C's claim on the ground, among others, that it would be inequitable and harmful to industrial relations at Fords.[474] The principle established here could be of general application, but only it would seem in extreme cases.[475]

§5. Double Insurance and Contribution

159. If an insured, whether deliberately or inadvertently, takes out policies on the same risk with more than one insurer so that he is doubly insured, he can at common law recover his entire loss from one insurer, although not of course from all, because of the principle of subrogation; that insurer then has the right in equity to sue the other insurers for a contribution.[476] In practice, the issue rarely arises in this way because of a standard condition in all indemnity policies providing that if there is any other insurance on the same property or risk, the insurer will not pay more than its rateable proportion of any loss or damage. This 'rateable proportion clause' does not affect the legal principles of double insurance, but prevents the insured from claiming all his loss from only one insurer. Where there is such a clause in both relevant policies, it also prevents one insurer from claiming a contribution from the other where the first

472. [1973] QB 793.
473. *See supra*. That agreement was strictly inapplicable since it applies only where one employee injures another person employed by the same employer.
474. Strictly this was the reasoning of only one of the judges, Lord Denning MR. The other majority judge decided the case on the basis of an implied term in the contract between Fords and C, which is perhaps legally more correct. *See* further, *Birds' Modern Insurance Law*, para. 17.16.
475. *Woolwich Building Society v. Brown, supra* at 629; *see also Enimont Supply S.A. v. Chesapeake Shipping Inc., The Surf City* [1995] 2 Lloyd's Rep. 242, where it was accepted that subrogation would not be equitable where the insurer had expressly agreed to a waiver of its rights.
476. It is essential, though, that the insurer claiming contribution sues in its own name: *Austin v. Zurich General Accident & Liability Insurance Company* [1945] KB 250.

has in fact paid more than its rateable proportion of a loss but was not legally obliged to.[477]

160. In order for there to be double insurance, it is essential that the policies[478] cover the same property or liability against the same risk and that they are taken out by or on behalf of the same insured. In *North British & Mercantile Insurance Company v. London, Liverpool & Globe Insurance Company*,[479] grain, the property of a bailor, was in possession of wharfingers, the bailee. Both bailor and bailee had policies of fire insurance covering the grain in this situation. The grain was destroyed in circumstances such that the bailee was legally liable to compensate the bailor. The bailee's insurer paid the damages and then sought a contribution from the bailor's insurer. It was held that they could not recover. The insured was not the same, and the bailee's insurance was paid not on behalf of the bailor but to cover the bailee's own legal liability. Had the loss occurred in a way that did not attribute legal liability to the bailee, the result would have been different. The bailee would still have been able to recover under their policy,[480] but would have held the money on trust for the bailor; the latter would then have been doubly insured and contribution would have applied.[481] This decision has been criticized as being inconvenient and too technical in its requirement of 'same insured or on behalf of the same insured', as quite commonly people with different interests in the same property do both insure it for its value. So contribution is often made applicable, sometimes by agreement between insurers, as is the case in fire insurance under the Rules of the Fire Officers' Committee,[482] or by a condition in policies which allows an insured to recover only the relevant proportion of a loss if the risk is covered elsewhere even if by a third party.

161. Where there is double insurance, problems can arise concerning the proportion of the loss payable by each insurer. In property insurances this depends basically upon the 'sum insured' in each policy. If they are the same, there are no difficulties; each insurer will bear an equal part of any loss. If the sums differ, but the risk covered is the same, each insurer will bear the proportion that his sum insured bears to the total of the sums insured. So if one insurer of particular property gives

---

477. *Legal and General Assurance Society Ltd. V. Drake Insurance Co. Ltd.* [1991] 2 Lloyd's Rep. 36. The Court of Appeal's holding, by a majority, that but for the presence of the clause, the first insurers would have been entitled to a contribution from the other insurers, even though the latter could have repudiated liability to the insured because they were not notified of the loss in breach of a policy condition, because the equitable basis of contribution overrode any unfairness to the second insurer, seems unsupportable in the light of the later Privy Council decision in *Eagle Star Insurance Co. Ltd. V. Provincial Insurance plc.* [1993] 3 All ER 1. *See also Drake Insurance plc v. Provident Insurance plc* [2003] EWCA Civ 1874, [2004] 2 WLR 530.

478. It is not essential that the type or scope of the policies is the same. For example, there could be double insurance as between a motor insurance policy and an employer's liability insurance policy, as in *Albion Insurance Co. v. Government Insurance Office of New South Wales* (1969) 121 CLR 342.

479. (1877) 5 Ch D 569. *See also International Energy Group Ltd v. Zurich Insurance plc* [2015] UKSC 33 at [57].

480. *See* para. 160.

481. *O'Kane v. Jones* [2003] EWHC 2158 (Comm), [2004] 1 Lloyd's Rep. 389.

482. For consideration of the agreements, *see* Lewis (1985) 48 MLR 275.

cover for GBP 10,000 and the other for GBP 20,000, the first will bear one-third and the second two-thirds of any loss. This approach is described as the 'maximum liability' approach because it uses the two or more insurers' maximum possible liabilities to work out the ratio. In liability insurances a different method is used because the figure governing the maximum possible liability of an insurer does not relate to the actual value of anything, premiums are not assessed, as they are in property insurance, largely on the basis of the sum insured and they do not increase pro rata according to the sum insured. Here the 'independent liability' method has been held to be correct, whereby the liability of each insurer for the particular loss is worked out quite independently of the existence of other insurance.[483] So, for example, if one insurer gives cover up to GBP 100,000 and the other up to GBP 10,000 and there is a loss of GBP 5,000, each would independently be liable for the full loss and so they share it equally. Only where the actual loss exceeds the lesser of the sums insured will the proportions not be equal. For example, if the loss in the example were GBP 20,000, the first insurer would, independently, be liable for GBP 20,000, the second for GBP 10,000. The first will therefore be liable for two-thirds, the second for one-third of the loss.[484]

162. Apart from the rateable proportion clause already referred to, other standard conditions in a policy may affect the operation of the principle of double insurance. One such provides that the insurer is not to be liable at all for a loss if the risk is covered by another insurer. If such a condition appears in just one of two or more policies, it will clearly be effective. If it appears in both, it could logically be argued that neither insurer is liable. This argument, however, is unlikely to be accepted as it has been held that a reasonable construction of such clauses is to exclude from the category of other insurance referred to in the condition any cover which itself is purportedly cancelled by the existence of other insurance; both insurers would thus be liable according to the relevant proportion.[485] An exclusion of liability in one policy in the event of there being other insurance will override a rateable proportion clause in the other policy, so that there is no double insurance.[486]

163. To protect themselves against the possibility of fraud, insurers sometimes insert conditions, particularly into property insurance policies, requiring the insured to disclose to them any other insurances taken out covering the same risk, and providing that the policy should be forfeited if this is not done.[487] For such a condition to operate, the other insurance must itself be effective insurance. If, for example, the second insurance provides that it does not come into force until the premium is paid, and that

---

483. *Commercial Union Assurance Company Ltd. V. Hayden* [1977] QB 804.

484. It is likely that the independent liability approach is the correct one in property insurances where the policies have different scopes.

485. *Weddell v. Road Transport & General Insurance Co.* [1932] 2 KB 563; *National Employers' Mutual Insurance v. Hayden* [1980] 2 Lloyd's Rep. 149; *Sobrany v. UAB Transtira* [2016] EWCA Civ 28. This assumes that the insured is entitled to recover under both policies and is not in breach of some term. If he is, he will be precluded from recovering from the relevant insurer and will recover only a proportion of his loss.

486. *National Farmers Union Mutual Insurance Society Ltd v. HSBC Insurance (UK) Ltd* [2010] EWHC 773 (Comm), [2011] Lloyd's Rep. IR 86.

487. Mere accidental overlap between policies will not bring such a condition into operation (*Australian Agricultural Co. v. Saunders* (1875) LR 10 CP 668); there must be clear double insurance of the same risk.

is never paid, there is no breach of a double insurance condition in the first policy.[488] Similarly if the second policy also contains a double insurance condition and the insured does not disclose the first policy to the second insurer, the first policy can logically never be affected as the second policy will never, by reason of the non-disclosure, be effective.[489]

488. *Equitable Fire & Accident Insurance Co. v. Ching Wo Hong* [1907] AC 96.
489. *Steadfast Insurance Co. v. F & B Trading Co.* (1972) 46 ALJR 10.

Chapter 6. Insurance and Third Parties

164. As was seen in an earlier chapter, one of the important consequences of the requirement of insurable interest is that generally the insured has an interest only up to the amount of his own loss. However, frequently a third party may also have an interest in the insured property. Common examples are the owner of goods in the possession of and insured by a bailee, the mortgagee of a house insured by the mortgagor, and the tenant of property insured by his landlord. In certain circumstances, the law allows the insured to recover for the benefit of the unnamed third party, either as well as for himself or solely for the third party. Provided first that the insured himself has an insurable interest, even though that may be a limited interest, he may be able to recover for the third party provided that this appears to be the result of the true construction of the policy. The answer then will depend upon how the insurance is expressed and how the interest of the insured is described.

The leading case is *Hepburn v. A. Tomlinson (Hauliers) Ltd.*[490] Tomlinsons were carriers, carrying a quantity of tobacco for the owners. Under the contract of carriage they were obliged to insure the goods which they duly did. The tobacco was stolen in circumstances which attached no legal liability to the carriers. They sought recovery under their insurance policy for the benefit of the owners. It was held that they were entitled to recover. On its true construction the insurance policy covered the goods and not merely the legal liability of the carriers. As bailees of the goods the carriers had an insurable interest in them, because of their potential legal liability if they were negligent and they could insure for the full value of the tobacco. As they did so insure, as bailees, the contract clearly entitled them to recover, although they would hold the insurance monies for the owners.

This is clearly, commercially speaking, a most convenient result and has been followed in another situation where commercial convenience was regarded as paramount, that of a global contractors' all risks insurance covering the interests of the owners of a site and all the contractors and subcontractors working thereon.[491] It does seem, however, that the principle will not easily extend to other cases of third party interests where it is much more likely that the normal insurance contract will, on its true construction, only cover the limited interest of the insured. Indeed this will be presumed if the insured was under no duty to insure on behalf of the third party and there is nothing more to show that he intended to.

165. A rather different situation is where the insured himself has no insurable interest in the loss that has occurred. He may recover if he can show that the requirement of insurable interest that is the normal implied requirement of a contract of indemnity

490. [1966] AC 451. *See also* the older decision in *Waters v. Monarch Fire and Life Assurance Co.* (1856) 5 E & B 870. However, in *North British & Mercantile Insurance Co. v. Moffat* (1871) LR 7 CP 25 the wording of the policy made it clear that bailees had insured only their own interest in the goods, and this possibility was confirmed in *Ramco (UK) Ltd v. International Insurance Co of Hannover Ltd* [2004] EWCA Civ 675, [2004] Lloyd's Rep. IR 606.

491. *Petrofina Ltd. v. Magnaload Ltd.* [1984] 1 QB 127. *See also Stone Vickers Ltd. v. Appledore Ferguson Shipbuilders Ltd.* [1991] 2 Lloyd's Rep. 288 and *National Oilwell (UK) Ltd. v. Davy Offshore Ltd.* [1993] 2 Lloyd's Rep. 582.

insurance has been dispensed with. This happened in *Thomas v. National Farmers' Union Mutual Insurance Society Ltd.*,[492] where, it seems, the insured held the monies recovered on trust for the landlord. Another good illustration is the decision in *Williams v. Baltic Insurance Association of London*,[493] where the plaintiff held a motor insurance policy on his car that included cover against his liability to third parties for personal injuries arising out of the use of the car. As is common, this cover was extended to other drivers, in this case to a friend or relative of the insured driving the car with the latter's consent. The plaintiff's sister, driving with his consent, negligently injured a third party and the plaintiff sought to recover the damages that she was liable to pay. He had no possible insurable interest in his sister's liability and was in no way himself liable. It was held, however, that he was entitled to recover. The general contractual requirement of insurable interest was excluded by the express undertaking by the insurer to extend the indemnity to other drivers.[494]

166. In the cases considered above, the monies recovered by the insured will be held for the third party.[495] The question then arises whether the third party himself could recover directly from the insurer. Since the Contracts (Rights of Third Parties) Act 1999 conferred on a third party the right to sue on a contract for his benefit, the previous problems regarding the application of the general principle of privity of contract[496] will not apply unless, as is possible, the application of that Act is excluded. In such a case the insured may be acting as agent for the third party and within his authority, when there is no problem.[497] If the insured acted in the absence of express authority, the third party may still be able to adopt the acts of the insured by ratification. In insurance, however, ratification is only possible if done before a loss; it is not effective after a loss has taken place. In *Grover & Grover Ltd. v. Matthews*,[498] Grover insured their factory at Lloyd's through their agent, B. When the policy expired, B, without authority, wrote to Lloyd's for a renewal. The factory was burnt down and only afterwards did Grover meet B and give him a cheque for the premium. It was

492. [1961] 1 WLR 386; *see* para. 81, *supra* .
493. [1924] 2 KB 282.
494. It was also regarded as important that the policy was one on goods and clearly outside the scope of the Life Assurance Act 1774. It seems that this would no longer be regarded as important, the modern authorities holding that the Act does not apply to any cases of indemnity insurance.
495. Whether on trust in the strict, so that the third party has an equitable claim to the money, or otherwise will depend upon the arrangement between the insured and the third party: *Re E Dibbens & Sons Ltd.* [1990] BCLC 577.
496. *Vandepitte v. Preferred Accident Insurance Corporation of New York* [1933] AC 70. Someone in the position of Williams' sister, however, has long had a statutory right (now under s. 148(7) Road Traffic Act 1988) to sue the insurer directly in respect of compulsory motor insurance.
497. Even if the agency was undisclosed: *Siu Yin Kwan v. Eastern Insurance Co. Ltd.* [1994] 1 All E.R. 213. *See also Talbot Underwriting Ltd v. Nausch, Hogan & Murray Inc* [2006] EWCA Civ 889, [2006] Lloyd's Rep. IR 531.
498. [1910] 2 KB 401. This decision is not free from difficulty, however; *see Birds' Modern Insurance Law*, para. 4.6.2, and it has more recently, *obiter*, been doubted: *National Oilwell (UK) Ltd. v. Davy Offshore Ltd.* [1993] 2 Lloyd's Rep. 582.

held that there was no contract of insurance, the purported ratification after loss being ineffective.[499]

167. There are further specific instances where the law allows a third party to claim on an insurance policy or in some other way protects third parties. These are described in the chapters below on Liability Insurance (Part III, Chapter 5) and Motor Vehicle Insurance (Part IV).

499. In practice where insurance of another's interest is common, such as those discussed or in a domestic situation where a policy may cover property belonging to the insured and of other members of his family, it is unlikely that insurers would rely upon technical points such as these to deny recovery.

Chapter 7. Termination of the Insurance Contract

168. The legal position concerning length and termination of the insurance contract differs quite considerably as between life insurance on the one hand and all other types on the other. There are no hard and fast rules, so that particular insurance contracts may very well stipulate their own terms varying from what can be regarded as the general position.[500]

§1. Life Insurance

169. There is a presumption that a contract of life insurance is entire, in other words it lasts until death or an earlier specified date, for example, if it is also an endowment policy.[501] The insurer therefore cannot cancel or refuse to renew it, provided that the premiums due are paid and any other conditions compiled with. Indeed it is invariably the practice for life insurers to provide 'days of grace' after the date due for the payment of the premium, so that if the premium is paid during that period, the contract is kept alive even if the life insured has already died.[502] If the premium is not paid within the days of grace or on the due date if there are none, the policy will lapse. Whether or not the insured is entitled when a policy lapses to a surrender value or a paid-up policy will depend entirely on the terms of the policy and the practice of the particular insurer.[503]

§2. Non-life Insurances

170. In most cases these will be contracts for a fixed period, in practice in the case of standard consumer and commercial insurances for a year. Each renewal, therefore, in law constitutes a fresh contract of insurance and the duties to make a fair presentation of the risk (in commercial policies) and not to make an actionable misrepresentation (in consumer policies) arise afresh. There is generally no obligation on an insurer to renew, nor to give reasons for non-renewal, nor to give notice of renewal.[504] In practice insurers do often send out renewal notices and allow the insured a period of 'days of grace', as in life insurance, in which to pay the premium for the

500. For example, insurance contracts tied to a construction project may be expressed to run for the length of the project.
501. *Stuart v. Freeman* [1903] 1 KB 47. Another possibility is that the policy is a term policy, i.e., expressed to last for a stated period.
502. *Ibid.*
503. For cancellation rights in respect of life insurance, *see* Part V, Ch. 4.
504. *Simpson v. Accidental Death Insurance Co.* (1857) 2 CB (NS) 257. It is perfectly possible for a policy to give a right of renewal to the insured, as in *Kirby v. Cosindit SpA* [1969] 1 Lloyd's Rep. 75.

new contract.[505] If days of grace are allowed, a loss within these but before the premium has been paid should be covered, provided that the premium is subsequently paid in time, as there is, as has been seen,[506] no legal requirement that the premium be paid before a binding contract of insurance exists. Non-life insurance policies often contain conditions giving the insurer the right to cancel the policy at any time during its occurrence. These conditions are valid even if no period of notice is prescribed and even if the insurer is not required to have good reason to cancel, provided that the risk insured against has not materialized.[507]

171. The ICOBS[508] confers general cancellation rights on consumer purchasers of general insurance contracts. These were required in respect of distance contracts,[509] but the FSA (now the FCA) took the opportunity to give them to all retail customers. In essence, apart from in respect of short-term contracts and travel insurance, all general insurance consumers must be offered the right to cancel for the fourteen-day period from the later of the conclusion (or renewal) of the contract and the consumer receiving the contractual terms and conditions required by ICOBS in a durable medium.[510] If the consumer is not told of the right to cancel, then there is no time limit. The consumer does not have to give reasons, and the notice is deemed served on the day it is sent. Where a consumer exercises the right to cancel, the insurer must repay any premium paid without delay and no later than thirty days after receiving notice of cancellation, subject to the consumer paying for services actually provided by the insurer, provided that he was told of what it might cost if he cancelled. This might be, for example, a situation where a motor policy is cancelled but the insured has already made a claim which has been partly indemnified by the insurer providing a hire car.

505. It is becoming common, in consumer insurance, for insurers to assume automatic renewal, at a stated premium and subject to proper disclosure, unless the insured notifies them otherwise.
506. *See* para. 93.
507. *Sun Fire Office v. Hart* (1889) 14 App Cas 98.
508. *See* para. 28.
509. Because of the Directive on distance marketing of financial services (2002/65/EC).
510. There is a longer thirty-day period for a pure protection contract, which is essentially term life insurance (this is not covered by the rules applying to most forms of life insurance).

Part III. Property and Liability Insurance

Chapter 1. Fire Insurance

172. Fire insurance is one of the oldest forms of insurance, becoming prevalent in the UK after the Great Fire of London in 1666. The modern fire policy, whether effected by a commercial concern or by an individual, still retains the same basic features of the old fire policy, although in practice, in both contexts, it is rare to find a fire policy by itself; rather the risk of loss by fire will be one component of a policy giving broader cover. This does not, of course, reduce the importance of describing the basic features of fire insurance, which clearly remains one of the most fundamental insurances on property.

§1. The Meaning of Fire

173. Clearly loss by the burning of property insured is covered by fire insurance,[511] and it does not matter in UK law whether the damage or loss is caused by a fire in a proper place as opposed to by a fire which has escaped from a proper place.[512] So, in *Harris v. Poland*,[513] the insured's goods were insured against loss or damage by fire. One day, as a security measure, she concealed her jewellery in the grate under coal which was ready for lighting. Later she inadvertently lit the fire without removing the jewellery which was damaged as a result. It was held that there had been a loss by fire. 'The risks against which the plaintiff is insured include the risk of insured property coming unintentionally in contact with fire and being thereby destroyed or damaged, and it matters not whether that fire comes to the insured property or the insured property comes to the fire.'[514]

However, it is clear that there must be actual ignition of the property insured, or of other properties in circumstances such that it can be said that fire was the proximate cause of the loss.[515] Damage from excessive heat without actual ignition is not enough.

511. *Harris v. Poland* [1942] KB 462. Of course, this does not cover deliberate loss by fire, as to which *see* para. 58.
512. UK law has never distinguished between a 'friendly fire' and a 'hostile fire'.
513. *Supra.*
514. [1942] KB at 468, per Atkinson, J.
515. In respect of the latter, *see* , e.g., *Symington v. Union Insurance Society of Canton* (1928) 97 LJKB 646, where water damage was held to be proximately caused by fire, having been effected in order to prevent a nearby fire from spreading; *see* para. 65.

In the old case of *Austin v. Drewe*,[516] the stock in a sugar refinery was insured against damage by fire. A flue passed up through all the floors of the refinery from a stove on the ground floor. At the top of the flue was a register, which was closed at night to retain heat, but opened when a fresh fire was lit in the morning. Inadvertently, one morning the register was not opened and as a result the intense heat in the flue damaged sugar being refined on the top floor. Although there were smoke and sparks, the fire itself was confined to the flue and the sugar did not ignite. It was held that there was no loss by fire.[517]

Damage from smoke arising from an unintended fire will be covered by a fire policy provided that the fire was the proximate cause of the loss.[518] However, smoke damage from a 'proper' fire is not covered. Damage caused merely by explosion or lightning is not damage by fire,[519] although in principle explosion caused by fire, or fire following an explosion or lightning, is covered,[520] because here there has been actual ignition.[521]

174. The basic cover afforded by fire or any other insurance of property is to compensate for the loss of or damage to the property itself, and not to compensate for any consequential losses such as loss of profits.[522] This can, though, be separately insured.[523]

§2. Standard Policy Cover and Exceptions

175. The standard fire policy wording in the UK[524] includes damage caused by lightning and explosion[525] of boilers and of gas.[526] It excludes loss or damage to the property caused by its igniting from its own spontaneous fermentation, combustion or heating.[527] There are a number of standard exclusions, which typically include riot,

516. (1816) 6 Taunt 436.
517. The same would apply, for example, in the event of excess heat causing a boiler to burst.
518. *The Diamond* [1906] P 282.
519. *Everett v. London Assurance Co.* (1865) 19 CB (NS) 126. As seen below, lightning damage is normally expressly covered separately.
520. Explosion resulting from fire is often expressly excluded from the standard fire policy and therefore has to be separately covered if desired.
521. *Stanley v. Western Insurance Co.* (1868) LR 3 Ex 71. This again is subject to the necessary causal link existing.
522. *Re Wright and Pole* (1834) 1 A & E 621.
523. *See* Ch. 2, *infra* .
524. As recommended by the Association of British Insurers.
525. As to the meaning of 'explosion', *see Commonwealth Smelting v. Guardian Royal Exchange* [1984] 2 Lloyd's Rep. 608, affirmed [1986] 1 Lloyd's Rep. 121. If 'explosion' is in fact excluded, this extends to loss suffered by an explosion occurring in the course of and caused by a fire: *Stanley v. Western Insurance Co., supra* , *Re Hooley Hill Rubber and Chemical Co.* [1920] 1 KB 257.
526. Unless the latter are caused by earthquake or subterranean fire.
527. This would not exclude resulting fire damage to other property. In the absence of an exclusion, such loss would probably be covered by fire risks.

civil commotion and war risks.[528] Policies issued by British insurers to insureds whose activities may take them to volatile areas of the world, for example, the Middle East, often contain more specific exclusions.[529] The term 'riot' is a technical term of the criminal law and must be construed accordingly so that it occurs whenever there are three or more people involved in a situation where violence *may* occur,[530] whereas 'civil commotion' denotes a stage between a riot and a civil war and means a general insurrection amounting to more than some disorder.[531] In modern times, it is possible to include cover for riot and civil commotion in a fire policy and indeed some standard policies include them automatically. However, it is never possible to include war risks in an ordinary policy; they must be separately insured and the appropriate premium paid. The classic wording in respect of war risks comprises 'war, invasion, act of foreign enemy, hostilities (whether war is declared or not), civil war, rebellion, revolution, insurrection or military or usurped power'. In addition, there may be an exclusion of 'terrorism'.[532] In addition to the exclusion of certain perils, it is conventional to exclude liability in respect of property that is more specifically insured, that is, when a special insurance covers a particular part of the overall property insured.

§3. Additional Insurable Risks

176. In addition to basic fire cover and the standard other perils conventionally covered under a fire policy, it is possible to add all or any number of a range of additional perils.[533] Some of these are catastrophe perils and are described separately in Chapter 9 of this Part. A second head concerns water and impact damage. This covers:

(1) damage caused by the escape of water from tanks, apparatus or pipes;[534]

---

529. *See* , e.g., *American Airlines v. Hope* [1974] 2 Lloyd's Rep. 301.

530. *London and Lancashire Fire Insurance Co. v. Bolands* [1924] AC 836; *see* para. 68. Compensation may be recovered from the police under statute: *see* the Riot Compensation Act 2016.

531. *Langdale v. Mason* (1780) Park, Insurance, Vol. 2, 965; *London and Manchester Plate Glass Co. v. Heath* [1914] 3 KB 411; *Cooper v. General Accident Fire and Life Assurance Corporation* (1923) 128 LT 481.

532. Clearly there is an element of overlap in some of these words, some of which have occasionally been the subject of litigation. So, the words 'military or usurped power' include both invasions from abroad and an internal rebellion (*Rogers v. Whittaker* [1917] 1 KB 942) an enemy air raid (ibid.) and repelling an enemy or suppressing a rebellion (*Curtis v. Mathews* [1919] 1 KB 425), but do not include a non-rebellious riot (*Drinkwater v. London Assurance Co.* (1767) 2 Wils KB 363) nor an act by a de facto government recognized by the British Government (*White, Child and Beney v. Simmons and Eagle Star Insurance Co.* (1922) 127 LJ 571). 'War' does not have a technical meaning and includes civil war (see, e.g., *Curtis & Sons v. Mathews, supra*).

533. In many domestic and commercial policies sold as packages, these are included in the standard package.

534. Damage caused by sprinkler leakage can be covered separately.

(2) storm damage;[535]
(3) storm and flood damage;[536] and
(4) impact damage, either by a third party's vehicle or animal or by both of the former and the insured's own.

The third head is subsidence insurance, which in practice covers both damage caused by subsistence (often following a long period of dry weather) and by heave (when the ground expands following the return of normal weather conditions). This type of insurance raises particular problems, particularly in ascertaining exactly when damage occurred.

177. It should be noted that, instead of a basic fire insurance with all or any of the above additional perils insured, it is possible to have 'all risks' insurance on property. This will cover any loss or damage arising accidentally except any not covered by ordinary wear and tear, inevitable depreciation or inherent vice and by any express exclusions.[537] In practice, express exclusions will both mirror the 'naturally occurring' perils excluded by the nature of all risks insurance and include specific risks which are never insured except by special arrangements, such as war and nuclear risks.

§4. Warranties and Conditions

178. Fire policies will invariably contain a number of standard warranties and conditions.[538] These often appear under the headings 'General Conditions' and 'Claims Conditions'. The latter will contain the obligations of the insured following a loss in terms of notice, etc. and including the express terms regarding fraudulent claims, subrogation, contribution and arbitration. All of these matters have been considered earlier in Part II. The General Conditions will in practice contain the following. The first is often merely repeating the general law in respect of the effect of material non-disclosure or misrepresentation.[539] The second is an 'alteration' clause providing that the insurance will be avoided unless the insurer consents to any alteration increasing

535. This excludes, *inter alia*, damage caused by rivers or the sea, etc. flooding as the result of a storm, although this can be covered by the next heading. Heavy rainfall without abnormal winds is not a 'storm' (*Oddy v. Phoenix Assurance Co. Ltd.* [1966] 1 Lloyd's Rep. 134), nor is an isolated gust of wind (*S & M Hotels Ltd. v. Legal and General Assurance Society Ltd.* [1972] 1 Lloyd's Rep. 157). *See also Anderson v. Norwich Union Fire Insurance Society Ltd.* [1977] 1 Lloyd's Rep. 293.
536. 'Flood' does not include the natural seepage of water; *see* *Young v. Sun Alliance & London Insurance* [1977] 1 WLR 104; *see* para. 67.
537. For the legal definition of 'all risks', *see* *British and Foreign Marine Insurance Co. v. Gaunt* [1921] 2 AC 41.
538. The following account deals with standard commercial fire policies. Domestic fire policies will have many of the provisions, although not usually all, although they may be worded and/or ordered differently.
539. It is not clear why this practice, which is of some antiquity, grew up. It adds nothing in legal terms and may be misleading since it is not worded to apply only to the period before commencement of the policy (although it can only apply then or on renewal) and does not make it clear that the duty of fair presentation arises on renewal.

the risk of damage[540] or arising by removal or the insured's interest ceasing to exist.[541] The third standard condition provides for any specific warranties to be continuing during the whole currency of the policy,[542] but mitigates the general law by providing in effect that breach of warranty shall bar a claim only in so far as it increases the risk of loss or damage.[543] The fourth condition imposes a general obligation to take reasonable precautions to prevent loss or damage.[544]

§5. Other Standard Provisions

179. In practice a fire policy will contain two further standard provisions. The first will be to impose average in the event of under-insurance,[545] although this is not always applied to domestic insurances. The second gives the benefit of the insurance to any purchaser of the property insured in the period between contract and completion.

This second provision is an attempt to deal with a rather unsatisfactory position that the general law reached in the situation where property insured by a vendor suffers an insured peril after he has contracted to sell the property to a purchaser, but before completion of the sale by the appropriate formal transfer of the legal title. After such contract, the purchaser obtains an equitable interest in the property, but this does not operate to give him any interest in the insurance proceeds.[546] Further, because the property is at the purchaser's risk from the date of contract, unless the contract provides otherwise, the insured vendor is entitled to enforce the contract against the purchaser. If he therefore recovers both the price of the property and the insurance monies, he must account to the insurers for the latter.[547] An attempt was made by statute to reverse this position,[548] but this was widely regarded as unsatisfactory and as a result insurers choose to provide contractually for the purchaser to have the benefit of insurance held by the vendor. As a result, in most cases there was somewhat unnecessary double insurance, since the wise purchaser would also insure.

More recently, it was recommended that the law concerning the risk of property between contract and completion should be changed, so that the risk remains with the vendor.[549] The law has not been formally changed, but standard conditions for the sale of land have been modified with this effect. The result should be that the position becomes much better and that the standard insurance provision referred to becomes unnecessary.

540. This is the modern 'increase of risk' clause discussed at para. 115.
541. Legally, the clause is probably a warranty in the sense described at para. 118.
542. Again, this is probably only confirmatory of the construction the law would reach anyway.
543. This may now be redundant given the provisions of the Insurance Act 2015. *See* para. 126.
544. As to this, *see* para. 64.
545. As to average, *see* para. 150.
546. *Rayner v. Preston* (1881) 18 Ch D 1.
547. *Castellain v. Preston* (1883) 11 QBD 380; *see* para. 154.
548. Law of Property Act 1925, s. 47, discussed in *Birds' Modern Insurance Law*, Ch. 11.
549. Law Commission Report No. 191, 1990.

§6. Specific Warranties

180. In commercial fire insurances, although not so often in domestic policies, it is usual for the insurer to control the risk by imposing specific warranties.[550] Typically these will involve an obligation on the insured to instal and maintain properly fire doors, fire alarms and, where appropriate, automatic sprinkler installations and other fire extinguishing appliances.

§7. Standard Optional Clauses

181. There is a wide range of other provisions that are used to a greater or lesser extent in fire policies. Typical such provisions are:

(1) those that will indemnify the insured against the cost of removing debris, dismantling or demolishing property and shoring up or propping property destroyed or damaged by fire;
(2) clauses extending cover to property temporarily removed from the premises;
(3) clauses providing that the interest of a third party such as a mortgagee, landlord or tenant is not prejudiced by any act or neglect of the insured (mortgagor, tenant or landlord) increasing the risk, provided that the third party notifies the insurer as soon as they know and pays any additional premium required;
(4) clauses waiving the insurer's subrogation rights against any parent or subsidiary company of the insured.

550. Whether or not these are warranties in the full sense described in para. 107, or merely clauses descriptive of the risk (*see* para. 114) will depend upon how they are construed in any particular case.

Chapter 2. Loss of Benefits Insurance

182. Loss of benefits insurance is normally referred to as consequential loss or business interruption insurance. As has been seen,[551] an ordinary indemnity insurance of property does not cover profits lost or expenses incurred by reason of the loss of the property.[552] For this reason, interruption insurance, which can cover any type of consequential loss, has become commonplace, either as an additional section to a property insurance policy or under a separate policy. The cover will be linked to the same perils as in a standard commercial property insurance policy, for example, fire, explosion, storm, flood, etc., but it is not sufficient for the peril to occur during the existence of the policy if the loss of profits occurs afterwards because the true peril insured against is the loss of profit not, for example, the fire.[553] In addition, cover is normally subject to what is called the material damage warranty, which requires that there must be a policy in force and a claim paid or admitted under it for material damage[554] caused by an insured peril before the interruption insurance is effective. The purpose of such insurance is to put the insured into the position he would have been in if the profits had been earned and he is therefore taxable on the indemnity received.[555]

183. Unless the policy is a valued policy, that is where the amount of indemnity is fixed as a certain sum per day or per week,[556] the measure of indemnity payable is based on the turnover of the business in the financial year preceding the loss.[557] From the turnover are deducted what are called the prime costs,[558] that is the costs of purchases, consumables and energy, which will not be incurred during the period of interruption, and the result is the basic indemnity. In substance, this will comprehend overhead expenses[559] and net profit. In addition, the policy will usually provide for increases in the costs of working in order to restore the business to normal trading as quickly as possible.[560]

---

551. *See* para. 65.
552. *Re Wright and Pole* (1834) 1 Ad & E 621; *Maurice v. Goldsborough Mort & Co* [1939] AC 452. Similarly, the loss of a market by reason of delay arising from an insured peril is not covered: *Lewis Emanuel & Son Ltd. v. Hepburn* [1960] 1 Lloyd's Rep. 304.
553. *Sexton v. Mountain* (1919) 1 LILR 507.
554. That is, the damage to the property.
555. *R v. Fir and Cedar Lumber Co. Ltd.* [1932] AC 441.
556. As to valued policies, *see* para. 197.
557. If there is no preceding year, because the business has not been running that long, the court has to do its best to assess what the turnover would have been: *Burts and Harvey v. Vulcan Boiler and General Insurance Co.* [1966] 1 Lloyd's Rep. 161.
558. Often described as the uninsured working expenses.
559. Wages and salaries, rent, etc., often referred to as standing charges.
560. For example, in *Henry Booth v. Commercial Union Assurance Co.* (1923) 14 LILR 114, there was insurance in respect of 'such sums as the insured shall necessarily pay for increase in the cost of working to continue the business for twelve months from the day of the fire'. It was held that the insured was entitled to both the extra cost of continuing in business and the cost of having to buy partly manufactured goods to replace those destroyed.

184. The insured is under a duty to take all reasonable steps to minimize his loss.[561] However, this does not require him to take on fresh premises nor, if he does, can the insurers at common law deduct profits made from the new premises from the amount of indemnity payable.[562] However, a standard term usually reverses this general point and allows deduction of such profits.

561. This is probably implied by the common law (*City Tailors Ltd v. Evans* (1921) 126 LT 439 at 443), but in any event is a standard term in such policies.
562. *City Tailors Ltd. v. Evans, supra* .

Chapter 3. Transport Insurance

185. The description 'transport insurance' is not one that is conventionally used in the UK, but it refers to insurances of goods in transit, whether by road, rail, sea or air. In the UK, the types of insurance concerned are recognized as goods in transit insurance, marine insurance and aviation insurance, of which the first two are considered in this chapter.[563]

§1. Goods in Transit Insurance

I. Description

186. The sort of goods in transit insurance effected will depend upon the legal relationship between the owner of the goods and the carrier of them, if they are different, and also whether the goods are being imported, exported or transported domestically.[564] If goods are being imported, they may be insured by a marine policy or an airfreight policy, as appropriate, up until the time that they reach their UK destination. Otherwise, they will be insured, if at all, as described below for domestic transit. Goods being exported may again be covered by the marine or air policy or they may be insured separately until they are loaded on the vessel or aircraft.[565] The regular exporter of goods will normally have a standing 'open cover' policy.

Standard contract terms covering the transport of goods domestically will normally impose some liability on the carrier in the event of loss due to the carrier's fault, and hence the carrier will normally effect liability insurance to cover this.[566] The well-advised owner will not be content with this and is likely himself to insure the goods under some form of all risks cover.[567] It is possible, though, and common for the carrier to effect insurance of the goods themselves and not just insurance of his potential legal liability in respect of them. This is because the law allows someone with a limited interest in goods to insure them and recover for their full value.[568] Whether or not this will apply in any particular case depends upon whether, properly

563. Aviation insurance is considered separately in Ch. 6, *infra* .

564. Goods being imported or exported will, in respect of their journey by road, normally be carried under the CMR Conventions under the Convention on Contracts for the International Carriage of Goods by Road.

565. This would be the normal course in the event of their sale under a fob contract.

566. In the event that the owner undertakes to insure, it has been held that the carrier's liability for negligence is excluded and that the owner's insurers will have no subrogation rights against him: *Coupar Transport (London) Ltd. v. Smith's (Acton) Ltd.* [1959] 1 Lloyd's Rep. 369.

567. Leading to double insurance in practice, although not often double insurance as a matter of law, since if the carrier is at fault in respect of a loss and is insured, his liability insurer will in law bear the loss. If the owner's insurer has indemnified the owner, it will have subrogation rights against the carrier (in effect, the latter's insurer). *See* para. 160.

568. *See* Part II, Ch. 6.

construed, the insurance was intended to cover more than the insured bailee's limited interest.[569]

One possible difficulty concerns the meaning of the words 'in transit'.[570] Subject to anything expressly to the contrary, the normal rule is that transit begins when the goods are received by the carrier,[571] so that if they are also insured while temporarily housed off the vehicle during the normal course of transit, which is the usual wording, they will be covered when stolen from the carrier's yard.[572] Transit will probably end when the goods have been unloaded off the vehicle and given into the custody of the recipient.[573]

II. Warranties, Conditions and Exceptions

187. There are a number of standard provisions in goods in transit policies that limit the insurer's liability either as exceptions or as warranties imposing obligations on the insured. It is very common to except liability for loss by theft occurring if the vehicle is 'left unattended' unless it is in a locked garage or secured yard. A vehicle is left unattended unless it is kept in the driver's view and he can give effective chase to anyone who attempts to make off with the vehicle or its goods.[574] However, a vehicle was 'attended' when it was left in a driveway for only a few seconds and was visible from a window.[575] If a vehicle can be left unattended only when in a locked garage, leaving it behind locked gates in a yard is not sufficient.[576] In practice the usual clause permits either garaging or leaving the vehicle in a locked yard which is fully enclosed,[577]

---

569. *Hepburn v. Tomlinson* [1966] AC 451; *see* para. 164. If the policy insures goods held 'in trust', this is not construed technically but merely refers to goods entrusted to the insured: *Waters v. Monarch Fire and Life Assurance Co.* (1856) 5 E & B 870 at 880; *Rigby (Haulage) Ltd. v. Reliance Marine Insurance Co.* [1956] 2 QB 468.
570. As to the words 'whilst in warehouse' or 'whilst in store', which may appear as additional cover, *see Leo Rapp Ltd. v. McClure* [1955] 1 Lloyd's Rep. 292 (warehouse means some sort of covered building, not a yard however secure); *see also Firmin and Collins Ltd. v. Allied Shippers Ltd.* [1961] 1 Lloyd's Rep. 633; *Wulfson v. Switzerland General Insurance Co. Ltd.* (1940) 163 LT 136.
571. *Kilroy Thompson Ltd. v. Perkins and Homer Ltd.* [1956] 2 Lloyd's Rep. 49.
572. *Crow's Transport Ltd. v. Phoenix Assurance Co. Ltd.* [1965] 1 WLR 383.
573. *Bartlett and Partners Ltd. v. Meller* [1961] 1 Lloyd's Rep. 487.
574. *Starfire Diamond Rings Ltd. v. Angel* [1962] 2 Lloyd's Rep. 217; *Ingleton Ltd. v. General Accident Fire and Life Assurance Corporation* [1967] 2 Lloyd's Rep. 179; *Sanger v. Beazley* [1999] Lloyd's Rep. IR 424. *See also Hayward v. Norwich Union Insurance Ltd* [2001] Lloyd's Rep. IR 410 regarding a clause against leaving keys in the ignition.
575. *Langford v. Legal and General Assurance Society Ltd.* [1986] 2 Lloyd's Rep. 103. The same applies if the driver is asleep inside: *Plaistow Transport Ltd. v. Graham* [1966] 1 Lloyd's Rep. 639.
576. *A Cohen & Co. Ltd. v. Plaistow Transport Ltd.* [1968] 2 Lloyd's Rep. 587.
577. In such a case it is no defence that the driver was obliged to leave the vehicle in order to comply with statutory requirements, e.g., relating to rest periods, since the driver should not have started the journey unless he had sufficient time to reach a proper parking place within the requirements: *Lowenstein & Co. Ltd. v. Poplar Motor Transport Ltd.* [1968] 2 Lloyd's Rep. 233.

and excuses non-attendance in day-time if the insured had no option but to leave the vehicle unattended and takes all reasonable safety and security precautions.

A standard condition or warranty requires the insured to take all reasonable precautions to protect and safeguard the goods, to use such protective appliances as may be specified in the policy and to maintain all vehicles, trailers, container and protective devices in good order. Such a term will be construed in accordance with the construction of such terms in insurance policies generally.[578] There may well be warranties relating to the reliability of employees.[579]

The standard conditions in goods in transit policies cover such matters as average, contribution and subrogation, cancellation and the claims procedure. Invariably such policies are subject to an excess and a limit expressed per any one loss.[580]

578. As to reasonableness clauses, *see* para. 58.
579. *See* , e.g., *Mint Security Ltd. v. Blair* [1982] 1 Lloyd's Rep. 188.
580. Discussion of all these can be found elsewhere in this work.

Chapter 4. Marine Insurance

188. As has been described earlier, marine insurance law follows in most respects the general insurance law, the notable fact being that it is codified in the Marine Insurance Act 1906. The account here will concentrate on the aspects of marine insurance that are particular to it and on the standard policies used. But first it is necessary to give a brief outline of the structure of the marine insurance industry in the UK.

§1. Structure of Marine Insurance Business in the UK

189. In the UK, marine insurance can be obtained from Lloyd's, the UK company market or the overseas market. Lloyds is also a centre for marine intelligence: the 'Lloyd's Shipping Index', published weekly, details vessels movements worldwide; 'Lloyd's Register and Lloyd's Confidential Index' gives details of vessels and their owners; while the 'Voyage Record' sets out a vessel's previous and current voyages. Business is placed at Lloyd's not directly but through a Lloyd's broker. It is the broker's job to present a 'slip' to Lloyd's underwriters (who act on behalf of syndicates) seeking their initials in order to underwrite a percentage or all of the risk.[581] The policy is prepared by the broker and submitted to the Lloyds Policy Signing Office for checking and signing. Another department, the Lloyds Underwriters' Claims and Recoveries Office, as the name suggests, handles claims. Lloyds are facilitated by the appointment of Lloyds' Agents throughout the world who provide information, conduct surveys and sometimes settle claims.

There is a strong company market in London and many of the companies are members of the Institute of London Underwriters (ILU). The Institute operates through committees, one of which is responsible for drafting and updating standard insurance clauses now in use throughout the world. In addition many risks can be covered by membership of a mutual insurance association or protection and indemnity club. Section 85 of the Marine Insurance Act specifically provides that where two or more persons mutually agree to insure each other against marine losses, there is said to be mutual insurance. There is nothing in principle that distinguishes insurance with such an association from insurance obtained from Lloyds or the company market.[582]

---

581. *General Reinsurance Corporation v. Forsakringsaktiebolaget Fennia Patria* [1983] QB 856, where it was held that on initialling, each broker was bound to the insurance contract for that amount overruling previous case law which suggested that the underwriter could withdraw up until the final initialling. *See also* para. 94.

582. *See* generally, Hill, Robertson and Hazelwood, *An Introduction to P & I*; Hazelwood, *P & I Clubs: Law and Practice*, and Braekhus and Rein, *Handbook on P & I Insurance* (3rd ed., Jeremy Kingsley).

§2. Marine Insurance Act 1906

190. The Marine Insurance Act 1906 (hereinafter called the '1906 Act') is a codification of the law relating to marine insurance,[583] and is the legal basis of marine insurance today. A marine insurance contract is defined in the 1906 Act as a contract which indemnifies against 'marine losses', that is losses incidental to a marine adventure.[584] Further, the 1906 Act specifies that a contract of marine insurance can be extended, either expressly or impliedly, to cover mixed sea and land risks thereby avoiding the need for separate insurance policies to cover both the land and sea journey.[585] The schedule to the 1906 Act contains a standard policy form, known as the Lloyd's SG Policy.[586] This policy was first adopted in 1779 and the wording of insurance companies' policies was substantially the same. Any amendments made were incorporated by attaching slips to the policy, or by writing in the margin of the policy. This resulted in the old policy form being laden with amendments, making interpretation very complex. Following severe judicial criticism and a critical report from the United Nations Commission on Trade and Development (UNCTAD),[587] since 1 January 1982 the Lloyd's SG policy has been replaced by the Lloyd's Marine Policy,[588] used in conjunction with the Institute of London Underwriters' Clauses.[589] The more important clauses for present purposes are:

583. *Container Transport International Inc. v. Oceanus Mutual Underwriting* [1984] 1 Lloyd's Rep. 476, at 490 per Kerr LJ; *see* further Chalmers, Marine Insurance Act 1906 (9th ed., 1983) where in the 'Introduction to First Edition of Digest (1901)' the draftsman stated that 'the object of [the 1906 Act] was to reproduce as exactly as possible the existing law, without making attempt to amend it'.
584. 1906 Act, s. 1. For further definition of a marine adventure *see* s. 3 especially subsection (2) which lists particular examples of a marine adventure: where a ship or goods are exposed to maritime perils, or where freight or other earnings are endangered by maritime perils, or any liability to a third party can be incurred by reason of a maritime peril. 'Maritime perils' means perils consequent on or incidental to the navigation of the sea, such as perils of the sea, fire, pirates, jettison, etc.
585. *See* , e.g., *Fuerst Day Lawson Ltd. v. Orion Insurance Co. Ltd.* [1980] 1 Lloyd's Rep. 656, where oil was insured on steamer and/or steamers and/or conveyances or any other method of transportation from 'anywhere to anywhere'; *H. Cousins & Co. Ltd. v. D and C Carriers Ltd.* [1971] 2 QB 230, where the relevant consignment was insured from Hong Kong to the Port of London, and thence by road to Scotland.
586. 'SG' stands for ships and goods.
587. *See* UNCTAD Official reports TD/B/590.
588. The policy itself does not contain the terms of the insurance contract, rather it is a schedule of information including: policy number, names of assured and vessel, period of insurance, subject matter insured, agreed value, premiums, etc.
589. The clauses were drafted by the Technical and Clauses Committee of the Institute of London Underwriters (ILU) and can be revised from time to time, to meet the needs of the insurance world. They contain the terms of the insurance contract – risks covered or excluded, duration of the policy, duties of the parties, measure of indemnity, assignment of policy, a choice of law clause, etc. The main clauses relate to cargo, hulls and freight, covering marine, war and strike risks, over a period of time or for a particular voyage. There are in excess of 150 clauses; the current ones are set out in the annual publication, 'Witherby's Reference Book of Marine Insurance Clauses'.

- Institute Cargo Clauses (ICC) A, B and C – (ICC A, B, C); Institute Time Clauses (Hulls) – (ITC (Hulls)); Institute Voyage Clauses (Hulls) – (IVC (Hulls)); Institute Time Clauses (Freight) – (ITC (Freight)); Institute Voyage Clauses (Freight) – (IVC (Freight)).
- The Lloyd's Policy and the relevant clauses together form the marine insurance contract.

§3. Insurable Interest

191. Because the marine insurance contract is a contract of indemnity, section 4(1) of the Act states that every contract of marine insurance by way of gaming or wagering is void. The section then codified the existing case law on the issue, so for example, a contract is deemed to be a wagering contract where the assured has no insurable interest or has no expectation of an insurable interest on entering the contract,[590] or where the policy is made with the terms 'interest or no interest' or 'without further proof of interest than the policy itself', or other similar terms.[591] The relevant time for determining whether the contract is an insurance contract or a wagering contract is the time the contract is concluded.

192. This is to be distinguished from the issue of whether or not the contract is a contract of indemnity – here the assured must have an insurable interest at the time of the loss.[592] Examples of insurable interests are given in the Act. These include defeasible and contingent interests,[593] and a partial interest.[594] A mortgagor has an insurable interest in the full value of the subject matter, while a mortgagee has an insurable interest only in respect of such sums due or to become due under the mortgage.[595] A master or crew member has an insurable interest in his wages.[596]

§4. Duty of Fair Presentation of the Risk

193. Sections 18, 19 and 20 of the Act, which codified the common law relating to the duty of disclosure of materials facts, disclosure by an agent of the assured and misrepresentation of material facts were totally repealed and replaced by the Insurance Act 2015, as that Act applies to marine insurance as well as non-marine insurance.[597] The Consumer Insurance (Disclosure and Representations) Act 2012 had already

590. 1906 Act, s. 4(2)(a).
591. 1906 Act, s. 4(2)(b). In the case of *Cheshire v. Vaughan* [1920] 3 KB 240, a PPI policy (policy proof of interest) was held to be void despite the fact that the insured may have had an insurable interest.
592. 1906 Act, s. 6.
593. 1906 Act, s. 7.
594. 1906 Act, s. 8.
595. 1906 Act. s. 14(1), (2).
596. 1906 Act, s. 11.
597. *See* paras 110 ff. Note also the statutory expression of the principle of utmost good faith in s. 17, which was modified by the 2015 Act.

reformed the law when a consumer takes out a marine policy. Particular examples in the marine context of what is considered material, a question that remains relevant under the 2015 Act, include the honesty of the assured,[598] and unusual terms of the relevant underlying contract.[599]

§5. General Rules

194. Section 22 provides that a contract of marine insurance is inadmissible as evidence unless it is embodied in a policy. The lack of a policy does not however invalidate the contract. Formal requirements are minimal. Sections 23 and 24 specify that the policy must contain the name of the assured and a signature of the insurer; and section 26 requires designation with reasonable certainty of the subject matter. Section 52 further provides that the issuance of the policy and the payment of the premium are concurrent conditions. Other documents are often issued, such as a certificate of insurance in the case of open cover and floating policies, or a cover note. Neither of these amounts to a policy,[600] and major differences exist between these documents and a policy. Only the policy sets out, in detail, the terms of the insurance, and only with a policy does the insured have a direct right of action against the insurer. Additionally, if a broker has not been paid, he has a lien on the policy only.

I. Classification of Policies

195. The 1906 Act classifies policies under various headings. Depending on the classification, the rules concerning the commencement of the risk, the terms implied, the duties of the parties and the methods of processing a claim all differ.

A. Voyage and Time Policies

196. Section 25 defines a contract to insure the subject matter 'at and from' or from one place to another, for example, 'from Hong Kong to London', as a voyage policy. This type of policy is most often used to insure cargo though it may be used to insure hulls. If however the contract is to insure the subject matter for a 'definite

598. *See The Kylie* [1983] 1 Lloyd's Rep. 444; *see* further *The Moonacre* [1992] 2 Lloyd's Rep. 501.

599. For contrast *see The Bedouin* (1894) P 1, where an off-hire clause was found to be usual in a time charter-party, and *Tate v. Hislop* (1885) 15 QBD 368, where an exemption clause was found to be unusual and hence should have been disclosed.

600. *See Diamond Alkali v. Bourgeois* [1921] 3 KB 443, and *Wilson & Holdgate v. Belgium Grain* [1920] 1 KB 1.

period of time' the policy is called a time policy.[601] This is the standard policy used to insure a ship. Accordingly, the ship is insured at all times within the period specified, usually one year, and cover is not dependant on issues such as when a voyage commences or ends. The main distinction is that under section 39(1) in a voyage policy there is an implied warranty that the vessel is seaworthy at the commencement of the voyage, whereas section 39(5) expressly provides that there is no equivalent warranty with a time policy. The rationale is that with a voyage policy, the insured is in control of the ship before it sails and therefore in a position to have it repaired, and made seaworthy if necessary. This may not be possible with a time policy where the ship may be at sea when the policy commences. Section 25 also allows for the possibility of a mixed time-voyage policy.[602]

B. *Valued and Unvalued Policies*

197. The 1906 Act also distinguishes between valued and unvalued policies.[603] A valued policy is one that specifies the agreed value of the subject matter insured.[604] The agreed valuation usually includes a profit factor in the form of a percentage of the agreed value. An unvalued policy does not specify an agreed value but sets a maximum limit within which the insurable value must be subsequently ascertained, when a claim is made.[605] Valued policies avoid disputes when a claim is made and are the norm today.

The significant difference between the two concerns the method of calculating the amount payable under the policy. Section 67 states that the sum the insured can recover in respect of a loss is called the measure of indemnity. Once the agreed value has been set, it forms the basis on which the total and partial loss claims will be calculated irrespective of changes in the market value. Section 68(1) provides that where there is a total loss the measure of indemnity is the sum agreed in the policy.

601. The meaning of the phrase 'time policy' was examined in *The Eurysthenes* [1977] QB 49. There the vessel was entered with a mutual insurance association on 17 Feb. 1972. According to the rules of the association, cover ran from the date of entry to noon 20 February of that particular or following year, when the policy year began, and continued thereafter from year to year until determined. The policy was still in existence in April 1974 when the vessel stranded. The Court of Appeal rejected the contention that the policy was not for 'a definite period of time' because it continued indefinitely until determined by either side. Instead the court held that the vessel was covered from 17–20 Feb. 1972, and again from 20 Feb. 1972 to 20 Feb. 1973, etc., each period representing a definite period of time.
602. In *The Al-Jubail IV* [1982] 2 Lloyd's Rep. 637, a vessel was insured 'for 12 months from and on the voyage from Singapore to the Persian Gulf, and whilst trading in the Gulf'. The court held this to be a mixed policy and also found that a warranty of seaworthiness applied although this point is laid down in the 1906 Act. The reasoning was based on the rationale for a warranty of seaworthiness in voyage policies, namely that the insured is in control of the vessel at the beginning of the voyage and in the best position to effect repairs, etc. The court also noted how the delivery part of the voyage resembled a voyage policy where a warranty of seaworthiness is implied by statute.
603. 1906 Act, s. 27(1).
604. 1906 Act, s. 27(2).
605. 1906 Act, s. 28.

Under a valued policy, and in the absence of fraud, the value fixed in the policy is conclusive evidence of the insurable value of the subject matter insured.[606] Despite this statement, cases in the past have concerned disputes as to the amount payable. So, for example, the agreed value was reopened where only part of the cargo insured for GBP 5000 was loaded,[607] and again under a freight policy where the value was based on a full cargo, because the ship sank with only a half cargo.[608] Rather than denying the conclusive nature of the valuation these cases can be viewed as scaling down to proportion the agreed value, while recognizing its conclusive nature, thus ensuring that the measure of indemnity is in proportion to the risk taken. With unvalued policies, there must be an inquiry into the value involving expert evidence, the production of invoices, estimates, etc. The means of ascertaining the insurable value is set out in section 16; for example, the value of a ship is its value at the commencement of the risk, including among other things its outfit, provisions and stores for the officers and crew, plus insurance charges. Regarding goods the insurable value is the 'prime cost'[609] of the property plus shipping expenses and insurance charges.[610]

C. Floating Policies

198. This is a type of insurance cover used in the export trade to cover goods, described in general terms, where the particulars are declared on shipment.[611] The insurance automatically covers each shipment that comes within the general description. A master policy is valued at a fixed sum, and each time there is a shipment the overall value of the policy is reduced by the value of the shipment. The insurer supplies a blank book of declaration forms, on which the shipper fills in the particulars of each shipment and sends them to the insurer. Cover is usually for one year, though this is not a time policy, rather it is a succession of voyage policies. Section 29 is the governing section. It provides among other things for the prompt making of declarations,[612] and

606. 1906 Act, s. 27(3); *see* , e.g., *Shaw v. Felton* (1801) East 109 where a ship insured for GBP 6,000 encountered bad weather and became a wreck. In trying to reach shore it sank. The insurers argued that the amount payable was the value of the ship when it was lost, that is, its value as a wreck. It was held that the value in the policy was conclusive. Any examination into the true value would be too burdensome and would lead to endless litigation. In *General Shipping v. British General* (1923) 15 Ll L R 175, the insurers claimed that the hull was grossly overvalued at GBP 5,000. It had been bought recently for approximately GBP 2,000, and its value at the time was GBP 1,500. The court held that, as the insurers were in a position to examine the value of the ship, but accepted the GBP 5,000 valuation along with the relevant premiums, the value was conclusive.

607. *Rickman v. Carstairs* (1833) 5 B & Ad 651.

608. *Forbes v. Aspinall* (1831) 13 East 323.

609. The term 'prime cost' is not defined in the 1906 Act; for interpretation of this phrase, *see Williams v. Atlantic Assurance* [1932] All ER Rep. 32 per Greer LJ at 40, and *The Captain Panagos* [1985] 1 Lloyd's Rep. 625.

610. As to the possibility of a claim in damages for late payment, see para. 143, *supra* .

611. 1906 Act, s. 29(1).

612. For example, if the declaration is made after notice of loss or arrival, the policy will be treated as an unvalued policy, the amount payable to be determined at the time of loss, 1906 Act, s. 29(4).

that any valuations must be honestly stated.[613] Today, in the export trade, floating policies have been replaced by open cover.

§6. Open Cover

199. There is no legislative provision for open cover. Nevertheless it has become the most popular means of effecting general cover for recurring shipments. It involves declarations followed by the issuing of insurance certificates. However insurance certificates are not insurance policies. Rather a certificate is a document by which the underwriter agrees to issue a policy within the terms of the cover. Often, there is no time limit – perpetual open cover – and no financial limit.

§7. Blanket Cover

200. Unlike the above two options, blanket cover does not involve declarations regarding individual shipments, hence avoiding excessive paperwork. This type of cover is most suitable for short voyages, frequent shipments and small quantities of cargo. It usually provides for a lump sum premium to cover all shipments over a period of time.

§8. Subject Matter of Insurance

201. The principal types of subject matter insured under a marine policy are ships,[614] goods[615] and freight.[616] Other examples include profits, wages, the liability of the shipowner to cargo owners, loans and disbursements.

613. 1906 Act, s. 29(3).
614. Rule 15 of the Rules for Construction appended to the First Schedule of the 1906 Act to assist in the interpretation of a marine policy states: 'The term ship includes hull, materials and outfit, stores and provisions for the officers and crew, and in the case of vessels engaged in a special trade, the ordinary fittings requisite for the trade … .'
615. Rule 17 of the Rules for Construction states: 'The term goods means goods in the nature of merchandise, and does not include personal effects or provision and stores used on board.'
616. Rule 16 of the Rules for Construction states: 'The term freight included the profits derivable by a shipowner from the employment of his ship to carry his own goods or moveables, as well as freight payable by a third party, but does not include passage money.'

§9. Attachment and Duration of Risk

I. Time Policies

202. There is no real difficulty in ascertaining when risk attaches under a time policy. In the Lloyd's Marine Policy Form, there is a space headed 'Voyage or Period of Insurance', where the commencement and termination dates of the risk are filled in, for example, 'noon 25 December 1992 to noon 25 December 1993'. There are no IST for cargo, but there are for hulls and freight. Two provisions of these Clauses warrant particular mention. They are the continuation clause[617] and the termination clause.[618] The continuation clause, a type of held covered clause, provides that where the vessel is at sea when the insurance expires, the subject matter insured – the vessel or freight – shall be held covered at a pro rata monthly premium to the port of destination provided previous notice is given to the underwriters. Similar to voyage policies where the vessel is insured throughout the voyage, the continuation clause provides protection where the vessel is still at sea due to unforeseen circumstances, for example, if the vessel is in distress or feared lost, in which case renewal would be difficult.[619] The termination clause specifies that the insurance shall terminate automatically on the happening of various events, for example, if the vessel changes class, or there are any changes in ownership, flag, or management. The rationale is that all these changes affect the risk undertaken and are material to the underwriters. This provision can be amended or excluded with the underwriters' written consent. Where the insurance is terminated the clause provides for a pro rata daily net return of premium.

II. Attachment and Duration of Risk under Voyage Policies

A. Hulls and Freight

203. The Schedule to the 1906 Act contains 'Rules for Construction of Policy' which apply to the Lloyd's SG Policy 'or other like form'. Rules 2–5 concern the attachment and duration of risk regarding voyage policies. Rule 2 states that where the subject matter is insured from a particular place, the risk does not attach until the ship starts on the voyage insured. Rule 3 states that where the subject matter is insured at and from a particular place and the ship is at that place in good safety when the contract is concluded, the risk attaches immediately. But if the ship is not at that place when the contract is concluded, the risk attaches as soon as it arrives there in good safety. In one case the vessel was insured 'at and from Havana to Greenwich' and the ship arrived at Havana but was damaged the next day. The court held that the ship was insured despite being damaged later, because it had arrived in good safety.[620] In another

617. ITC (Hulls) Clause 2; ITC (Freight) Clause 3.

618. ITC (Hulls) Clause 4; ITC (Freight) Clause 5.

619. In practice, renewal of insurance is usually negotiated well before the termination date, often up to months in advance, so the usefulness of this clause is diminished.

620. *Haughton v. Empire Marine Insc* (1866) LR 1 Ex 206.

case, where the vessel arrived at the port of commencement in a damaged condition, it was held that the ship was not in good safety so the risk did not attach.[621]

The relevant provisions in the 1906 Act are sections 42–49. Section 42, recognizing the above rules, provides that if the subject matter is insured under a voyage policy, it is not necessary that the ship should be at the port of commencement when the contract is concluded. Further, section 42(1) implies a condition that the adventure must be commenced within a reasonable time and if it is not so commenced, the insurer may avoid the contract.[622] Other provisions affecting the attachment of risk provide that if the port of departure,[623] or the destination,[624] is specified in the policy, and the vessel leaves from or arrives at different ports, the risk does not attach. The remaining sections state that, unless otherwise provided, the insurer is discharged from liability if there has been a change of voyage,[625] or an unjustifiable deviation[626] or delay.[627] The Institute Clauses usually provide otherwise, as explained in the following paragraphs.

204. In Lloyd's Marine Policy, under the section headed 'Voyage or Period of Insurance', it is specified the particular voyage to be insured. For example, 'from Hull to Le Havre', or 'at and from Hull to Le Havre until moored and twenty-four hours in good safety'.[628]

205. As far as commencement is concerned, Clause 1.1 IVC (Hulls) simply states: 'The vessel is covered subject to the provisions of this insurance *at all times* (emphasis added) … .' None of the other clauses sheds further light on this subject of attachment of risk. Similar rules apply to chartered freight as to hulls,[629] but with other types of freight, risk attaches pro rata as goods are shipped, subject to the proviso of readiness to receive cargo.[630] This applies, for example, in the liner trade.

206. As far as continuation is concerned, as noted previously, sections 45–49 list circumstances where the insurer is discharged from liability unless contrary provision is made, as in Clause 2 of IVC (Hulls) and Clause 3 of IVC (Freight). These are held covered clauses in case of deviation or change of voyage, provided notice is given to the underwriter and there is agreement as to amended terms of cover and additional premium. Beyond what is specified in the policy, Clause 1.2 states that there is no cover for towage unless customary (hulls and freight), and transhipment is not covered (hulls only), unless previous notice is given to the underwriters and amended terms of cover and additional premium is agreed.

207. The insurance cover terminates at the end of the voyage as specified in the policy. At what point in time a voyage ends is not always easy to assess and terms

621. *Parmeter v. Cousins* (1809) 2 Camp 235.
622. *De Wolf v. Archangel* (1874) LR 9 QB 451.
623. 1906 Act, s. 43.
624. 1906 Act, s. 44.
625. 1906 Act, s. 45.
626. 1906 Act, ss 46, 49.
627. 1906 Act, ss 48, 49.
628. This wording is taken from the Lloyd's SG policy and was commonly used. The twenty-four hours was needed to ensure that the ship was in good safety. There is no reference to such a period in the modern policy form.
629. *See Foley v. United Fire and Marine Insc* (1870) LR 5 CP 155 and *Beckett v. West England Marine Insurance* (1871) 25 LR 739.
630. Rules for Construction, Rule 3.

such as 'moored and twenty-four hours in good safety' are often included to clarify the point.

B. Cargo

208. The transit clause, Clause 8, is identical to ICC A, B and C. It deals specifically with the duration of the risk and is based on what became known as the warehouse-to-warehouse clause.[631]

The clause begins: 'The insurance attaches from the time the goods leave the warehouse or place of storage at the place named therein for the commencement of the transit … .' Reference must be made to the Marine Policy which will specify the warehouse or place of storage under the heading 'Voyage or Period of Insurance'.[632] It seems that the goods are not covered by the transit clause while they are in the warehouse, or indeed while they are in the process of being loaded. Only when they have left the warehouse does risk attach. Some guidance on this point can be found in the American case of *Plata v. Lancashire*,[633] where a clause with identical wording was used. The cargo was tallow which was loaded by means of a pipeline from onshore tanks onto the ship. It was held that risk did not attach to that portion of the cargo which had not left the tanks; it was not in transit. However, the court did not go so far as to say the tallow should actually have passed into the ship's tanks before risk attached. Rather at some intermediate point, described as 'beyond the point of return', where there was a 'physical separation', the risk attached. On the facts this amounted to passing a gauge pump.

The lack of any case law on the ICC transit clause leaves many questions unanswered. For example, what if goods leave the warehouse mentioned therein and are taken to packers as part of the transit? Insurance practice is to say that risk does not attach until they leave the packers' premises on the basis that before packing, goods

631. This extended the cover under the old SG Policy which insured cargo only from when it was put on board the ship. Extensions became usual to cover lighters bringing cargo from the shore to the ship, and further to cover the journey to the docks thereby giving rise to mixed land and sea risks. The same problem existed at the end of the voyage, where under the SG Policy cover continued until the cargo was 'discharged and safely landed'. Again the period from dock to warehouse had to be separately insured. This lead to the development of the warehouse-to-warehouse clause where risk attached on leaving the warehouse, continued throughout the transit, and terminated on delivery to the other warehouse. Clause 8 of the ICC is the modern equivalent.

632. The old warehouse-to-warehouse clause did not specify 'the place named therein' rather it spoke of the risk commencing from the time the goods left the shipper or manufacturer's warehouse. The scope of this term was addressed in *Re Traders and General Insurance* (1924) 18 Ll L R 450, where goods were insured on a voyage from Antwerp. The goods had been manufactured at a Belgium inland town, carried to Antwerp and stored in a warehouse. Before the ship arrived, the goods were damaged by fire. The assured argued that the insurance commenced on leaving the manufacturer's warehouse inland, though this place was not mentioned. The court held otherwise, the insurance commenced when the goods left the Antwerp warehouse. Shipper's or manufacturer's warehouse refers to where the voyage commences, otherwise one could trace back indefinitely. The new wording of Clause 8 is a welcome clarification on this point.

633. [1957] 2 Lloyd's Rep. 347.

are not fit to be shipped. A similar problem arises regarding containers. The usual pattern is that goods are packaged into containers at the manufacturer's warehouse, and then transported to a container terminal to await the ship. The question is, does cover commence on leaving the manufacturer's warehouse or the container terminal? Again current practice favours the former. It is worth noting that Clause 19 provides that the insurance is subject to English law *and practice*, and therefore the above conclusions seem justified.

209. Clause 8 states that the insurance cover 'continues during the ordinary course of transit ... '. Clause 8.3 further provides that the insurance shall remain in force during delay beyond the control of the assured, any deviation, forced discharge, reshipment and transhipment and during any variation of the adventure. The insurance terminates on the happening of one of three events. First under Clause 8.1.1; 'on delivery to the consignee's or other final warehouse or place of storage at the destination named therein'. Words similar to these were litigated in *John Martin v. Russell.*[634] In this case, goods were discharged from the vessel and placed in a transit shed on the quay where they were damaged. The question was whether the insurance was still operative or had the cargo reached 'the consignee's or other final warehouse'. The court found that a transit shed constituted a warehouse, and the reference to 'consignee's' warehouse did not require the consignee to own the warehouse, it was enough that the consignee used the shed for storage. Regarding the word 'final', the court found that the transit shed was not a final warehouse rather a transit warehouse so the warehouse-to-warehouse clause was still operative. The clause as it is now worded, including place of storage, clarifies this point, so that on reaching the transit shed, cover would cease.

Second, Clause 8.1.2 refers to: 'any other warehouse or place of storage, whether prior to or at the destination named therein which the assured uses for storage other than in the ordinary course of transit, or for allocation or distribution'. This contemplates termination before or at a different place than the end of the voyage as specified. The effect of this clause is illustrated in *Safadi v. Western Assurance,*[635] where under an old warehouse to warehouse clause, goods were to be delivered inland to Damascus via Beirut. The insured stored the goods in Beirut thinking the insurance would not lapse until the goods arrived at Damascus. The court held that the goods were no longer in the ordinary course of transit and therefore were not covered. There was a similar finding in a case where the goods were stored elsewhere than the final destination for a period of five months.[636]

Third, Clause 8.1.3 provides for the termination of insurance on the basis of a time limit. If the insurance has not already lapsed under the above clauses, it will lapse under Clause 8.1.3 on the expiry of sixty days. Under the common law, insurance expired after a reasonable time.[637] At the beginning of the twentieth century, a thirty-day limit was introduced and this was extended to sixty days during World War II. The set limit avoids the problem of deciding what is a reasonable time. Under Clause 8.2, if once discharged the cargo starts on a new transit, the insurance terminates on

634. [1960] 1 Lloyd's Rep. 554.
635. (1933) 46 Ll L R 110.
636. *Industrial Waxes v. Brown* [1958] 2 Lloyd's Rep. 626.
637. *Allagar Rubber v. National Benefit* (1922) 10 Ll L R 564.

the commencement of the transit to the new destination. Finally, Clause 8.3 referred to above, provides that the insurance remains in force despite delay, deviation, etc. However, this clause does not operate to extend cover beyond Clauses 8.1 and 8.2. Also while insurance continues despite delay, loss caused by delay is not covered (*see infra*).

§10. Risks

I. Included in a Marine Policy

210. Out of a long list of potential risks covered by a marine insurance policy, the following more important ones will be examined in some detail.

211. Perils of the Sea: Section 1 of the 1906 Act speaks of a marine insurance contract indemnifying against losses incidental to a marine adventure. Section 3 then defines marine adventure, which includes being 'exposed to maritime perils', which in turn is defined, in part, as 'perils of the sea'. It is important to note that sections 1 and 3 do not govern any particular policy, rather they determine whether the policy comes within the Act. What risks are actually covered depends on the individual policy.

The Lloyd's SG policy used the term 'perils of the sea'. Today both the ITC (Hulls) and (Freight), and the IVC (Hulls) and (Freight), list perils of the sea as a risk covered. However, no reference to perils of the sea is made in the ICC. There, Clause A covers all risks, so perils of the sea are impliedly insured against, but Clauses B and C, Subclause 1 (similar though not identical) list specific causes of loss, synonymous with perils of the sea but fail to mention that term. For example, Clause 1.1.2 refers to vessels being 'stranded, grounded, sunk, or capsized'.

The Rules for Construction offer some guidance as to the meaning of the phrase 'perils of the sea'. Accordingly, the term refers 'only to fortuitous accidents, or casualties of the seas. It does not include the ordinary action of the winds and waves.' The leading case in this area is *The Xantho*,[638] where a ship was lost due to a collision with another ship. The House of Lords held that the collision had been a peril of the sea. An extract from Lord Herschell's judgment is illuminating on the point:

> I think it clear that the term 'perils of the sea' does not cover every accident or casualty which may happen to the subject-matter of the insurance on the sea. It must be a peril 'of' the sea. Again, it is well settled that it is not every loss or damage of which the sea is the immediate cause that is covered by these words. They do not protect, for example, against that natural and inevitable action of the winds and waves, which results in what may be described as wear and tear. There must be some casualty, something which could not be foreseen as one of the necessary incidents of the adventure. The purpose of the policy is to secure an indemnity against accidents which may happen, not against events which must happen.

638. (1887) 12 App Cas 503.

In the case of *Hamilton, Fraser v. Pandorf*,[639] the House of Lords held that damage caused by sea water which entered by a hole in a pipe which had been gnawed by rats was damage caused by perils of the sea.[640] In a later case, overheating due to the ventilators being closed because of heavy seas damaged rice. Again it was held that the damage was caused by a peril of the sea.[641] However, damage caused by a burst boiler was held not to be a peril of the sea.[642]

212. Scuttling: Doubt has been raised as to whether or not scuttling is a peril of the sea. In *Samuel v. Dumas*,[643] the master scuttled the ship, and it sank due to the incursion of sea water, arguably a peril of the sea. However, it was held that perils of the sea referred to fortuitous accidents and casualties, and the real cause of the loss was the deliberate conduct of the master in scuttling the ship. The problem here was that the claimant was an innocent mortgagee. The Clause 8 then in force was amended so that '… the Assured's right of recovery hereunder shall not be prejudiced by the fact that the loss may have been attributed to the wrongful act or misconduct of the shipowners or their servants, committed without the privity of the Assured … '. Despite criticism in *The Salem*,[644] that the provision was misdrafted in that it spoke of the insured's right to recovery, where in fact due to *Samuel v. Dumas* the insured had no right to recover, it was widely accepted that the amended Clause 8 succeeded in reversing the effect of *Samuel v. Dumas*. However, there is no equivalent to Clause 8 in the current ICC. This leaves open the effect of scuttling upon innocent parties such as mortgagees or cargo owners. The ICC A covers 'all risks', and there is no exclusion for scuttling, but ICC B and C do not cover all risks. Instead they list specific examples such as vessels being sunk or capsized only. This does not amount to scuttling. Even more importantly, in the general exclusion clause, Clause 4.7 excludes insurance cover for deliberate damage to or destruction of the subject matter insured by the wrongful act of *any person or persons*. Based on this provision, it seems that scuttling is not a risk insured against under the ICC B and C. To obtain cover in these circumstances a malicious damage clause should be added.

213. The Inchmaree Clause – Hulls and Freight only: It has been held that the explosion of a boiler is not a peril of the sea.[645] This finding was contractually reversed by what is known as the Inchmaree Clause. The present Inchmaree Clause can be found in ITC (Hulls), Clause 6.4 and IVC (Hulls) 4.2, which covers damage caused by accidents in loading, discharge or shifting of cargo or fuel, bursting of boilers, breakage of shaft, or any latent defect in the machinery or hull,[646] negligence of master, officers, crew or pilot, etc.

639. (1887) 12 App Cas 518.
640. It had previously held that damage caused by rats gnawing cargo was not a peril of the sea, *see Laveroni v. Drury* (1852) 8 Exch 166.
641. *Canada Rice Mill v. Union Marine Insurance* [1941] AC 55.
642. *Scindia v. London Insurance* [1937] 1 KB 639.
643. [1924] AC 431.
644. [1983] 1 All ER 745.
645. *Scindia v. London Insurance*, *supra* .
646. In *The Caribbean Sea* [1980] 1 Lloyd's Rep. 338, the policy contained an Inchmaree Clause. As the vessel was proceeding through the Panama Canal, it grounded and damage was caused to the ship. The vessel later sank in open sea. Goff J held this to be caused by a latent defect in the hull and therefore covered.

214. Other marine risks covered include loss or damage caused by fire or explosion, earthquake or other Act of God, jettison, discharge of cargo at port of distress (cargo only), or violent theft or piracy (hulls and freight only).[647]

II. Risks Excluded in a Marine Policy

215. The ITC have an identical general exclusion clause which lists various grounds on which liability is excluded; some have been mentioned already. Examples include loss or damage attributable to wilful misconduct of the assured, ordinary wear and tear, insufficient packing, inherent vice or delay. More specifically, under the cargo, hulls and freight clauses there are almost identical clauses for war exclusions, strike exclusions and nuclear exclusions. For ICC B and C, and the hulls and freight clauses, there is a malicious acts exclusion. Any loss or damage caused by these risks can be separately insured against using the specifically drafted clauses, which mirror almost exactly the relevant exclusion clauses.

216. An interesting exclusion clause can be found in the freight clauses, known as the 'charter freight' clause.[648] It provides that the insurance does not cover any claim consequent on the loss of time whether arising from a peril of the sea or not. The clause is based on the case of *Bensuade v. Thames and Mersey Insurance*,[649] where due to a shaft breaking on the first day of the voyage the ship had to return to port, frustrating the charter-party, which was cancelled. The shipowner claimed the loss of freight was due to the breakage and therefore was covered by an Inchmaree type clause. The court held that the loss was caused by delay which had led to the frustration and hence was not covered. More recently, the case was reaffirmed in *The Playa de les Nievas*,[650] where again the vessel broke down within hours of the commencement of the voyage. The vessel went off-hire, and the plaintiffs claimed for loss of hire from their insurers. They in turn denied liability on the basis that the loss was consequent on loss of time and therefore excluded. The insurers succeeded at first instance, lost on appeal where the Court of Appeal identified the effective and dominant cause as the breakage, but succeeded in the House of Lords.

§11. Excluded Losses

217. Loss caused by perils insured against is covered even though it would not have happened but for the misconduct or negligence of master or crew, but section 55(2)(a) also provides that the insurers are not liable for loss or damage attributable to the wilful misconduct of the assured. Also excluded is loss caused by delay, though the delay is caused by a peril insured against.[651] Finally the insured is not covered for

647. For a definition of piracy, *see The Andreas Lemos* [1983] 1 All ER 590.
648. *See* ITC (Freight) Clause 14 and IVC (Freight) Clause 12.
649. [1897] AC 609.
650. [1978] AC 853.
651. 1906 Act, s. 55(2)(b).

ordinary wear and tear, etc.[652] All these exclusions are effective unless the policy provides otherwise.

I. The Doctrine of Proximate Cause

218. Section 55, headed 'Included and Excluded Losses', provides that the insurer is liable if the loss is proximately caused by a peril insured against. The doctrine of proximate cause was once referred to 'the nearest cause in time'. In *Cory v. Burr*,[653] the ship was seized and lost because of the master smuggling goods. If the loss was caused by seizure, that is, the restraint of princes, this would be covered. However, if the loss was caused by smuggling, the loss would not be covered. The House of Lords held that the cause was seizure – the nearest in time.[654] This case forms the basis of section 55(2)(a) of the 1906 Act, which provides that the insurer is liable for loss proximately caused by perils insured against even though the loss would not have occurred but for the misconduct or negligence of the master and crew. As late as 1903, the cause 'nearest in time' was said to be the proximate cause. However, two subsequent House of Lords' decisions indicate a move away from the nearest in time to find the *effective* cause of the loss. The first of these is *Samuel v. Dumas*,[655] where the ship was scuttled. There were two possible causes: the intrusion of sea water which was covered as a 'peril of the sea' or the actual scuttling which was not covered. The court found that the true cause was not the perils of the sea, but the scuttling. In the second case, *The Coxwold*,[656] in order to lessen the possibility of attack from enemy submarines during World War II, the master ordered the ship to follow a zigzag course, technically amounting to a deviation. As a result of the unusual current, the ship was swept onto a sandbank and stranded. If stranding was the cause of the loss, the ship was covered but if the loss was caused by the instructed deviation, that is, a war risk, the loss would not be covered. The House of Lords held that the proximate cause was the instructed deviation. Viscount Simon spoke in terms of 'the effective and predominant cause'.[657] This reflects the position in non-marine insurance.[658]

Lastly, section 55 applies 'unless the policy otherwise provides'. It has been suggested that the ICC B and C have abandoned the doctrine of proximate cause because both clauses speak in terms of the insurance covering loss or damage 'reasonably attributable' to various factors. 'Attributable to' when compared with 'caused by' (which is used in IVC and ITC (Hulls)) is clearly a term capable of wider meaning. Why use different words if not to convey a different meaning? Others argue that it was not the intention of the drafters of the clauses to change long-established principles

652. 1906 Act, s. 55(2)(c).
653. (1883) 8 App Cas 313.
654. Other examples of nearest in time include: *Greenock SS v. Maritime Insc* [1903] 1 KB 367; and *Powell v. Gudgeon* (1816) 5 M&S 431.
655. [1924] AC 431.
656. [1942] AC 691.
657. *Ibid.*, at 698.
658. *See* para. 66.

of marine insurance law. But again we are left to surmise, until a case raising this point comes before the courts.

II. The Burden of Proof

219. The burden of proof that the loss comes within the policy lies on the insured.[659] Once this has been established, the burden shifts to the insurer to prove that the risk is excluded.[660]

§12. Particular and General Average Losses

220. Particular average loss is defined in section 64 as a partial loss of subject matter insured, caused by a peril insured against which is not a general average loss. Section 66 in turn defines a general average loss as a loss caused by or directly consequential on a general average act. This involves the notion that where there is a common danger and some part of the vessel or the cargo is sacrificed for the common good, the person who has suffered that loss can claim general average contribution from those who benefited from the general average act.[661] For example, if during a storm the captain had to jettison the deck cargo to prevent the vessel sinking, then the owners of the deck cargo could claim general average contribution from the shipowner and other cargo owners to compensate for their loss.

The question is whether these types of losses are covered by the contract of insurance. While the Lloyd's SG Policy did not cover partial loss in certain circumstances,[662] the Institute Clauses cover all partial losses, though it is possible to contract out of this. The measure of indemnity is calculated according to sections 69–71, subject to provisions in the policy. So, for example, where a ship is damaged, but not totally lost, the measure of indemnity where the ship has been repaired is the reasonable cost of the repairs, where the ship has only been partially repaired the measure of indemnity is reasonable cost plus reasonable depreciation, and where the ship has not been repaired

659. *The Popi M* [1985] 2 All ER 712; *The Marel* [1994] 1 Lloyd's Rep. 624.

660. *Golodetz v. Czarnikow-Rionda* [1980] 1 WLR 495 at 513.

661. General average is a doctrine of maritime law dating back to Ancient Rhodes and Roman Law. It is founded in restitution not contract law. The only connection between general and particular average is one of terminology. Today a clause is usually inserted in the contract of affreightment incorporating the York-Antwerp Rules, which are a standard set of rules governing general average. First formulated in 1877, the last revision was in 1974. They determine when contributions are payable and what amount to contribute. A general average claim is permitted under the York-Antwerp Rules where temporary repairs have been effected: *The Bijela* [1994] 2 All E.R. 289.

662. At the end of the Lloyd's SG Policy is a memorandum, which lists specific types of cargo. Some cargoes (corn, fish, etc.) are 'warranted free from average unless general'. According to Rule 13 of Rules for Construction average unless general is a partial loss, so these goods are warranted free from partial loss, only a total loss of these cargoes is covered. Other types of cargo such as sugar, hemp are 'warranted free from average under five pounds per cent'. This is known as a franchise, whereby any claim less than 5% is excluded, avoiding small claims.

and has not been sold the measure of indemnity is an amount equal to reasonable depreciation.

221. In relation to general average, rather than claiming from each other, parties claim on their insurance, hence avoiding the complications of average adjustment. The insurer on payment of the insurance money is subrogated to the rights of the assured under the contract of insurance, and may pursue the relevant claims. Any general average loss incurred, or any general average contribution paid can be recovered under the insurance,[663] subject to express provisions of the policy.

The Institute Clauses cover general average.[664] Regarding hulls and freight the relevant clauses provide that the assured may recover in respect of the whole loss without first enforcing their right of contribution from other parties. In relation to the cargo clauses, an identical clause provides that the insurance covers general average, adjusted and determined by the contract of affreightment.

§13. Partial Loss and Total Loss

222. This distinction is made in section 56(1) and is relevant to the measure of indemnity. Total loss is further subdivided into actual total loss or constructive total loss in subsection (2).

223. Actual total loss occurs where the subject matter insured is destroyed, or so damaged that it ceases to be the thing insured, or where the assured is irretrievably deprived of it.[665] A salutary example of actual total loss is given in section 58; where a ship is missing and after a reasonable time no news of it has been received, then an actual total loss may be presumed. Other examples of actual total loss include a case where moulds for light fittings were immersed in water during transit, rusted, and became totally useless for their purpose, even though in form they still looked the same.[666] In another case, a cargo of dates became immersed in sewage. The court held that vegetable matter of some use existed but the dates no longer existed in the sense referred to in the insurance policy, and so there was an actual total loss.[667] Again where a perishable cargo was sold by the master to avoid deterioration, it was held that there was an actual total loss of freight by the shipowner because freight was payable on delivery.[668]

224. Constructive total loss, however, occurs where although the physical subject matter still exists, for practical purposes it has lost its value. A comprehensive definition can be found in section 60.[669] Two types of loss are envisaged in section 60(1). The first is where the subject matter is reasonably abandoned on account of a total loss

663. 1906 Act, s. 66(5).
664. ICC Clause 2; ITC Hulls/Freight Clause 11 and IVC Hulls/Freight Clause 9.
665. 1906 Act, s. 57.
666. *Berger v. Pollock* [1973] 2 Lloyd's Rep. 442.
667. *Asfar v. Blundell* [1896] 1 QB 123.
668. *Milles v. Fletcher* (1779) 1 Doug KB 231.
669. *Petros M. Nomikos v. Robertson* (1939) 64 Ll L Rep. 45 where the House of Lords held that the whole of s. 60 is a definition, and not merely subs. (1) followed by illustrations in subs. (2) as had previously been suggested.

appearing to be unavoidable. So for example, if in a storm the ship was sinking, it would be reasonable to abandon the ship and this would be a constructive total loss; if the ship sank it would become an actual total loss. The second and more usual type of constructive total loss occurs because the subject matter could not be preserved from actual total loss without an expenditure that would exceed its value when the expenditure would be incurred. In determining whether there is a constructive total loss of this sort, the value of a wreck cannot be added to the cost of repairs in order to come within section 60. Thus in *Hall v. Hayman*,[670] the break-up value of the ship was United States Dollars (USD) 14,000; repairs would have amounted to USD 30,500. The repaired value would have been USD 34,000, and the insured sought to include the cost of repair in order to claim the vessel was a constructive total loss. The court held that the value of the wreck could not be taken into account. This approach is followed in the Institute Clauses where nothing in respect of damaged or break-up value of the vessel or wreck shall be taken into account.[671]

Where there is a constructive total loss, according to section 61 the insured can treat the loss as a partial loss, or abandon the subject matter and treat it as an actual total loss.

225. As far as abandonment is concerned, the relevant provisions are sections 62 and 63. The insured is required to give notice of abandonment.[672] No particular form is required,[673] but notice must be given with reasonable diligence.[674] The insurer can then accept or reject the notice.[675] Where there is a valid abandonment, the insurer is entitled to take over the interests of the insured and all proprietary rights;[676] for example, the insurer is entitled to any freight that has been carried, or where the ship is carrying the owner's goods, the insurer is entitled to remuneration under the contract of carriage.[677]

§14. Warranties

226. Warranties are standard terms in marine insurance contracts included to benefit both parties. They allow the insurer to limit the risk, which in turn reduces the premium. Defined in section 33(1) of the 1906 Act as a 'promissory warranty', subsection (3) states that a warranty is a 'condition which must be exactly complied with, whether

670. [1912] 2 KB 5.
671. ITC (Hulls) Clause 19; IVC (Hulls) Clause 17.
672. 1906 Act, s. 62(1).
673. 1906 Act, s. 62(2).
674. 1906 Act, s. 62(3).
675. 1906 Act, s. 62(4)–(9).
676. 1906 Act, s. 63(1).
677. 1906 Act, s. 63(2).

it be material to the risk or not'.[678] However, a breach of warranty no longer has the effect by statute of automatically discharging the insurer from liability, [679] and the section 11 of the Insurance Act 2015 described earlier may affect the operation of a breach.[680] Note that, as these provisions can be excluded in a non-consumer insurance contract, clear express provisions in a marine policy may have the same effect as previously.

Section 33(2) provides that warranties can be express or implied. If the former, they must be 'included in, or written upon, the policy, or must be contained in some document incorporated by reference into the policy'.[681] The 1906 Act contains some examples of warranties, for example, it states that where a ship is expressly warranted neutral there is also an implied condition that as far as the assured can control, it shall be properly documented,[682] or in a voyage policy there is an implied warranty that the ship is seaworthy,[683] or there is an implied warranty that the adventure insured against is lawful.[684]

Other examples include warranties that the ship will sail on or before a particular date,[685] that the ship will depart on a particular date,[686] that the ship's class is maintained,

678. This is sometimes referred to as the doctrine of strict and literal performance. An example of its application can be found in *Overseas Commodities v. Style* [1958] 1 Lloyd's Rep. 546, where the policy covered tins of canned pork, and contained the following; 'warranted all tins marked by manufacturers with a code of verification of date of manufacture'. Some tins were not marked in this manner. When the insured claimed for damage to the tins, the insurer successfully argued discharge from liability due to breach of warranty. The court went further and refused to allow a claim for a proportion of those damaged tins properly marked. *See* further Gilman, J.C.B., et al. *Arnould's Law of Marine Insurance and Average* 632 (14th ed.).

679. *See* *The Good Luck* [1991] 3 All ER 1 as to the effect of the now repealed final sentence of s. 33(3), discussed in para. 118.

680. *See* generally paras 118–127.

681. 1906 Act, s. 35(2).

682. 1906 Act, s. 36(2); there is no implied warranty as to a ship's nationality or that its nationality will not be changed during the voyage; *see* s. 37.

683. 1906 Act, s. 39, but s. 40 states that there is no implied warranty that the goods are seaworthy. Also if the subject matter is warranted 'well', or 'in good safety' on a particular day, s. 38 provides that it is sufficient if it be safe at any time during that day. Due to the fact that a cargo-owner has no control over the seaworthiness of the vessel, the position that a cargo-owner would not be insured in these circumstances is altered by ICC Clause 5 where the underwriters waive breach of this warranty unless the assured is privy to the unseaworthiness.

684. 1906 Act, s. 41. The rationale behind this provision can be found in *Redmond v. Smith* (1844) 7 Man & G 457 at 474 where Tindal CJ said: 'A policy on an illegal voyage cannot be enforced, for it would be singular if the original contract being invalid and, therefore, incapable to be enforced, a collateral contract founded upon it could be enforced.' For problems raised by statutory illegality, *see* *James Yachts Ltd. v. Thames and Mersey Marine Insc. Co. Ltd.* [1977] 1 Lloyd's Rep. 206; *St John Shipping Corp. v. Rank* [1957] 1 QB 266 and *Archbalds v. Spanglett* [1961] 1 QB 374.

685. *See* , e.g., *Ridsdale v. Newnham* (1814) 3 M & S 456; *Bouillon v. Lupton* (1863) 15 CBNS 113; *Nelson v. Salvador* (1829) Dan & Ll 219; and *Sea Insurance Co. v. Blogg* [1898] 2 QB 398.

686. *See* , e.g., *Moir v. Royal Exchange Insurance* (1815) 3 M & S 461.

or that the subject matter is partly uninsured;[687] regarding containers the policy could contain the words 'warranted full container load', in order to prevent damage to the cargo by 'stuffing' the container with other shipper's goods.

§15. Premiums

227. The premium is the consideration paid by the insured in return for the promise by the insurer to pay money in the case of certain events. The law assumes the payment of a premium, so the omission of a reference to premium in the contract will not vitiate the contract. Where the policy states premium or additional premium to be arranged, and it is not, section 31 states that a reasonable premium is payable. What is reasonable depends on the market and insurance practices. In *Hewitt v. London General Insurance*,[688] the vessel deviated to such an extent that a 'held covered clause subject to additional premium to be arranged' came into effect. The parties failed to agree on a figure, so the court had to decide. The effect of the deviation was to add 10% to the cost of the voyage but apart from a longer journey there was no extra risk. Had the issue been decided before the deviation, no extra premium would have been payable. Based on these facts the court held that no extra premium was payable.

Section 52 governs when the premium is payable and unless otherwise agreed, the payment of the premium and the issuance of the policy are concurrent conditions. But the validity of the insurance contract is not dependent on the issuance of the policy.[689]

228. Another important issue in this area relates to the return of premium. This can be regulated by agreement or, in default, by law. Examples of the former include ITC (Hulls) Clause 4 where there is provision for a pro rata daily net return of premium if the insurance is automatically terminated due to the happening of various events, such as change of classification, ownership or flag, etc. Another example is to be found in Clause 22, which provides for premium returns for lay-up or cancellation. Beyond these agreements, section 84 of the 1906 Act states that the premium is not returnable unless there is a total failure of consideration. What amounts to a 'total failure' therefore needs to be examined in greater detail. Subsection (3) provides a litany of circumstances where the consideration has failed including where the policy is void,[690] where the subject matter has never been imperilled,[691] or where the assured has had no insurable interest throughout the currency of the risk.[692] Section 84(2) distinguishes between partial failure and total failure of an apportionable part of the premium. In the latter

687. *See* , e.g., *General Insurance Company of Trieste v. Cory* [1897] 1 QB 335 and *Roddick v. Indemnity Insurance* [1895] 2 QB 380. *See also* ITC (Hulls) Clause 21.2 and IVC (Hulls) Clause 19.2.
688. (1925) 23 Ll L R 243.
689. *See* 1906 Act, s. 21.
690. 1906 Act, s. 84(3)(a).
691. 1906 Act, s. 84(3)(b).
692. 1906 Act, s. 84(3)(c).

case, a proportionate part of the premium is returnable.[693] Premium may be considered apportionable where it is calculated according to a measure of cargo, for example, 'GBP 5 premium per ton'.

§16. Sue and Labour Clauses

229. Section 78(4) of the 1906 Act states that it is the duty of the assured and his agents to take such measures as may be reasonable for the purpose of averting or minimizing a loss.[694] A similar statement of this duty can be found in ICC Clause 16, ITC (Hulls) Clause 13 and IVC (Hulls) Clause 11. There are two views as to the effect of this duty. One is that a breach simply allows the insurer to claim from the insured any loss the breach has caused.[695] What is probably the better view is that a failure to sue and labour wholly deprives the insured of his claim, as that, rather than an insured peril, becomes the real cause of the loss.[696] It seems unlikely that this would impose an obligation to litigate, as in practice subrogation[697] allows the insurer to take over the insured's rights, hence avoiding this issue.

§17. Assignment

230. Due to the chequered history in this area, a marine insurance policy can be assigned in equity, under the Law of Property Act 1925, section 136, or under the Marine Insurance Act 1906, section 50. Under section 136, written notice of assignment is needed but there is no time limit for notice. Under section 50, assignment is effected by endorsement or other customary manners.[698] A policy can be assigned before or after the loss,[699] but to be effective the assignor must have an interest at the time of assignment.[700] Assignment may be expressly prohibited.[701] Marine insurers are sensitive to changes in ownership of vessels, because it may affect the risk, to such an extent that under the Institute hulls and freight clauses any change in ownership results in an automatic termination of the insurance cover, unless the underwriters agree to the

693. Cases which illustrate instances where premiums are returnable include *Forbes v. Aspinall* (1811) 13 East 323 which concerned a freight policy, due to the fact that only some goods were on board when the ship was lost and *Rickman v. Carstairs* (1833) 5 B & Ad 651, where there was a valued policy on goods but a considerable portion of the cargo was not shipped at the time of the loss.
694. For detailed examination, *see* Rose, *Failure to Sue and Labour*, JBL 190 (1990).
695. *The Vasso* [1993] 2 Lloyd's Rep. 309.
696. *National Oilwell (UK) Ltd. v. Davy Offshore Ltd.* [1993] 2 Lloyd's Rep. 583; *Netherlands v. Youell* [1997] C.L.C. 938.
697. *See infra* para. 231.
698. For the meaning of other customary manner *see* *Baker v. Adam* (1910) 15 Com Cas 227; *Safadi v. Western Assurance* (1933) 46 Ll L R 140.
699. 1906 Act, s. 50(1).
700. 1906 Act, s. 51, *see* further *North of England Oil-Cake Co. v. Archangel* (1875) LR 10 QB 249.
701. 1906 Act, s. 50(1).

contrary in writing.[702] The hulls and freight clauses contain a similar 'assignment clause' which states that no assignment is binding unless a dated notice of assignment, signed by the assured, is endorsed on the policy and the policy is produced before payment of claim or return of premium.[703] In contrast cargo policies are usually freely assignable and as cargo changes hands frequently, so too do policies. Normally the policy can be assigned by blank endorsement, and no notice need be given to the insurers. An assignee acquires the same rights as the assignor against the insurer and any defence the insurer had against the assignor, can be used against the assignee.[704] The ICC does not contain a similar provision, though Clause 11, the 'insurable interest clause', requires that any person claiming under the policy have an insurable interest at the time of the loss.

§18. SUBROGATION

231. Section 79 provides that where there is a total or partial loss of subject matter insured, the insurer is entitled to take over the interests of the assured and is subrogated to all the rights and remedies of the assured, once he has paid the insured. Most problems arise where liability against third party is greater in tort than under the policy. The issue is whether the insurer is entitled to the windfall. In light of more recent cases this seems unlikely.[705]

Sister-ships can cause problems in this area. In the case of *Simpson v. Thomson*,[706] it was stated that the insurance company takes over the rights of the insured but does not gain additional rights. The case involved a collision between sister-ships and the insured sought to claim on the policy. The court found that the insurance company was strictly confined to the right of the assured, and because the assured could not sue himself, the insurance company was also prevented from recovering in this way. The Institute Clauses seek to avoid this ruling by use of 'the sister-ship clause', ITC (Hulls) Clause 9 and IVC (Hulls) Clause 7, which allow the assured to claim as if the other vessel was the property of others.

702. ITC (Hulls) Clause 4 and ITC (Freight) Clause 5.
703. ITC (Hulls) Clause 5; IVC (Hulls) Clause 3; ITC (Freight) Clause 6; and IVC (Freight) Clause 4.
704. 1906 Act, s. 50(2).
705. *See Yorkshire v. Nisbet* [1962] QB 330, in contrast *see Thames & Mersey v. British & Chilean SS* [1916] 1 KB 30. *See* further *Lord Napier and Ettrick v. Hunter* [1993] 2 WLR 42. The points are fully discussed in Part II at paras 137–142.
706. (1877) 3 App Cas 279.

Chapter 5. Liability Insurance

232. Insurance against the insured's potential legal liability to a third party, whether in contract or tort, is commonplace. In a number of instances, such insurance is required to be effected by statute and this is treated separately.[707] This chapter is concerned with the principles applicable to all liability insurances, which range from such effected by private insureds, commonly as a part of a standard household insurance policy, which will cover their potential liability as, for example, occupiers of their houses, to such policies effected by commercial concerns. The latter may insure separately against their liability in respect of products manufactured or sold, liability under environmental law and so on, or, again, liability cover may be a part of a broader insurance policy.[708] While the particular cover afforded and the exceptions to it will vary from type to type, and be a matter of construing the appropriate words in accordance with general principles of construction,[709] there are a number of general features of liability insurance that are examined here. There follows brief separate consideration of professional indemnity insurance, which is the only type of liability insurance apart from those governed by statute in respect of which it can be said that there are special legal rules.

§1. Nature of the Cover

233. There is no mandatory wording for the basic cover provided by a liability policy, but in practice the policy will usually refer to the insured being covered in respect of sums which he 'shall become legally liable to pay'. It is quite clear that this covers only sums paid out by the insured when he was legally liable to the third party. He cannot recover in respect of a settlement made on a purely ex gratia basis,[710] but can do so if a settlement was agreed when he was in fact legally liable.[711] The fact that the insured has been adjudged legally liable to the third party is not of itself determinative of the insured's rights against his liability insurer.[712] Unless expressly excluded, which it often is, liability includes liability in contract, and if there is concurrent liability in contract and tort, any exclusion for contractual liability is inapplicable as cover for

707. *See* Part IV on Motor Vehicle Insurance and Part V, Ch. 1 on employer's liability insurance.

708. For example, the standard contractors' all risks policies and goods in transit policies will have liability insurance components as well as property insurance components.

709. *See* para. 66.

710. *Corbin v. Payne*, The Times, 11 Oct. 1990. *See also Smit Tak Offshore Services Ltd. v. Youell, The Mare* [1991] 2 Lloyd's Rep. 420, where the broader words in a general liability policy – 'any liability they may incur' – were held to mean only 'any legal liability which they may incur'.

711. *Peninsular & Orient Steam Navigation Co v. Youell* [1997] 2 Lloyd's Rep. 136; *Structural Polymer Systems Ltd v. Brown* [2000] Lloyd's Rep. IR 64.

712. *Omega Proteins Ltd v. Aspen Insurance UK Ltd* [2010] EWHC 2280 (Comm), [2011] Lloyd's Rep. IR 186.

tort liability takes priority.[713] Where the cover refers to a 'claim', this means a claim made by a third party against the insured.[714]

234. It is common in certain types of liability policy to limit the cover further by reference to liability for a loss caused by or arising out of an accident.[715] The meaning of the word 'accident' in this context has given rise to a number of cases[716] from which it can be said that in general, the act must be both unexpected and unintended from the point of view of the insured. However, in considering what is the degree of foresight necessary to prevent the insured from recovering, it appears that the courts have taken a stricter view in the case of injury to third parties than in the case of property damage.[717]

As far as injury cases are concerned, a famous decision is that in *Gray v. Barr*.[718] The insured B, on discovering one day that his wife was not at home, suspected her to be with the plaintiff's husband G (with whom she had previously had an affair) and he set off for the latter's house with a loaded shotgun in order to frighten him. When he arrived there, he and G were involved in a struggle on the stairs as the result of which two shots were fired from the gun, the second one killing G. B was acquitted of murder and manslaughter, but held liable to pay damages in tort to the plaintiff. He claimed that his insurers were liable to indemnify him under a policy which provided such an indemnity if the loss was 'caused by accident'. The majority of the Court of Appeal held that at what happened was not an accident within the policy, on the ground that the death of G was a foreseeable consequence of B's intentional act of taking a

713. *Jan de Nul (UK) Ltd v. Axa Royale Belge SA* [2002] EWCA Civ 209, [2002] Lloyd's Rep. IR 589.

714. *Thorman v. New Hampshire Insurance Co.* [1988] 1 Lloyd's Rep. 7. The word 'claim' has a different meaning when appearing as a limit on the sum insured under a liability policy; *see* para. 245.

715. In this context, even an intended act by an insured may be accidental from the point of view of the third party victim, but it is clear that this is irrelevant and indemnity will not be provided if what the insured did was not from his point of view an accident.

716. *See also* the cases on the meaning of the word in the context of personal accident policies; *see* Part V, Ch. 2.

717. In addition, the courts have been somewhat confused as to the relevance in liability insurance of cases decided under the former Workmen's Compensation Acts. Clearly these cases must be a relevant factor when the wording of a policy is the same as that used in the Acts, in other words 'injury or damage caused by accident'. But workmen's compensation policies were construed more liberally than other insurance contracts because they were the system of first party insurance established for the benefit of employees before the days of state insurance under the social security system. For example, death or injury from natural phenomena has been held covered under a workmen's compensation policy, whereas it would not be so regarded under a personal accident policy. While workmen's compensation cases may be useful, therefore, they should not be binding authorities.

718. [1971] 2 QB 554.

loaded shotgun into the G's house.[719] The decision is not free from criticism,[720] but stands as authority for the meaning of accident in this sort of context.

So far as property damage is concerned, the Australian decision of *Robinson v. Evans* [721] is a good example of the use of what is thought to be a sensible test, that the event must be unintended and unexpected from the point of view of the insured.[722] Here the plaintiff (a market gardener) sued the defendant (a brick manufacturer) for damages for the destruction of his crop of brussel sprouts. The plaintiff's claim, which involved two separate incidents, was settled and the dispute concerned the defendant's claim to be indemnified by its public liability insurers, the terms of the policy providing indemnity in respect of accidental damage only.[723] The court found that the damage to the plaintiff's crop was caused by the emission of fluoride. In respect of the first incident, the defendant's managing director knew about the danger, and it was held that this claim was not for accidental damage. While it may have been unintended by the defendant, it could not be said to be wholly unexpected because of the managing director's knowledge. The test to be applied was whether an ordinary reasonable sensible man, in the position of the insured (or, in this case, its responsible officers), would or would not have expected the occurrence. The second incident arose after the defendant had built a much higher stack on its chimney which it was genuinely believed would cure the problem, but which did not. It was held that the defendant's insurers were liable to indemnify it in this respect. This damage was unintended and unexpected and hence accidental.

235. A further issue in this context may concern the relevance of natural causes. In *Mills v. Smith*,[724] a householder's liability policy indemnified the insured against liability for 'damage to property caused by accident'. This insured was held liable in damages to a neighbour for settlement damage to the neighbour's house caused by the root action of a tree in the insured's garden taking water from the soil on the neighbour's land. It was held that this was caused by accident. The learned judge was clearly disposed to give a wide meaning to these words in a householder's policy and the insured obviously did nothing that was intended or expected in any way. However, it could be argued that the real cause of the insured's liability was entirely natural, namely

---

719. The case was decided also on public policy grounds, as to which *see* para. 68.

720. It may be thought that the opinion of the trial judge ([1970] 2 QB 626) and of Salmon, L.J., in the Court of Appeal to the contrary is to be preferred; and note also the critical comment in *Marcel Beller Ltd. v. Hayden* [1978] QB 694. There was no intention to fire a shot or to kill. Most people would surely regard what happened as an 'accident' therefore, and to introduce questions as to prior acts is to bring in a confusing distinction between means and results which has been said to bedevil a related area, that of the meaning of accident in the context of personal accident policies; *see* Part V, Ch. 2.

721. [1969] VR 885.

722. Compare the Canadian decision in *Canadian Indemnity Co. v. Walkem Machinery & Equipment Ltd.* (1975) 52 DLR (3d) 1, where the court allowed recovery in respect of an unintended but highly foreseeable and risky 'accident'. In doing so, it relied very heavily on English workmen's compensation cases, arguably wrongly and in a quite different context. *See* Hasson (1976) 14 Osgoode Hall L.J. 669.

723. In fact the policy's actual wording was 'damage caused by accidental means', but the court sensibly rejected the distinction between means and results; *see* further, Part V, Ch. 2.

724. [1964] 1 QB 30.

the action of the tree roots, albeit there was an 'accident' when the neighbour's foundations dropped. The judge considered that there were two questions to be answered on the facts. The first was whether there had at any moment in time been some unexpected event leading to damage. Here the settlement was this event, being more than the natural movement of foundations. The second was what was the cause of this. His answer was that it was the action of the roots of the tree and that this meant that the insurers were liable.[725] It should be noted that changes in wording might make a difference to the result in such a case. If, for example, the policy had provided an indemnity in respect of damage 'caused by *an* accident' or 'caused by accidental means', it would have been more difficult to reach the same result.[726] Accident by itself is much more capable of a wide meaning than 'an accident', and 'accidental means' implies that the entire causal history must be accidental.[727]

§2. Insolvency of the Insured

236. At common law, if an insured went bankrupt, or, if a company, went into liquidation, after a claim was made against him by a third party, any money paid by his insurers after the commencement of the bankruptcy or liquidation to indemnify the insured against the claim went towards the general assets of the bankrupt or insolvent company, and were not entitled to be claimed by the third party.[728] This injustice was remedied by the Third Parties (Rights Against Insurers) Act 1930, which has been replaced with effect from 1 August 2016 by the 2010 Act with the same title. Because the latter Act applies only prospectively, that is to liabilities arising only on or after that date, this account considers the 1930 Act first.

In essence, the Act statutorily subrogates the third party to the position of the insured. Section 1(1) provides that where a liability insured goes bankrupt[729] having incurred a liability to a third party,[730] his rights against the insurer under the contract of insurance in respect of the liability 'shall, notwithstanding anything in any Act or rule of law to the contrary, be transferred to and vest in the third party to whom the

725. The case is not free from difficulty. If the real cause of the loss was the action of the tree, that was surely natural and not 'caused by accident'. If it can be supported, it must be on the ground that the event must be looked at solely from the point of view of the insured, ignoring underlying 'natural' factors. If, so far as he was concerned, the event was unexpected and unintended, then the loss was caused by accident.

726. *See* [1964] 1 QB 30 at 36.

727. Although as noted *supra* , the decision in *Robinson v. Evans* rejected the applicability of a distinction between means and results.

728. *Re Harrington Motor Co.* [1928] Ch. 105. The third party had merely the right to prove in the bankruptcy or liquidation as an ordinary creditor along with all the other ordinary creditors of the insured, because he had no rights in respect of the contract between insured and insurer.

729. If the insured is a company, the same applies if the company becomes insolvent within the meaning of the Insolvency Act 1986. This covers situations where a company goes into liquidation, administration or receivership.

730. Liability includes any contractual liability: *Re OT Computers* [2004] EWCA Civ 653, [2004] Lloyd's Rep. IR 669.

liability was so incurred'.[731] It is impossible to contract out of the section's provisions,[732] but it is possible to circumvent the Act by providing that the insurer's liability arises only when the insured himself has paid the third party.[733]

Section 2 casts upon the insured who becomes insolvent the duty to inform the third party who has a claim of any relevant insurance. This duty arises on the occurrence of one of the insolvency events covered by section 1(1) and is not dependent on the insured's liability being established.[734] Section 3 provides that settlements made between the insurer and the bankrupt or liquidated insured are of no effect as regards the third party.[735] If the total insurance fund available is insufficient to pay all the claims made by third parties, the fund is distributed on a first come, first served basis.[736]

237. The years since 1930 saw a number of decisions which tended to restrict the effectiveness of the Act so far as third parties were concerned. It is clear first of all that the insured's right to sue the insurer is transferred to the third party only when the liability of the insured has been established by judgment or settlement, although there is a contingent transfer of rights, as explained below. In *Bradley v. Eagle Star Insurance Co. Ltd.*,[737] the House of Lords confirmed earlier decisions[738] to the effect that the third party gets no better rights than the insured, and the latter's rights arise only when his liability to the third party has been determined or agreed. The correct procedure in this sort of case is for the third party to obtain the leave of the court to bring proceedings against the bankrupt insured. Only when these proceedings have been determined can the insurer be liable under the 1930 Act.[739] However, the third party gets some contingent rights on insolvency, in particular the information rights under section 2.[740]

238. A further limit on the effectiveness of the 1930 Act is that the third party obtains his rights under it subject to the conditions of the policy. Thus a standard condition is likely to forbid the insured making any admission of liability without the

731. By s. 1(2), the same applies where the insured dies insolvent.
732. Section 1(3).
733. *Firma C Trade SA v. Newcastle Protection and Indemnity Association, The Fanti* and *Socony Mobil Oil Co. Inc. v. West of England Shipowners Mutual Insurance Association (London) Ltd, The Padre Island* [1990] 2 All ER 705. This decision concerned standard 'pay to be paid' clauses in the rules of shipowners' mutual protection clubs and is in practice likely to be so confined. *See* further Birds [1990] JBL 512.
734. *Re OT Computers Ltd, supra* . *See* further below.
735. Section 3 does not affect settlements made before bankruptcy, even in respect of a liability already incurred by the insured: *Normid Housing Association Ltd. v. Ralphs* [1989] 1 Lloyd's Rep. 289.
736. *Cox v. Bankside Members Agency Ltd.* [1995] 2 Lloyd's Rep. 437.
737. [1989] AC 957.
738. Especially *Post Office v. Norwich Union Fire Insurance Society Ltd.* [1967] 2 QB 363.
739. If the insured was a company, it is possible for the company to be restored to the register for these purposes under the Companies Act 1985, s. 651.
740. *Re OT Computers, supra* . *See also Centre Reinsurance International Co. v. Freakley* [2005] EWCA Civ 115, [2005] Lloyd's Rep. IR 303, and *Financial Services Compensation Scheme Ltd v. Larnell* [2005] EWCA Civ 1408, [2006] Lloyd's Rep. IR 448, where it was held that the rule that limitation periods ceased to run at the date a winding up applied to a claim under the Act.

insurer's consent,[741] and the third party is subject also to this term.[742] Except in compulsory motor insurance and, to a lesser extent in employer's liability insurance, where insurers' rights are more circumscribed by statute,[743] any defence that the insurers have against the insured under the insurance contract is available against the third party. So courts have disallowed third party's claims under the Act where the insured was guilty of non-disclosure or breach of warranty,[744] where the insurers had the right to avoid liability because of a fraudulent claim,[745] and where there was a breach of condition requiring immediate notification by the insured of legal proceedings instituted against it.[746] Further, the courts have upheld the insurers' right, under the policy, to insist upon arbitration as a condition precedent to their liability.[747] However, insurers cannot simply claim to set off against the amount due to the third party any premiums due but unpaid by the insured.[748] The third party is bound by any limitations in the policy regarding the amount of indemnity provided.[749]

239. As indicated above, the 1930 Act has been replaced by the Third Parties (Rights Against Insurers) Act 2010, but only as regards liabilities incurred after it came into in force on 1 August 2016. The 2010 Act followed a review by the Law Commissions.[750] As well as completely redrafting what is section 1(1) of the 1930 Act, the 2010 Act reflects changes in insolvency law by widening the scope of the application of the scheme to include situations where an insured facing financial difficulties enters into various voluntary arrangements with his or its creditors.[751] Perhaps, in practice, most importantly, it removes the need for the third party to issue proceedings both

741. *See infra* .
742. *See* the *Norwich Union* case, *supra* .
743. *See* Part IV and Part V, Ch. 1.
744. *See* , e.g., *McCormick v. National Motor and Accident Ins. Union Ltd.* (1934) 43 LlLR 361.
745. *Total Graphics Ltd v. AGF Insurance Ltd* [1997] 1 Lloyd's Rep. 599.
746. *Pioneer Concrete (UK) Ltd. v. National Employers Mutual General Insurance Association Ltd.* [1985] 1 Lloyd's Rep. 274. *See also Farrell v. Federated Employers' Insurance Association Ltd.* [1970] 1 WLR 1400, although the actual decision in this case in the context of employers' liability insurance is overruled by the Employers' Liability (Compulsory Insurance) Regulations; *see* Part V, Ch. 1. However, the third party will not be prejudiced if the insured cannot comply with a condition because of the insolvency: *Saunders v. Royal Insurance Inc* 1999 SLT 358.
747. *Freshwater v. Western Australian Assurance Co.* [1933] 1 KB 515; *Smith v. Pearl Assurance Co.* [1939] 1 All ER 95. These decisions have been overruled by statute (s. 148(5), Road Traffic Act 1988) so far as motor insurance is concerned (*see Jones v. Birch Bros* [1933] 2 KB 597), but the principle holds good for other liability insurances. *See Socony Mobil Oil Co. Inc. v. West of England Ship Owners Mutual Insurance Association* [1984] 2 Lloyd's Rep. 408.
748. *See Murray v. Legal & General Assurance Society* [1969] 3 All ER 794, where it was held that the rights and liabilities of the insured transferred to the third party are only those rights and liabilities in respect of the liability incurred by the insured to the third party. The right to claim premiums was a general right, not dependant on any term of the policy. It would appear that the effect of this decision would be reversed if there were an express term in a liability policy that it was a condition precedent to the liability of the insurer for any particular claim that all premiums owing under the policy before the claim arose were duly paid.
749. *Averando (UK) Ltd v. National Transit Insurance Co Ltd* [1984] 2 Lloyd's Rep. 613.
750. Law Com. No. 272, Scot Law Com. No. 184, 2001, CM 5217.
751. This category is extended by Sch. 2 of the Insurance Act 2015 and s. 19 of this Act allows the Secretary of State to amend it further if necessary, as had indeed been done.

against the insolvent insured and then against the latter's insurers. This will remain an option, but alternatively the third party will be able to sue the insurer for a declaration as to either or both the insured's liability to him or the insurer's potential liability to him. This will become the second situation[752] where the law will permit an 'action directe' against an insurer. It will also remove the need for the third party to apply to have an insured company restored to the register. The Act expressly covers voluntarily incurred liabilities, and it gives the third party much greater rights to information about the insurance, which are set out in detail in Schedule 1.

240. As recommended by the Law Commissions, although the Act continues to allow the insurer to raise defences such as non-disclosure, misrepresentation or breach of warranty by the insured, to set off against the third party the amount of any liability of the insured to it, and to apply any excess to the third party's claim, it does reform the current law in other important respects. So, section 9 applies where transferred rights are subject to a condition, whether under the contract of insurance or otherwise, that the insured has to fulfil. Anything done by the third party which, if done by the insured, would have amounted to or contributed to fulfilment of the condition is treated as if done by the insured. This will allow the third party, among other things, to give notice and particulars of a claim. Further, transferred rights are not subject to a condition requiring the insured to provide information (other than giving notice of a claim) or assistance to the insurer if it cannot be fulfilled because the insured is a body corporate that has been dissolved or an individual who has died. Transferred rights are not subject to a condition requiring the prior discharge by the insured or the insured's liability to the third party,[753] although in marine insurance this applies only to the extent that the insured's liability is in respect of death or personal injury.

§3. Admissions of Liability and the Conduct of Proceedings

241. A standard term found in all liability insurance policies concerns admissions of liability by the insured and the insurers' conduct of proceedings against the insured.[754] The standard wording is as follows:

> No admission of liability or offer or promise of payment, whether expressed or implied, shall be made without the written consent of the insurer, which shall be entitled at its own discretion to take over and conduct in the name of the insured the defence or settlement of any claim.[755]

752. The other is in respect of compulsory motor insurance, as described in Part IV.
753. Thus reversing the decisions in *The Fanti* and *The Padre Island* (*see* para. 236).
754. Another standard condition concerns the insured's obligation to take reasonable care; this is considered in para. 58.
755. Some policies, particularly professional indemnity policies, may have in addition a clause providing that proceedings by the third party are not to be contested unless a Queen's Counsel so advises (the 'QC clause'). As to this, *see* *West Wake Price and Co. v. Ching* [1957] 1 WLR 45.

In respect of the conduct of proceedings, although the words appear to give the insurer absolute discretion as to what is done, it is clear that this discretion is controlled. The insurers have 'the right to decide upon the proper tactics to pursue in the conduct of the action,[756] provided that they do so in what they bona fide consider to be the common interest of themselves and their assured'.[757] A blatant ignoring of the interests of the insured occurred in *Groom v. Crocker*[758] where, quite without foundation and knowing of its inaccuracy, the solicitors acting for the insurers admitted to the third party claimant that the insured had been negligent. It was held that this was a clear breach of duty and the insured was entitled to damages for breach of contract and to damages in tort for libel.[759] That *Groom v. Crocker* did not, however, establish a very strict limit on the insurer's discretion is evident from the latter case of *Beacon Insurance Co. v. Langdale.*[760] Here the insurers did not admit that their motor insured was negligent, but without his knowledge they settled the third party's claim with a strict denial of liability and then sued the insured for the GBP 3 excess for which the policy provided. It was held that they were entitled to succeed. They had acted quite properly, had made an advantageous settlement and denied liability.[761]

The result is that the insurers can settle with the third party so long as they do not unjustifiably admit liability, and, possibly, so long as they do not unjustifiably settle beyond the policy limits or refuse a settlement offer by the third party within these limits. There is no English authority on this latter point, but the question has been much litigated in the United States of America where there are decisions holding that if a liability insurer refuses an offer of settlement by the third party within the policy limits, and the latter subsequently recovers more than the sum insured in a civil action against the insured, the insurer is liable for the whole amount.[762] It is thought that such conduct on the part of an insurer in the UK would also entail civil liability as a breach of the duty to act in good faith laid down by *Groom v. Crocker*. However, it is clear that the standard condition does not oblige the insurers to take over the insured's defence,[763] so that there can be no basis for any liability on the insurers if they choose not to do so, other than to indemnify the insured within the limits of the policy if the latter is in fact adjudged legally liable to the third party.

---

756. Including the appointment of solicitors to represent the insured. However, the insurers cannot compel the insured to accept legal representation: *Barrett Bros v. Davies* [1966] 1 WLR 1334.
757. Lord Greene MR in *Groom v. Crocker* [1939] 1 KB 194 at 203.
758. *Supra.*
759. The contract damages, however, were only nominal, as the insurers had paid the third party the sum he claimed, and the court declined to award damages for injury to reputation or feelings. Such an award may now be possible.
760. [1939] 4 All ER 209.
761. The decision appears harsh and the niceties of paying up but with a denial of liability may be lost on some insureds. The defendant continued to deny that he was liable and would not therefore see why he should have to pay anything until the contrary were proved. Furthermore, such evidence as there is from the report suggests that the third party recovered sufficient to cover him only for his out of pocket expenses and not for the fairly severe injuries he recovered, implying that it was by no means certain that the insured was liable.
762. *See* especially, *Crisci v. Security Ins. Co.* 66 Cal (2d) 425 P (2d) 173 (1967).
763. In contrast, American policies often do; *see* the discussion by Stephen, J., in *Distillers Co. v. Ajax Insurance Co.* (1974) 48 ALJR 136, esp. at 147.

242. If insurers do take control of proceedings under the standard condition, they are not necessarily thereby prevented from subsequently denying liability to indemnity the insured, for example, for a non-disclosure or breach of warranty or condition by the insured discovered only at a later date. If, however, the insurers do discover such a right to avoid liability, but continue to act for the insured, they will be deemed to have waived their right.[764] Similarly, provided that they do not clearly admit liability, the insurers' conduct of the defence of the insured does not prevent them from subsequently alleging that the event that occurred was not in fact within the cover provided by the policy.[765]

243. The part of the standard condition that prohibits admissions of liability, etc. without the insurer's consent is important and regarded by insurers as essential for the protection of their interests.[766] In principle, it should not matter whether or not the insurer has in fact been prejudiced by an admission by its insured, for example, if there can be no doubt whatsoever as to the latter's legal liability.[767]

244. The question may arise whether an insurer is still entitled to rely upon this condition if in fact it elects not to have anything to do with the insured's defence against the third party. The essence of the condition is that it prohibits the insured from settling without consent. If the insurer refuses to consent, the insured will be compelled to let the matter go to litigation unless he can argue that by refusing to have anything to do with his defence the insurer has forfeited its right to rely upon the condition. This question, which has never been considered in the English courts, produced a difference of opinion in the High Court of Australia in *Distillers Co. Ltd. v. Ajax Insurance Co. Ltd.*[768] The dispute arose out of the manufacture of drugs containing thalidomide, which the insured had distributed in Australia. These drugs were taken by pregnant women and, allegedly owing to the negligence of Distillers, caused severe damage to their unborn foetuses. Distillers had public liability cover with Ajax, the policy containing the relevant condition. Upon being sued for negligence, Distillers wished to consider compromising with the third parties, but Ajax refused to consent to this, at the same time refusing to conduct Distillers' defence. By a majority,[769] it was held that the insurers were entitled to refuse consent without incurring any liability. The decision

---

764. *Evans v. Employers' Mutual* [1936] 1 KB 505.

765. *Soole v. Royal Insurance Co* [1971] 2 Lloyd's Rep. 332. The insurers' conduct in defending the insured did not amount to an unequivocal representation that they would indemnify him regardless, because no insurer when it takes over the defence of its insured can be sure that it will be liable in the long run. For example, the third party's claim might fail. The insurer's conduct of the defence is merely an indication that the proceedings may give rise to a liability to indemnify the insured. Compare *Hansen v. Marco Engineering (Aust) Pty. Ltd.* [1948] VLR 198, an Australian case, where it was held that the insurer was estopped.

766. What is perhaps slightly disturbing about this standard condition is its width and the fact that an insurer could rely on a fairly casual 'it's my fault' said or written to the third party by the insured to avoid liability, despite the lack of any real prejudice to their position.

767. *Terry v. Trafalgar Insurance Co.* [1970] 1 Lloyd's Rep. 524.

768. (1974) 48 ALJR 136.

769. Gibbs, J., dissenting, preferred to follow an Irish case (*General Omnibus Co. Ltd. v. London General Insurance Co. Ltd.* [1936] IR 596) and held that the two aspects of the standard condition were linked, so that the right to rely upon the condition applied only where the insurer in fact conducted the insured's defence.

appears correct in principle, but Stephen, J., in an important judgment, made it clear that the decision would not confer upon an insurer an arbitrary power to refuse consent. He referred in particular to the sort of case where a conflict between insured and insurer might arise, where the claim against the insured is above the sum insured under the policy and the insured is anxious to settle below that figure whereas the insurer would gain little from a settlement close to the limit and might prefer to fight the case. He said that in such a case, the insurer must exercise its powers under the policy with due regard to the interests of the insured.[770] The position must depend on a reasonable estimate of the third party's claim. If that has every chance of succeeding, it would be improper for the insurer to refuse to consent to a settlement substantially within the policy limits. If, on the other hand, the third party's claim is doubtful, and the only reason or a principal reason why the insured wishes to settle is to avoid bad publicity attendant on being sued, the insurer would be justified in refusing its consent. The result is that if the insurer refuses its consent and leaves the insured to act alone, but the latter enters into a quite reasonable settlement, the insurer will be liable to indemnify him regardless of the breach of condition.

§4. Sums Insured and Costs

245. It has just been noted how the sum insured in a liability policy may be of great importance in the context of an admission of liability condition. More generally, while the sum insured obviously puts the limit of the insurer's liability, and is commonplace except in relation to personal injury aspects of motor insurance where statute does not allow it,[771] it may be expressed in different ways. For example, the policy may have a limit applying to any one contractual period, regardless of the number of claims made, or the limit may apply to each accident or each occurrence or each claim, with no global maximum. The first sort of limit causes no problems, and it has been held that where the limit is per accident, each separate claim by a third party arises out of a separate accident.[772]

If, however, the limit is expressed to be per occurrence, then it seems that the number of occurrences is the number of times the insured is negligent. If there is only one negligent act, there is only one occurrence. So, the policy limit will apply regardless of how many individual claims may be made by third parties as a result.[773] The same construction applies where the limit applies 'per claim', that is, that claim means claim by the insured against the insurer rather than claim by each third party against the

770. Following *Groom v. Crocker, supra* , on the analogous point already discussed *supra* .
771. *See* Part IV.
772. *See South Staffordshire Tramways v. Sickness and Accident Assurance Association* [1891] 1 QB 402 where a policy indemnifying the insured against liability for accidents caused by vehicles had a limit of '£250 in respect of any one accident'. One of the insured's trams overturned injuring forty passengers. It was held that each passenger had an accident and therefore the insurers was potentially liable for 40 x GBP 250.
773. *See Forney v. Dominion Insurance Co. Ltd.* [1969] 1 WLR 928.

insured.[774] This was also the construction adopted in a case where the relevant limit was contained in an excess clause in a liability policy.[775]

246. Liability policies invariably include in their cover any costs incurred by the insured, in addition to the damages he is liable to pay. This would not usually include the costs of the insured in successfully defending a claim as the provision as to costs normally applies only where the insurer is liable to indemnify the insured,[776] but the insured will in general recover these from the plaintiff third party. Costs though will normally be limited, for example, by being included together with damages in the sum insured, or by being limited to the same proportion which the indemnity provided bears to the insured's loss where the latter exceeds the former because it is greater than the sum insured by the policy.

§5. Insurers' Duty to the Victim

247. Frequently in practice liability insurers will negotiate directly on their insured's behalf with the latter's victim. For obvious reasons, but to the potential detriment of the victim, they will seek to keep their liability as low as possible and may well induce the victim to agree to a settlement for an amount below his legal entitlement. Where the victim so relies on the insurers, it is likely that a fiduciary relationship will arise and that the settlement will be voidable on the ground of undue influence unless the insurers either inform the victim of the desirability of seeking independent advice or make an offer that is realistic in respect of the victim's loss.[777]

§6. Professional Indemnity Insurance

248. There is a wide range of policies available insuring professionals against their potential liability in contract and tort.[778] Of increasing importance in recent years are the 'master policies' effected by some professional bodies to cover all their members against potential liability. These may exist in place of or in addition to individual policies, but the basic principles applicable are the same as those applicable to individual policies.

---

774. *Haydon v. Lo & Lo* [1997] C.L.C. 626. *See also* cases where the limit applied with respect to 'causes' or 'events': *Caudle v. Sharp* [1995] LRLR 80; *Cox v. Bankside Members Agency Ltd.* [1995] 2 Lloyd's Rep. 437. As to the construction of the phrase 'single act or omission' in the context of an excess or deductible, *see Lloyds TSB General Insurance Holdings v. Lloyds Bank Group Insurance Co Ltd* [2003] UKHL 48, [2003] Lloyd's Rep. IR 623.
775. *Trollope & Colls Ltd. v. Haydon* [1977] 1 Lloyd's Rep. 244.
776. *Cross v. British Oak Insurance Co.* [1938] 2 KB 167 at 174.
777. *Horry v. Tate & Lyle Refineries Ltd.* [1982] 2 Lloyd's Rep. 416; *see* Merkin (1983) 46 MLR 91. The contract of settlement may also be voidable for misrepresentation: *see Saunders v. Ford Motor Co. Ltd.* [1970] 1 Lloyd's Rep. 379.
778. A requirement to insure has been imposed upon an increasing number of professions either by statute, e.g., in respect of insurance intermediaries and estate agents, or by the rules of the profession, e.g., in respect of solicitors and accountants.

The basic purpose of professional indemnity insurance is to afford cover in respect of the liability of the insured for negligence by himself or his employees.[779] Thus, there is no indemnity against loss due to negligence where that does not cause a liability.[780] In addition, the basic indemnity does not cover situations where the loss is caused by the dishonesty of the insured[781] or an employee.[782] In practice this general principle, which in respect of the insured himself arises out of public policy,[783] is expressly confirmed in the policy wording. The standard words of cover provide indemnity in respect of 'any negligent act, error or omission'. It has been held that the word 'negligent' qualifies only the word 'act' so that cover is available in respect of non-negligent errors or omissions.[784] In practice this is unlikely to matter, since in virtually all cases the liability of a professional person is dependent on negligence, whether arising out of a breach of contract or otherwise.

249. Many professional persons carry on their business in partnership and liability attaches to the partnership as well as to the individual. Potential problems could arise concerning the liability of the partnership for negligence by a partner who has since retired. As a result, it is usual for the policy to contain a clause covering predecessors in business of the current partners,[785] although this will not cover the individual liability of a retired partner. It is also a feature of professional liability that negligence claims may be made some time after the allegedly negligent act or error. Normally the policy will provide that it covers claims made during its currency regardless of when the actual negligence occurred and, in addition, that the insured is protected so long as he gives immediate notice of any occurrence which may give rise to a claim against him even if the actual claim occurs later and outside the period of insurance. Of course, in addition to a standard notice provision,[786] the general duty of fair presentation[787] will require that the insured inform the insurer on original application or on renewal of anything which might give rise to a claim against him.

---

779. However, the policy may cover non-negligent liability where that exists: *Wimpey Construction UK Ltd. v. Poole* [1984] 2 Lloyd's Rep. 499; *Lumbermen Mutual Casualty Co v. Bovis Lend Lease Ltd* [2005] Lloyd's Rep. IR 74.

780. *Walton v. National Employers Mutual General Assurance Ass. Ltd.* [1974] 2 Lloyd's Rep. 385, where the insured repaired the loss so that the third party had no negligence claim against him. It is possible for one subsidiary of a group to have an effective claim against another subsidiary so that the latter's liability can be covered by its professional indemnity policy: *Wimpey Construction UK Ltd. v. Poole, supra* .

781. *Haseldine v. Hosken* [1933] 1 KB 822.

782. For example, *Davies v. Hosken* [1937] 3 All ER 192; *West Wake Price & Co. v. Ching* [1957] 1 WLR 45; *Johns v. Kelly* [1986] 1 Lloyd's Rep. 468. However, modern policies may provide cover in respect of the fraud or dishonesty of employees, except where this could have been discovered or suspected by the insured: *see* *MDIA Ltd v. Swinbank* [1999] Lloyd's Rep. IR 516.

783. *See* para. 68.

784. *Wimpey Construction UK Ltd. v. Poole, supra* .

785. *See* , e.g., *Maxwell v. Price* [1960] 2 Lloyd's Rep. 155, which gave a broad construction of such a provision to cover the acts of a partner before he joined the partnership.

786. *See* para. 136.

787. *See* para. 111.

250. The standard conditions in professional indemnity policies are those already described as common to all liability insurances. A usual addition in this instance, though, is the 'QC clause', providing, for the protection of the reputation of professionals, that the insured cannot be required to contest any legal proceedings against him unless a Queen's Counsel so advises.[788]

788. *See West Wake Price & Co. v. Ching* [1957] 1 WLR 45.

Chapter 6. Legal Aid Insurance

251. In the UK, legal aid is available to some persons as a matter of right from the State, in respect of both civil and criminal litigation. However, it is subject to a means test and the limits have become much tighter in recent years, and state legal aid has been abolished in a large number of situations, with the consequence that interest in private insurance against legal costs has increased considerably.[789] In the UK, this is known as legal expenses insurance. This sort of insurance has been available for some time as part of the standard cover under liability insurance policies, which pay the cost of defending civil actions brought against the insured.[790] Legal expenses insurance policies by themselves or as a separate part of a broader policy, for example, a motor policy or standard commercial policy packages, go further and generally indemnify in respect of:

(1) the costs of defending criminal charges;
(2) the costs of defending civil actions; and
(3) the costs of recovery in respect of civil actions brought by the insured, for example, in tort or contract.

Such insurance is subject to the general principles described elsewhere in this work. The special provisions concern the choice of lawyer to represent the insured and the resolution of differences as to the insured's chances of success. In respect of the former, the standard term provides that the insurer can reject the first nomination by the insured, but not the second.[791] In respect of the latter, if the insurer considers that the insured has no chance of success, there is provision for arbitration to resolve the difference by an independent lawyer. A further feature of legal expenses insurance is the standard provision by the insurer of a telephone helpline, often available on a twenty-four-hour basis.

789. There was once also some doubt as to the legality, on public policy grounds, of such insurance.
790. *See* para. 230.
791. There may also be provision for nomination by the President of the Law Society, which the insurer is bound to accept.

Chapter 7. Aviation and Space Insurance

252. Insurance in respect of liability as regards passengers, baggage, cargo and third parties is compulsory under Regulation 785/04 of the European Parliament and Council,[792] supplemented by the Civil Aviation (Insurance) Regulations 2005.[793] Subject to exemptions for state aircraft and various kinds of small aircraft, the requirements apply to all air carriers and aircraft operators flying within, into out of or over the territory of a Member State. In most cases he insured risks must include acts of war, terrorism, hijacking, acts of sabotage, unlawful seizure and civil commotion. Various minimum amounts of cover are required in respect of the different liabilities.

Standard policies cover both the aircraft[794] and third party and passenger liability while the aircraft is in flight,[795] taxing on the ground or moored.[796] There will be onerous warranties requiring the insured to comply with current air navigation and airworthiness regulations.[797]

792. 21 Apr. 2004, OJ L138.
793. SI 2005/1089. It is thought that these rules will be retained when the UK leaves the European Union in March 2019.
794. Aviation hull insurance.
795. 'In flight' will normally cover taxing preparatory to take-off, if this is not covered separately: *Dunn v. Campbell* (1920) 2 LlLR 98.
796. If the cover operates while the aircraft is 'over' certain territories, this is effective only when it is in the air: *Banque Sabbag v. Hope* [1974] 2 Lloyd's Rep. 301.
797. For modern cases construing aspects of aviation policies, *see Banque Sabbag v. Hope* [1974] 2 Lloyd's Rep. 301 and *Pan American World Airways v. Aetna Casualty Co.* [1975] 1 Lloyd's Rep. 77.

Chapter 8. Theft and Embezzlement Insurance

253. Separate policies insuring property against theft or embezzlement by themselves are unusual, but such cover within a broader policy on property, for example, a household insurance policy, is commonplace.

The first very important consideration is that the cover is usually defined by reference to 'theft' and other words that have a defined meaning under the criminal law. Here the general rule of construction which dictates that such words are to be construed in their technical meaning[798] applies, so, in particular, 'theft' is to be construed according to its meaning under the Theft Act 1968.[799] Some circumstances of theft may be excluded, in particular theft by the insured's employees or by members of the insured's household or by the insured's customers.[800] Theft cover in commercial policies is often restricted to theft consequent upon entry to or exit from the relevant premises by 'forcible and violent means' or following some violence to or assault on the insured or his employees. In *Dino Services Ltd. v. Prudential Assurance Co. Ltd.*,[801] thieves stole the keys to the insured's business premises from his car which he had parked overnight and used the keys to gain entry to the premises from which they stole a substantial amount of property. It was held that the insured was not entitled to recover. Although the thieves' entry was forcible,[802] it was not violent which requires such as the breaking down of a door or the forcing open of a window.[803]

254. Theft insurance policies will normally contain warranties relating to precautions to be taken by the insured, for example, with regard to security devices such as a burglar alarm, or a general requirement to take reasonable care.[804] It is usual also to impose a term that the insurance ceases if the premises are left unoccupied for more than a specified period of time unless the insurers are notified of the unoccupancy. Unoccupancy relates to the absence of a physical presence in the building insured, so that if in fact no one is regularly and daily present therein, it is unoccupied,[805] unless

---

798. *See* para. 62.

799. *Grundy (Teddington) Ltd. v. Fulton* [1981] 2 Lloyd's Rep. 666. *See also Dobson v. General Accident Fire & Life Assurance Corp plc.* [1989] 3 All ER 927 where a household policy insured goods against 'loss by theft' and leading criminal law cases were used to decide that there was a theft when the insured sold property to a rogue in return for a cheque which proved to be a forgery.

800. For cases on the meaning of these phrases, *see Saaqi and Lawrence v. Stearns* [1911] 1 KB 426 and *Lake v. Simmons* [1927] AC 487.

801. [1989] 1 All ER 427.

802. Even a minimal amount of force, such as turning a key in a lock, will suffice.

803. Following the earlier cases of *Re George and Goldsmiths and General Burglary Insurance Association Ltd.* [1899] 1 QB 595 and *Re Calf and Sun Insurance Office* [1920] 2 KB 366. The Court of Appeal in *Dino Services* was critical of the insurers for their wording and for taking the point as a defence, although it is thought that the criticism was somewhat harsh.

804. As to the latter, *see* para. 58.

805. *See* , e.g., *Marzouca v. Atlantic and British Commercial Insurance Co. Ltd.* [1971] 1 Lloyd's Rep. 449.

the absence is merely temporary, for example, by reason of the insured being on holiday,[806] or at work during the day.

255. UK law and practice does not recognize embezzlement insurance as such. However, cover against losses caused by an employee is widely available under fidelity insurance policies. These are effected by employers to cover theft, embezzlement and other losses caused by employees and are subject to all the normal rules of insurance law.[807] In practice a policy will either cover particular named employees or be of a floating nature covering all employees. The only usual special feature of fidelity insurance is that it covers all losses during the period of indemnity, even if they are discovered after the insurance has ceased, provided that this is within a certain period, for example, two years of the cessation of the insurance or the cessation of employment of the employee concerned.

806. *Winicofsky v. Army and Navy General Insurance Co.* (1919) 88 LJKB 111.
807. Including the technical rule of construction where appropriate. All the reported cases on fidelity policies are referred to in *MacGillivray on Insurance Law*, 12th ed., paras 31-028–31-038.

Chapter 9. Agricultural Insurance, Hail Insurance and Livestock Insurance

256. There are no special principles governing these types of insurance. Standard agricultural insurance packages available to farmers[808] will include property insurance against the usual risks of fire, theft, etc. on buildings and stock, interruption insurance and liability insurances of various kinds as appropriate.[809] The principles examined elsewhere will govern such insurances. These standard policies will cover crops against fire, flood and related perils. Hail insurance is available, especially for fruit and hops, as additional cover. Again, in legal terms it is only a particular type of property insurance to which the usual general principles apply.

257. Livestock insurance policies deserve a little more consideration.[810] There are a number of different forms in use covering all kinds of risks[811] to horses, cattle and other animals.[812] A policy may mirror a personal accident policy for humans,[813] or it may cover accidental death or injury arising in particular circumstances such as when animals stray or are being transported.[814] Notwithstanding the similarities that such policies may have to life or personal accident policies on humans, they are invariably not valued policies but ordinary polices of indemnity providing for the payment on death of the market value of the animal up to a stated limit or sum insured. If a policy covers both death and injury, but an animal is so seriously injured that the proper course is to slaughter it immediately, the loss will be treated as a death within the policy.[815] It is frequently required that a qualified veterinary surgeon must certify the claim at the time it is made or shortly afterwards.[816]

808. Fish farmers have their own packages – aquacultural insurances.
809. Especially employers' liability and public and products liability.
810. For the few reported cases on these policies other than those mentioned here, all of which turned on particular wordings not necessarily in use today, *see* *MacGillivray on Insurance Law*, paras 27-038–27-042.
811. Apart from death and accident, third party liability, veterinary fees and loss by theft are usually covered.
812. Breeding animals, e.g., racehorses, are covered under what is conventionally described as bloodstock insurance. Domestic pet animals can also be insured against various risks including death, accident and the costs of veterinary fees.
813. As in *Burridge v. Haines* (1918) 87 LJKB 641. As to these, *see* Part V, Ch. 2.
814. The latter insurance is usually included in a standard agricultural insurance policy. The broader risks are separately insured.
815. *Shiells v. Scottish Assurance Corporation Ltd.* (1889) 16 R 1014. It was also held in this case that where slaughter is required to save the animal from unnecessary suffering, a term requiring the written consent of the insurer before slaughtering does not apply.
816. Breach of this requirement can be waived as in *Burridge v. Haines, supra* , where the insurer repudiated the claim immediately (and wrongly) before the insured had the chance to obtain a veterinary report.

Chapter 10. Catastrophe Insurance

258. This chapter examines briefly the principles applicable to the insurance of nuclear risks and natural catastrophes. There are no special principles governing the insurance of natural catastrophes such as earthquakes.[817] If such protection is required, it will be added as an extra risk to a standard fire policy. The legal principles will then be the same as apply to fire policies and insurance policies in general.

259. Nuclear risks, on the other hand, are governed by special arrangements,[818] although again it would not be true to say that there are any special principles of law applying thereto. In line with international conventions, the law on third party liability of operators of nuclear installations is governed by the Nuclear Installations Acts 1965 and 1969, as amended by the Energy Act 1983.[819] These Acts require satisfactory insurance of liabilities before a licence to operate a nuclear installation is granted. Such de facto compulsory insurance is provided by the British Insurance (Atomic Energy) Committee comprising insurance companies and members of Lloyd's, whose policy covers: (a) the liabilities arising under the nuclear legislation[820] for the relevant 'cover period';[821] (b) other legal liabilities;[822] and (c) legal and other costs in dealing with claims under (a) or (b).

In practice also, although this is not in any way compulsory, the standard policy issued by the Committee also covers 'material damage'. This is basically fire insurance of the installation[823] with the addition of insurance against:

(a) loss or damage resulting from excessive temperature within the nuclear reactor consequent upon a sudden uncontrolled, unintentional and excessive increase or release of energy or upon the failing of the cooling system; and
(b) destruction or damage: (i) of the outside surface of the external nuclear reactor shield or of the primary cooling circuit; (ii) of any of the property insured which is outside the nuclear reactor shield or primary cooling circuit; and (iii) by radioactive contamination occasioned by or happening through any accidental escape of radioactivity from the nuclear reactor or from anything which is on the site but is not within the nuclear reactor.

817. Serious earthquakes, as opposed to occasional tremors in some areas, are unknown in the UK.
818. Though where the risk concerns nuclear materials in transit, these are covered by some appropriate form of transport insurance, e.g., a marine insurance policy.
819. Basically liability, which is limited to GBP 20 million, or GBP 5 million for small nuclear installations, is strict.
820. Limited to the amounts stated in the previous note.
821. In practice this is the lifetime of the institution in question unless there is a change in ownership or substantial claims have to be paid; in the latter event, a fresh cover period may be required by the Government for the required indemnity.
822. That is, what is covered by the standard public liability insurance policy.
823. In the standard form as described in Ch. 1, *supra* . It may also be possible for the Committee to provide consequential loss insurance in the form described in Ch. 2, *supra* .

Chapter 11. Credit Insurance

260. This chapter is concerned with the types of insurance contract that protect a person from potential purely financial loss occasioned by his debtor being unable to repay his debt. Conventionally, this type of insurance is referred to as credit or guarantee insurance. Contracts under which a creditor is protected against the consequences of his debtor being unable to repay his debt can be either contracts of insurance or contracts of guarantee or suretyship. The distinction, which is not always easy to apply, is important for a number of reasons. These include the following:[824]

(1) A contract of guarantee must be evidenced in writing,[825] whereas a non-marine insurance contract can be oral.[826]
(2) A contract of guarantee is not a contract of the utmost good faith, whereas of course an insurance contract is such.[827]
(3) A surety who has paid the creditor can sue the debtor in his own name, whereas an insurer who has indemnified his insured has merely the right to be subrogated to the rights of the insured.[828]
(4) If the debtor discharges his debt, the surety is automatically also discharged from liability; this is not necessarily so in respect of an insurer.[829]

261. The distinction between contracts of credit insurance and contracts of guarantee depends on a number of elements[830] and the description attached to the contract is not necessarily conclusive. The first element is the motive of the parties; generally an insurer takes business for money, whereas a surety enters into a guarantee as a friend, often for no consideration. Second, the method of business differs in that a surety will usually be asked to undertake the guarantee by the debtor, whereas an insurer deals with the creditor as insured and not normally directly with the debtor. Third, a surety is usually fully conversant with the risks he is being asked to assume, or at least in as good a position as the creditor to discover them. In contrast, an insurer is not in such a position and relies on disclosure by the creditor.[831] Fourth, a surety

824. *See* further, *MacGillivray on Insurance Law*, para. 32-040.
825. Under s. 4 of the Statute of Frauds 1677.
826. *See* para. 84.
827. *See* para. 59.
828. As to subrogation, *see* para. 153.
829. In addition, the business of the giving of contracts of guarantee is not regulated under the Financial Services and Markets Act.
830. The leading authority is the judgment of Romer, L.J., in *Seaton v. Heath* [1899] 1 QB 782 at 792–793. There are many other cases where the distinction has been considered and applied. These are summarized in *MacGillivray*, para. 32-041. For an excellent detailed consideration of the distinction, *see* Blair, *The Conversion of Guarantee Contracts*, 39 MLR 522 (1966).
831. If, therefore, there is evidence that the 'guarantor' relied on the creditor to tell him about the risk, the contract is likely to be one of insurance (*Kreglinger and Fernau Ltd. v. Irish National Insurance Co. Ltd.* [1956] LR 116), whereas evidence that the debtor approached the guarantor is likely to lead to the conclusion that the contract is of guarantee (*Workington Harbour and Dock Board v. Trade Indemnity Co.* [1937] AC 1).

promises to pay the original debtor's debt, whereas an insurer promises to a sum of money on a specified event[832] which is an independent obligation possibly differing from the original debt both as to amount and as to when it is to be paid. The latter incidents will indicate insurance rather than guarantee.[833]

262. The forms of credit insurance vary from insurance of a particular debt to insurance of debts in general, possibly including any incurred after the policy is effected. The insured may be in the business of providing credit or may, for example, be a one-off creditor, perhaps as a surety or guarantor. Similarly, the event actually insured against may vary from the non-payment or a debt at the due date or within a specified time thereafter[834] to insolvency of the debtor.[835] Frequently, credit insurance policies are used as additional security by banks and other lenders in respect of loans they make.[836]

263. The usual incidents of insurance contracts apply to credit insurances, so that in particular, the insured is under a duty to disclose material facts, for example, the financial standing of an insured surety,[837] and the insurer on indemnifying the insured will be subrogated to the insured's rights to claim against the debtor and any security given by the latter in respect of the debt.[838] The policy may provide that the insurer is liable to pay the whole debt, once the debtor is in default, or alternatively that the insured must recover what he can from the debtor and the insurer is only liable for the unrecovered balance. There will normally be a condition precluding the insured from unilaterally agreeing to any arrangements that modify his rights or remedies against the debtor.[839]

832. *Dane v. Mortgage Insurance Corp.* [1894] 1 QB 54.
833. *Re Law Guarantee Trust and Accident Society* [1914] 2 Ch. 617.
834. In which case, the reason for non-payment to the insured is irrelevant: *Mortgage Insurance Corp. v. Inland Revenue Commissioners* (1887) 57 LJQB 174.
835. Other causal factors may be required, as, for example, in *Waterkeyn v. Eagle Star Insurance Co. Ltd.* (1920) 5 LILR 42, where insolvency had to arise directly from damage or destruction of the premises and contents of specified banks through riot, war, etc. The subject matter of the insurance was money deposited in Russian banks, for the loss of which the insured claimed following the Russian revolution and the confiscation of the banks' property. As there was no evidence that the premises or contents of the banks had been damaged or destroyed, the claim failed.
836. In this context, if the insurer discovers something material about the debtor, he is under a duty to disclose it to the insured: *see Banque Financière de la Cité v. Westgate Insurance Co.* [1991] 2 AC 249.
837. *Seaton v. Burnand* [1900] AC 135.
838. *Dane v. Mortgage Insurance Corp, supra* .
839. If, under insolvency legislation, the debtor comes to some compromise or arrangement with his creditors, this may impact on a particular creditor/insured's rights under his insurance policy. If the creditor assents in breach of the policy condition, the insurer will be entitled to repudiate liability. If, however, the creditor does not assent, but is nonetheless bound by the compromise or arrangement, he will still be entitled to payment from the insurer (who will be subrogated to the creditor's rights against the debtor). If the effect of a compromise or arrangement is to extinguish the creditor's rights against the debtor, albeit perhaps replacing them with new rights, the insurer will no longer be liable, unless there is a specific provision in the insurance contract governing that additional risk: *Shaw v. Royce Ltd.* [1911] 1 Ch. 138.

Chapter 12. Technical Insurance

264. In British practice, the type of insurance primarily subsumed by the title of this chapter is usually called contractors' all risks insurance[840] or construction insurance. This can cover any building project, ranging from the construction of major buildings to the construction of such as ships. The essential features are that the contractor, the person primarily responsible for the building, is covered in respect of both the property in question, the contract works, generally including the necessary plant, machinery and equipment, and liability that may be incurred as a result of the building operations. It is thus in practice both a property and a liability insurance.[841] Underpinning most such policies will be the contract effected between the employer and the contractor[842] which, in any project of any size, is likely to follow one of the standard forms of contract available for building and engineering projects.[843] A policy may be drafted to cover one specific project and if so, the duration of the policy is likely to be the duration of the project.[844] Alternatively, the policy may cover a number of projects over a stated period.[845]

265. A standard feature of contractors' all risks insurance, in which respect it appears unique in British insurance practice, is the habit of having many more than one insured under the policy.[846] In practice, the contractor will be the principal insured, but this will generally be jointly with the employer. Further, the policy will expressly insure subcontractors and other interested persons, bringing them all within the definition of the 'insured'. The latter may not actually be named, though. The British courts have only relatively recently had to consider the implications of such co-insurance and indeed have not yet been presented with an opportunity to deal with the full ramifications.[847]

840. The use of 'all risks' is a misnomer, since such insurances are rarely all risks in the conventional sense.
841. There are likely to be quite separate parts of the one policy covering these different aspects.
842. And, more than likely, subcontracts between the contractor and subcontractors.
843. The principal such contracts are the *Institute of Civil Engineers Conditions of Contract* and the *Standard Form of Building Contract 1980* (also known as JCT 80).
844. If, as is common, the building project runs beyond the time originally agreed, the insurance contract will require extension. Sometimes this is available at the option of the insured on payment of an additional or increased premium, but if it is not, fresh insurance will have to be arranged, and the insurer cannot be obliged to accept the additional cover. In *Jones Construction Co. v. Alliance Insurance Co.* [1961] 1 Lloyd's Rep. 121, where there was a provision for extension 'in respect of which the insured shall have paid and the insurers accepted the premium required', it was held that the requirement for the insurers to accept additional premium of necessity implied that they were not required to accept any extension.
845. In the latter event, it is unlikely to be required that the contracts covered are in ICE or JCT standard form, provided of course that the contract in question is an appropriate building contract: *see* *Rowlinson Construction Ltd. v. Insurance Company of North America (UK) Ltd.* [1981] 1 Lloyd's Rep. 332.
846. There are many other examples of such co-insurance involving two or three insureds, but in a construction insurance there could be tens or even hundreds of insureds.
847. For a consideration of these, *see* Birds, *Insurable Interests*, in *Interests in Goods* (Palmer & McKendrick, 2d ed., Lloyd's of London Press 1998).

However, it seems clear that, if there are no words indicating otherwise, each of the co-insured will be entitled to recover in respect of a loss exceeding his own proprietary interest in the property lost, holding the excess for the benefit of the others involved.[848] Insurers who have indemnified one insured in respect of a loss caused by the negligence of a co-insured are not entitled to subrogation rights in the name of the former against the latter.[849] Furthermore, for certain purposes the courts are likely to treat such co-insurance as consisting of separate contracts between the insurer and each co-insured, so that the non-disclosure of material facts or the making of a fraudulent claim by one of the latter will not prevent an innocent co-insured from recovering.[850]

266. In most other respects, construction insurances are simply ordinary property and liability insurances, as appropriate, and the general law of insurance will apply to them. One particular aspect, however, deserves brief further consideration. This is the standard practice of excluding from the insured risks losses that arise from faulty or defective workmanship, materials or design.[851] The use of words like 'faulty' or 'defective' raise the problem as to whether they apply only where it can be shown that someone was actually at fault. Where a policy covering the construction of a bridge excluded loss or damage arising from 'faulty design' and the piers of the bridge were swept away by exceptionally heavy flood waters, it was held that the insurers could rely upon the exception, notwithstanding that the design of the bridge was the best available at the time.[852] The fact that no one was at fault was irrelevant; the design was faulty since otherwise the piers would never have collapsed.[853]

---

848. *Petrofina Ltd. v. Magnaload Ltd* [1984] 1 QB 127. *Quaere* whether this is in fact a necessary or sensible principle; *see* Birds, *supra* .
849. *Ibid.*; *Stone Vickers Ltd. v. Appledore Ferguson Shipbuilders Ltd.* [1991] 2 Lloyd's Rep. 288. *See* the general discussion and other authorities cited in para. 157.
850. *Samuel v. Dumas* [1924] AC 431; New *Hampshire Insurance Co v. MGN Ltd* [1997] LRLR 24; *Arab Bank plc v. Zurich Insurance Co* [1999] 1 Lloyd's Rep. 262; *FNCB Ltd v. Barnet Devanney (Harrow) Ltd* [1999] Lloyd's Rep. IR 459.
851. This is because insurers regard these risks as more properly covered, if at all, by other types of insurance.
852. *Queensland Government Railways and Electric Power Transmission Pty. Ltd. v. Manufacturers' Mutual Life Insurance Ltd.* [1969] 1 Lloyd's Rep. 214, a decision of the High Court of Australia, but of highly persuasive authority in England.
853. If the word 'faulty' is used to qualify 'workmanship', it might be read as meaning negligent.

Part IV. Motor Vehicle Insurance

§1. Compulsory Cover

267. For many years in the UK, some form of motor vehicle insurance has been compulsory. What the law requires at present is that anyone who uses or causes or permits another to use a motor vehicle on a road or other public places must be insured against liability to pay damages for death or bodily injury or property damage caused by or arising out of the use of the vehicle.[854] The exact scope of this requirement will be considered shortly. The requirement in respect of property damage was introduced only at the end of 1988, pursuant to the Second EC Directive on Motor Insurance,[855] although in practice most motor policies have long covered third party property damage. It should be noted that the EC Directives, of which there were five, now consolidated in Directive 2009/103/EC, only require that civil liability in any Member State is covered by insurance and do not affect the nature of that liability, which in the UK is of course based on fault.[856] However, it is equally clear that it is in respect of motor vehicle insurance, together with the general regulation of insurance discussed in Chapter 2, that EU law has become of particular importance in insurance law. As well as the provisions derived from EU law that are described throughout this chapter, and European Court of Justice (ECJ) cases construing aspects of the Directives, note the establishment, pursuant to the Fourth Directive,[857] of the Motor Insurers' Information Centre, which is required to keep information about all vehicles normally based in the UK and the insurance arrangements applying to them, so that information can be provided to victims of accidents.[858] The Fifth Directive[859] was implemented on 11 June 2007 and

854. Road Traffic Act 1988, ss 143 and 145.

855. Directive 84/5, O.J. L8/17. This was implemented first by regulations and then consolidated in the Road Traffic Act 1988. Pt VI of the latter contains the provisions regarding compulsory motor vehicle insurance. The history of these provisions since 1930 is usefully set out in *Norman v. Aziz* [2000] Lloyd's Rep. I. R. 52 at 54-6.

856. In contrast in some Member States there is some form of strict liability, for example, where passengers are injured. As to the requirements of EU law in this respect, *see* *Ferreira v. Companhia de Seguros Mundial Confianca SA* [2000] All E.R. (D.) 1197.

857. Implemented by the Motor Vehicles (Compulsory Insurance) (Information Centre and Compensation Body) Regulations 2003, SI 2003/37.

858. There are equivalent institutions throughout the European Economic Area.

859. Directive 2005/14/EC.

increased the minimum cover required in respect of liability for property damage. The EU law was consolidated in Directive 2009/103/EC.[860]

268. As is well known, the UK is scheduled to leave the European Union in March 2019. Together with aspects of the law governing the regulation of insurers, motor vehicle insurance law is the predominant part of UK insurance law that has been substantially affected by EU law, as can be seen from the introductory remarks above. However, it seems likely that the provisions implementing EU Directives and Regulations will remain part of domestic UK law in any event, and relevant decisions of the ECJ made before the date of departure, though not afterwards, will probably continue to be applicable in UK law.

It has long been conventional to sell motor policies under particular labels, although these have no legal significance. Thus, a 'comprehensive' policy will generally, in addition to what is compulsory, cover first party property damage, that is insurance of the vehicle as goods against loss, and first party injury, that is in effect a personal accident insurance under which the insured who is killed or injured when involved in an accident in his vehicle will receive a stated sum. It often also covers personal effects in the vehicle.[861] The other common form of motor policy which does not just cover third party liability is the third party, fire and theft policy; in addition to third party liability, this covers insurance of the vehicle itself but limited to those losses caused by fire or theft.

In practice a motor policy may not just cover the insured or policyholder himself. The policy may extend either to named others or possibly to anyone driving the car with the insured's permission, and may also cover the insured driving other vehicles. In addition, there are various categories of use, for example, 'social, domestic and pleasure purposes' and 'business purposes', adopted by insurers, which determine the uses to which the vehicle can be put while remaining covered. These matters are examined later in this Part. Also of special importance in the field of motor insurance are excesses and no-claims and loyalty bonuses. Excesses have been described earlier.[862] No-claims bonuses provide for specified reductions in premiums if no claim, or no relevant claim, is made during the previous year.[863] 'Knock-for-knock' agreement used

---

860. It has been obvious for some time that UK law did not fully implement the EU Directives. The UK Government was challenged on this in *Roadpeace v. Secretary of State for Transport* [2017] EWHC 2725 (Admin); although most of the claim was unsuccessful, this was only because the court recognized that the Government was taking steps to amend the law.

861. In addition, there are usually special provisions regarding windscreen damage whereby the insured may be able to have a broken windscreen replaced and only claim later, and without prejudice to his no-claims bonus. Some policies now provide for the insured to be entitled to claim the cost of hiring an alternative vehicle while his is being repaired, and there are special policies available to people over particular ages.

862. *See* para. 144.

863. The practice of offering no-claims bonuses has spread to other forms of insurance in recent years. Loyalty bonuses tend to allow for an unlimited number of claims over a longer period without their being lost. Technically, there may be difficulties in showing a legal entitlement to such bonuses since motor policies, like other indemnity policies, are of limited duration and each renewal is a separate contract. As to possible arguments around these difficulties, *see Birds' Modern Insurance* Law, para. 5.7.3.

to be common in the motor insurance industry, but have fallen out of favour in recent years.[864]

I. The Scope of Compulsory Cover

269. Part VI of the Road Traffic Act 1988,[865] which governs the compulsory aspect of motor insurance, as well as defining these obligations, also provides special protection to the injured third party from the strict contractual rights of the insurer as against the insured. The basic obligations will be examined at this stage and the latter aspect will be considered later. Subject to the exceptions in section 144,[866] section 143 provides that a person must not use, or cause or permit any other person to use, a motor vehicle on a road or public place, unless there is in force a policy which complies with the Act covering the required third party risks or a security in relation to those risks.[867] The requirements are stated in section 145.

First, the policy must be issued by an authorized insurer, which means for this purpose a person carrying on motor insurance business in Great Britain who is a member of the Motor Insurer's Bureau.[868] It is now perfectly lawful for a motor policy to be issued by any foreign insurer, subject only to the requirement of MIB membership. The required risks are:

(1) insurance against liability in respect of death or bodily injury to any person or damage to property caused by or arising out of, the use of the vehicle on a road or public place in Great Britain;[869]

864. *See* para. 157.
865. This consolidated earlier legislation dating originally from 1930.
866. These are described later.
867. Securities, which it seems are rarely used, are governed by s. 146. This requires that they are given by either: (1) an authorized insurer; or (2) by some body of persons which carries on in the UK the business of giving securities of a like kind and has deposited and keeps deposited with the Accountant General of the Supreme Court the sum of GBP 500,000 in respect of that business. The security must consist of an undertaking by the giver of it to make good, subject to any conditions specified in it, any failure by the owner of the vehicle or such other persons or classes of persons as may be specified in the security duly to discharge any liability which may be incurred by him or them which is a liability required under s. 145 to be covered by an insurance policy.
868. As to the MIB, *see* para. 274.
869. This does not mean that the user has to be insured against his potential liability to the driver, e.g., because he has negligently let him drive an unsafe vehicle; the driver is not within the words 'any person': *Cooper v. Motor Insurers' Bureau* [1985] QB 575; *R v. Secretary of State, ex p. National Insurance Guarantee Corp plc*, *The Times*, 3 Jun. 1996. *See also Bretton v. Hancock* [2005] EWCA Civ 404, [2005] Lloyd's Rep. IR 454, which is discussed at para. 269, *infra*. Liability to passengers is covered even if the vehicle is not designed to carry them: *Farrell v. Motor Insurers Bureau of Ireland* C-365/05, ECJ. Liability for deliberate acts should be covered: *EUI Ltd v. Bristol Alliance Ltd Partnership* [2012] EWCA Civ 1267.

(2) insurance against any liability in the other EC Member States which those States require;[870] and
(3) insurance against liabilities in respect of emergency treatment.[871]

Where a vehicle is normally based in one EC Member State, and used in another, the compulsory insurance cover must be in accordance with the law requiring the greater cover.[872]

Heading (1) does not, however, require insurance in respect of the following:

(a) the liability of an employer to an employee in respect of death or bodily injury arising out of and in the course of his employment, provided that in respect of someone carried in or upon a vehicle or entering or getting on to or alighting from a vehicle,[873] the exception does not apply unless there is effective cover under the Employers' Liability (Compulsory Insurance Act) 1969;[874] because employers' liability policies are no longer required to cover these risks,[875] in practice they are likely to be covered by a motor policy;[876]

870. *See also* the Motor Vehicles (Compulsory Insurance) No. 2 Regulations 1973, SI No. 2143, as amended by SI 1974/791, SI 1974/2186 and SI 1987/2171, which also provide that it is an offence for someone exempted from s. 143 by s. 144 to use a GB-registered vehicle in another Member State without the compulsory insurance required by that State (Reg. 5), and that someone with a policy issued in another Member State in respect of a vehicle normally based there is exempted from s. 147(2) (policy to be issued by an authorized insurer) and s. 147(1) (the requirements for certificates) (Reg. 8). The latter exclusion (Reg. 8) also applies in respect of vehicles from the non-EEC European States listed in Reg. 2(1).

871. This liability arises under s. 158. Where medical or surgical treatment is immediately required as a result of bodily injury (including fatal injury) to a person caused by or arising out of the use of a motor vehicle on a road and such emergency treatment is effected by a legally qualified medical practitioner, the person who was using the vehicle at the time of the event out of which the injury arose must, on a claim being made under s. 159, pay a fee and expenses to the practitioner or the hospital. If the person using the vehicle was not the tortfeasor who caused the accident, he can recover the money paid from the tortfeasor. The claim under s. 159 may be made orally at the time when the emergency treatment is effected; if not so made, it must be made by written request served on the user of the vehicle within seven days of the treatment.

872. Amendments made to s. 145 by the Motor Vehicles (Compulsory Insurance) Regulations 1992 (SI 1992/3036), implementing the Third EC Directive on Motor Insurance 90/232.

873. This does not cover someone such as a policeman trying to stop a vehicle by opening the door: *Miller v. Hales* [2006] EWCA 1529 (QB), [2007] Lloyd's Rep. IR 54, nor an employee in a hoist incorporating an elevating platform: *Axa Insurance plc v. Norwich Union Insurance Ltd* [2007] EWHC 1268 (QB), [2008] Lloyd's Rep. IR 122.

874. The requirement of effective employers' liability cover, rather than a blanket exemption of employers' liability risks, was inserted as s. 145(4A) by the 1992 Regulations.

875. The Employers' Liability (Compulsory Insurance) Regulations 1998, SI No. 2573, Sch. 2, para. 14.

876. A policeman is not an employee: *Miller v. Hales, supra* .

(b) cover in respect of property damage of more than GBP 1,200,000 'caused by, or arising out of, any one accident involving the vehicle';[877]
(c) liability in respect of damage to the vehicle;
(d) liability in respect of damage to goods carried for hire or reward in or on the vehicle or in or on any trailer drawn by the vehicle;[878]
(e) liability of a person in respect of damage to property in his custody or under his control;[879] and
(f) any contractual liability.[880]

270. The basic obligation arising from the words of section 143 cited above has been the subject of considerable case law. One problem used to be the meaning of the word 'road', when the obligation to insure was limited to use of a vehicle on a road. In particular, this would not normally include a car park.[881] However, section 143[882] was amended by the insertion of 'public place', which clearly includes a car park.[883] Insurance is required when part of a vehicle is on a public road after being driven from private property.[884]

The major problem has been the meanings of the words 'use' and to 'cause' or 'permit' use in section 143. 'Use' includes the leaving of a car on a road or other public places, even though it is incapable at present of being mechanically propelled.[885] It has also been held to cover the case of someone who left their car because it had run out of fuel and caused an accident when they crossed the road for help.[886] However,

877. Section 161(3) provides that any reference to an accident includes a reference to two or more causally related accidents. The limit was increased to GBP 1,200,000 by the Motor Vehicles (Compulsory Insurance) Regulations 2016, SI 2016/1193. Most policies on private vehicles do not have a limit though commercial policies often do. A limit was adopted in order to mitigate the effect on the MIB (*see* below) in cases of uninsured drivers. Note that there is a broad construction of 'accident' in this sort of context; *see* *South Staffordshire Tramways Co v. Sickness and Accident Assurance Association* [1891] 1 QB 402, where a liability policy effected by a tramway company had a limit of '£250 in respect of any one accident'. It was held that when a tram overturned injuring forty passengers, each passenger suffered an accident and therefore the insurer's maximum liability was forty times GBP 250.
878. This does not exclude liability in respect of goods carried gratuitously, although the next exception may do so.
879. For example, the belongings of passengers. It is unclear how far this exception goes. It would probably apply to luggage in the boot of a car, although it can hardly apply to items of clothing or other things on the person of a passenger.
880. Section 145(4).
881. *See* the decision of the House of Lords in *Cutter v. Eagle Star Insurance Co Ltd* [1998] 4 All E.R. 417. A hotel forecourt habitually used by the public as a road was held to be a road: *Bugge v. Taylor* [1941] 1 K.B. 198, but compare *Thomas v. Dando* [1951] 2 K.B. 620. *See also Evans v. Clarke* [2007] Lloyd's Rep. IR 16.
882. And other relevant provisions of the 1988 Act.
883. The Motor Vehicles (Compulsory Insurance) Regulations 2000, SI No. 726. Difficult questions as to what is a 'public place' might still, though, arise.
884. *Randall v. Motor Insurers' Bureau* [1968] 2 Lloyd's Rep. 553.
885. *Elliott v. Grey* [1960] 1 QB 367. It is otherwise if the vehicle is totally immovable: *Thomas v. Hooper* [1986] R.T.R. 1.
886. *Dunthorne v. Bentley* [1999] Lloyd's Rep. IR 560.

the word is not so wide as to include, for example, the normal case of someone being a passenger in a motor vehicle,[887] or asking another to transport some goods in his car, even though it could perhaps be said colloquially that that person was using the other's car. In the context of the Road Traffic Act, use implies an element of controlling, managing or operating the vehicle at the relevant time.[888] Use does not cover a situation where a vehicle has stopped to pick up a passenger who is injured when crossing the road in an attempt to reach the vehicle.[889] 'Use' should be interpreted to include any use that is consistent with the normal function of the vehicle[890] and therefore includes repair work required to put a vehicle into good working condition.[891] There can be more than one person using a vehicle at any given time within the statutory meaning. So, in *Leathley v. Tatton*,[892] it was held that a passenger involved in a criminal adventure with others to steal and take away a car was using the car for the purposes of section 143, and in *O'Mahony v. Joliffe*,[893] in respect of a passenger who was enjoying a joint escapade with the unlicensed and uninsured driver of a motor cycle that was untested and untaxed.[894] In *Bretton v. Hancock*,[895] a passenger who had an interest in a car was held to be a user.

Whether someone causes or permits another to use a vehicle is a question of fact. Clearly it is so if, for example, X allows Y to drive his car. The word 'cause' involves an express or positive mandate to use a car in a particular way, whereas 'permit' is looser, and merely denotes an express or implied licence to use a vehicle.[896] In *McLeod v. Buchanan*, a man appointed his brother as manager of his farm and bought him a car that was insured for business and private use. The car having proved unsatisfactory, the man authorized his brother to buy a van instead; this was insured for business use only, but was in fact used for private purposes. It was held that the man had permitted his brother to use the van while uninsured. The van was given to him for the same purposes as the car, and the brother was not told not to use it for private purposes. In *Lyons v. May*,[897] a garage owner was driving a car back from the garage after repair, at the request of the car's owner. It was held that the latter had

887. *B. (A Minor) v. Knight* [1981] R.T.R. 136; *Hatton v. Hall* [1999] Lloyd's Rep. IR 313.
888. *Brown v. Roberts* [19651 1 QB 1 at 15, per Megaw J. Here the passenger in a car was negligent in opening her door and thereby injured a pedestrian. It was held that she was not using the car in the statutory sense, because she had no control over the vehicle, so the driver was not therefore causing or permitting her to use it and thus not liable in damages for breach of statutory duty in not insuring her against her potential liability.
889. *Slater v. Buckinghamshire County Council* [2004] Lloyd's Rep. IR 432.
890. *See* the decision of the European Court of Justice in *Vnuk v. Zavarovalnica Triglav DD* (C-162/13).
891. *R & S Pilling v. UK Insurance Ltd* [2017] EWCA Civ 259.
892. [1980] R.T.R. 21. *See also Cobb v. Williams* [1973] R.T.R. 113 and *Stinton v. Stinton* [1995] R.T.R. 167; compare *B. (A Minor) v. Knight* [1981] R.T.R. 136.
893. [1999] Lloyd's Rep. IR 321.
894. This point is especially important in the context of the MIB Agreements where the same words are construed in the same way; *see* para. 291.
895. [2005] EWCA Civ 404, [2005] Lloyd's Rep. IR 454, discussed at para. 269.
896. Lord Wright in *McLeod v. Buchanan* [1940] 2 All E.R. 179 at 187.
897. [1948] 2 All E.R. 1062.

caused or permitted the use of the car. In contrast, in *Watkins v. O'Shaughnessy*,[898] an auctioneer sold a car which the purchaser drove away immediately without, to the auctioneer's knowledge, being insured. It was held that the auctioneer had not caused or permitted the use of the car because, having sold it, he no longer had any control over it. In *Thompson v. Lodwick*,[899] a driving instructor was held not to have caused or permitted his pupil to use the vehicle when the latter owned it.

271. Section 143 requires that there be in force a 'policy' of insurance. A policy exists for these purposes even though it is voidable.[900] Policy includes a cover note.[901] However, it has been decided that the existence of a contract of insurance by itself is not enough to satisfy the statute. In *Roberts v. Warne*,[902] the relevant policy did not cover the particular driver who was using the car, although a cover note had been arranged to effect this and when this expired, the insurers clearly regarded the driver as covered.[903] The driver was convicted for using the car without insurance and the owner for causing or permitting this. It was held that, even if the insurers were contractually bound to cover the driver, which may well have been the case, the policy did not cover him and hence there was no policy as section 143 requires. It is thought that this decision is wrong.[904] There seems no reason to read the word 'policy' as meaning anything other than a legally enforceable contract of insurance. Even an enforceable oral contract should suffice.[905]

272. In addition to the requirement under section 143 to have a policy, section 147 provides that the policy is of no effect unless and until the insurer delivers to the insured a certificate of insurance.[906] Notwithstanding this wording, it has been held[907] that a third party was not precluded from suing the insurers under section 151,[908] where a certificate was issued subsequently to the accident but expressed to be retrospective

---

898. [1939] 1 All E.R. 384.
899. [1983] R.T.R. 76.
900. For example, for non-disclosure or misrepresentation: *Adams v. Dunne* [1978] R.T.R. 281. Avoidance for one of these reasons does not amount to avoidance *ab initio* for criminal law purposes: *Goodbarne v. Buck* [1940] 1 K.B. 771.
901. Section 161(1), although it must be contractually binding, *see Taylor v. Allon* [1966] 1 QB 304.
902. [1973] R.T.R. 217.
903. There were severe communication difficulties at the time because of a postal strike.
904. *See also* (1973) Crim. L.R. 244.
905. That this is the better view seems to be supported by the decision in *Ackman v. Policyholders Protection Board* [1992] 2 Lloyd's Rep. 321, where the Court of Appeal held that the word 'policy' in the Policyholders Protection Act 1975 had no special meaning and meant simply a contract of insurance.
906. *See* s. 147(2) for the certificate of security when the obligation is satisfied by a security rather than by insurance. Where a policy or security is cancelled, the insured must, within seven days, surrender the certificate or, if it is lost or destroyed, make a statutory declaration to that effect: s. 147(4). The contents of certificates are prescribed by the Motor Vehicles (Third Party Risks) Regulations 1972, SI No. 1217, as amended, which require the registration mark of the vehicle, the name of the policyholder, the dates of commencement and expiry of the cover, the person or persons entitled to drive and the limitations as to use. Insurers must keep full records of certificates issued and must issue a fresh certificate on request in the event of loss or destruction. Certificates can be delivered electronically: s. 147(1A)-(1E).
907. *Motor and General Insurance Co v. Cox* [1990] 1 W.L.R. 1443.
908. *See* para. 271.

to a time before the accident, and where a cover note had been issued before the accident. Certificates constitute the easily checkable evidence of compliance with the insurance obligation; in particular they must be produced in order to obtain a road fund licence for a vehicle.[909] While the certificate or parts of it may be incorporated into the contract of insurance or policy, for example, concerning the permitted user of the vehicle, if there is any conflict between the two, the policy prevails, and the certificate itself is not a contract of insurance.[910]

II. Exemptions from Section 143

273. Section 144 provides for a number of exemptions from the obligation to insure under section 143. The first is in respect of a vehicle owned by a person who has deposited and keeps deposited in court the sum of GBP 500,000 at a time when the vehicle is being driven under the owner's control.[911] A sum deposited under section 144(1) cannot be used to discharge any other liabilities of the depositor so long as there are undischarged liabilities that would require to be insured against under section 145.[912] Section 144(1) is supplemented by the Motor Vehicles (Third Party Risks Deposits) Regulations 1967 (SI No. 1326), which provide the detail as to the making of deposits and allow for withdrawal of them in appropriate cases, for example, when the depositor satisfies the court that he intends to comply with section 143 in some other way or ceases to own a motor vehicle.

274. Second, Part VI of the 1988 Act contains a number of other exemptions. The whole of Part VI does not apply:

(1) to invalid carriages;[913]
(2) to tramcars or trolley vehicles operated under statutory powers; nor
(3) to vehicles in the service of the Crown.

By section 144(2), section 143 does not apply:

(1) to a vehicle owned by county and other councils and other local government bodies when the vehicle is being driven under the owner's control;
(2) to police vehicles being driven under the owner's control;
(3) to vehicles being used for salvage purposes;

909. Section 156.
910. *Biddle v. Johnston* [1965] 2 Lloyd's Rep. 121.
911. Section 144(1). In 1984 about 14,000 vehicles were the subject of deposits which are intended to be an indication of the solvency of depositors who will therefore be able to meet tort claims from their own resources. 'Being driven under the owner's control' means being driven by the owner or by a servant of the owner in the course of his employment or otherwise subject to the control of the owner: s. 161(1).
912. Section 155(1).
913. Defined as a mechanically propelled vehicle with a weight of not more than 5 cwt which is specially designed and constructed and not merely adapted for the use of a person suffering from some physical defect or disability and is used solely by such person.

(4) to army or air force vehicles; and
(5) to National Health Service vehicles.

III. Sanctions for Failure to Insure

275. The consequences of a failure to comply with the obligation to insure under section 143 are potentially twofold. First, it is a criminal offence of strict liability.[914] Second, commission of the offence is a breach of statutory duty and anyone who suffers loss as a result can sue in tort for damages. The importance of this is not against the negligent driver, who would be liable in negligence anyway, but against someone who used the car with him or caused or permitted him to use it. The meanings of these expressions, as already discussed, may therefore be of importance in this context as well as in the criminal context. In *Monk v. Warbey*,[915] the defendant owner of a car lent it to a friend who permitted another to drive. Neither of the latter was insured. It was held that the plaintiff, who had been injured by the negligence of the driver, could sue the owner.[916] It would appear that the owner's insurer, assuming that he has one, might be liable in such circumstances to indemnify him against this liability, as the standard policy wordings do not require the insured to be driving, but indemnify him against 'legal liability ... arising from an accident caused by, through or in connection with the insured car'. Since 1946, the Motor Insurer's Bureau indemnifies such uninsured drivers,[917] but it has been held that this does not remove the action for breach of statutory duty. In the case in question, *Corfield v. Groves*,[918] judgment was awarded against the owner subject to the proviso that if the MIB did satisfy the judgment, it could not be enforced against the owner. In practice, therefore, this action is really only relevant if for some reason the MIB is not liable, for example, because of a failure to comply with one of the conditions precedent to their liability.[919]

However, a claim under the principle of *Monk v. Warbey* does not comprehend a claim for pure economic loss. In *Bretton v. Hancock*,[920] the claimant B had an ownership interest in the vehicle being driven by her uninsured fiancé, in which she was a passenger. An accident for which the latter was found 25% to blame and the other driver 75% caused the death of the fiancé and injury to the other driver, the defendant H, who brought a counterclaim against B for breach of statutory duty. It was held that although B, because of her interest, had been using the car within the meaning of section 143, a user was not bound to insure against the liability of one

914. Subject to the defences in s. 143(2), which provide for no liability if a person proves: (1) that the vehicle did not belong to him and was not in his possession under a contract of hire or loan; (2) that he was using the vehicle in the course of employment; or (3) that he neither knew nor had reason to believe that there was no valid insurance or security.

915. [1935] 1 K.B. 75.

916. This action is 'in respect of personal injuries' and therefore the limitation period under the Limitation Act 1980, s. 11, is three years: *Norman v. Ali* [2000] Lloyd's Rep. 395.

917. *See* para. 274.

918. [1950] 1 All E.R. 488.

919. In *Norman v. Aziz* [2000] Lloyd's Rep. IR 52, an attempt to argue that *Corfield v. Groves* was wrongly decided was rejected.

920. [2005] EWCA Civ 404, [2005] Lloyd's Rep. IR 454.

tortfeasor to contribute with another tortfeasor in respect of their joint liability to the user. Because the Road Traffic Act was only concerned with third party risks, the principle operated only when the victim was the claimant and there was an essential difference between the claim of the primary victim and the claim of the joint tortfeasor, which was only in respect of the other tortfeasor's right of indemnity or contribution.

§2. Common Terms and Exceptions

276. The standard terms and conditions that are found in motor vehicle policies are important to compulsory and non-compulsory insurance alike, because, even though, as will be seen, some of them may not be enforceable against a third party victim where insurance was compulsory, they may remain of effect between insurer and insured so that the insurer who has had to pay the third party may be entitled to recover this sum of money from the insured. The standard terms will be considered under three headings: standard extensions; limitations on use; and terms relating to the condition of the insured vehicle.

I. Standard Extensions

277. It is common for motor policies to insure people other than the insured or policyholder driving the car or vehicle in question. For example, cover may extend to the spouse of the insured, to particular named drivers or drivers identified by a class, or, most widely, to anyone driving the vehicle on the insured's order or with the insured's permission. Only the last sort of extension can give rise to legal problems, but before examining these, one important point of general interest relates to the status of the other driver in terms of the contract between insured and insurer.

At common law, the insured can enforce the contract in so far as it confers a benefit on a third party, there being in effect a waiver of any requirement of insurable interest.[921] The latter though cannot enforce the contract himself.[922] Now, however, the common law seems redundant in this context, for two reasons. First, section 148(7) of the 1988 Act provides:

> Notwithstanding anything in any enactment, a person issuing a policy of insurance under section 145 of this Act shall be liable to indemnify the persons or classes of persons specified in the policy in respect of any liability which the policy purports to cover in the case of those persons or classes of persons.

Thus, the third party can enforce the contract directly, subject, of course, to any right in the insurer to avoid liability,[923] and he is not dependent on the owner insuring as his

921. *Williams v. Baltic Insurance Association of London* [1924] 2 K.B. 282.
922. *Vandepitte v. Preferred Accident Insurance Corp of New York* [1933] A.C. 70.
923. *Guardian Assurance v. Sutherland* [1939] 2 All E.R. 246.

trustee or agent.[924] In effect, he is by statute a party to the contract.[925] Second, the third party can now in the alternative rely on the Contracts (Rights of Third Parties) Act 1999.[926]

278. The question of whether, other than in obvious cases, someone is driving with the insured's permission has occasioned some difficulties. It seems that the law would not sanction a permitted driver himself giving effective permission to another so that the other is covered, in the absence of the insured's direct consent.[927] That the insured can become the third party and recover as such if injured by the negligence of someone whom he permitted to drive the car is well established. In *Digby v. General Accident Fire and Life Assurance Corp*,[928] the insured's policy covered anyone driving with her permission. She gave such permission to her chauffeur and was then, as a passenger, injured by his negligent driving. It was held that the insurers were liable to indemnify the chauffeur in respect of his liability to the insured. Permission may be expressly or impliedly limited to a particular class of use of the vehicle. In *Singh v. Ratour*,[929] the driver had borrowed a van belonging to an association of which he was a member, the representative of the association believing that he had borrowed it for the purposes of the association. In fact he had borrowed it to attend a private social function. The driver sought an indemnity against the consequences of his negligence from his own insurers under a term in the policy that permitted him to drive vehicles belonging to another 'provided he [had] the consent of the owner'. The Court of Appeal held that he was not entitled to recover, as the consent was impliedly limited to use for the purposes of the association.

Permission once given can obviously be revoked. In the absence of such revocation, it appears that permission continues even when the insured dies. In *Kelly v. Cornhill Insurance Co*,[930] the insured gave permission to his son to drive the insured car and soon afterwards died. Some eight months later the son was involved in an accident, the policy period not having expired. By a bare majority, the House of Lords held that the son was entitled to sue under the policy, the permission of his father not having been revoked by his death.[931] While there are obvious difficulties in saying that permission continues in such a case in the absence of its renewal by the insured's personal representatives, in whom the ownership of the car and policy will have vested,

924. *Tattersall v. Drysdale* [1935] 2 K.B. 174.
925. It was undecided, before it was compulsory to insure against property damage liability, whether the statute covered only the compulsory aspects of a motor policy. It is now an academic point except where a policy provides more cover than s. 145 requires, e.g., unlimited cover in respect of property damage cover rather than the GBP 1,000,000 limit allowed.
926. *See* para. 166.
927. *See* the Canadian case of *Minister of Transport v. Canadian General Insurance* (1971) 18 DLR (3d) 617, where a son of the insured who was permitted to drive the car in question purported to give permission to a friend. It was held that the friend was not insured. It seems likely that an English court would reach the same conclusion; *see* *Morgans v. Launchberry* [1971] 2 QB 245 at 253.
928. [1943] A.C. 212.
929. [1988] 2 All E.R. 16.
930. [1964] 1 All E.R. 321.
931. It is noteworthy that there was little merit in the insurers' defence, as under the policy the father was expressly precluded from driving; it had been effected solely for the son's benefit.

the result is sensible, since otherwise a permitted driver could automatically and without his knowledge become uninsured, even, for example, in the course of a particular journey. The decision implies that the insured's personal representatives in such a case would have the power to revoke the permission. Otherwise it must continue only until the expiry of the policy. It would appear that revocation of permission is effective only when actually communicated to the person given permission.

A purchaser of a car, however, cannot be claiming to drive with the former owner, the insured's, permission, unless the insurers expressly consent. Here the insured ceases to have any insurable interest in the car, his policy lapses and is not assignable.[932]

II. Limitations on Use

279. Insurers have well-established categories of permitted use of an insured vehicle, and these are enforceable even against a third party.[933] These vary from, for example, use covering only social, domestic and pleasure purposes and use by the insured for travel to and from his place of business, to use by the insured in person or use by others in connection with the insured's or his employer's business. The cost of motor insurance premiums is affected by the permitted use, which is generally stated on the motor insurance certificate. Few legal difficulties can arise over some of the distinctions adopted, but in one respect there is a body of case law.

280. If an insured is covered for social, domestic and pleasure purposes and not for business use, or at least only for travelling to and from work,[934] the distinctions become important and not always easy to apply.[935] It must depend on the facts of the particular case and the 'essential character'[936] or 'primary purpose'[937] of the journey. In *Jones v. Welsh Insurance Corporation*,[938] the policy covered social, etc. purposes and used in connection with the insured's business, which was stated in the schedule to be that of motor mechanic. In addition, the insured farmed a few sheep, really as a hobby but with the aim of making a small profit. He was carrying some sheep when the relevant accident occurred. It was held that the insurers were not liable. The insured was carrying on the business of sheep farming; this was not stated in the schedule and thus the cover did not apply. In *Wood v. General Accident Fire & Life Assurance Corp*,[939] the relevant accident happened when a garage proprietor was being driven in his own car by one of his drivers to a firm with which he intended to negotiate a

932. *Peters v. General Accident Fire & Life Assurance Corp* [1938] 2 All E.R. 267; *see* para. 75.
933. As will be seen below, many provisions in contracts of motor insurance cannot be relied upon against a third party.
934. Travelling to work is not a social, domestic or pleasure purpose; it must be separately covered (*see* *Seddon v. Binions*, below).
935. As was pointed out in *Seddon v. Binions* [1978] 1 Lloyd's Rep. 381 at 384–385, there will be cases falling each side of the line when a phrase such as social, domestic and pleasure purposes is used, and it is impossible to state any firm principle under which it can be predicted on which side of the line a particular case will fall.
936. Per Roskill L.J., *ibid.*
937. Per Megaw L.J. *ibid.*, at 387.
938. [1937] 4 All E.R. 149.
939. (1948) 65 T.L.R. 53.

business contract. It was held that, though it was convenient and comfortable for him to make the journey like this, the car was not being used for social, etc. purposes. In *Seddon v. Binions*,[940] a father who helped his son occasionally on Sundays in the latter's business of carpet layer was driving home, in his son's car, his son's only employee who had toothache. Having delivered the latter, the father intended to go home for his lunch. The father's own policy covered his driving of other cars but only for social, etc. purposes. The son's insurers had paid in respect of the accident that occurred and were claiming a contribution from the father's insurers. It was held that the latter were not liable, the essential purpose of the journey being a business one, namely the father transporting his son's employee back from work. However, in *Keeley v. Pashen*,[941] where a mini-cab driver had dropped off his last passengers of the day and was driving home, the purpose of his journey became for social, etc. purposes.[942] The fact that he reversed towards the passengers after they had alighted in order to frighten them, because they had seemingly been drunk and abusive towards him, was merely an incidental episode and could not be classed as a separate journey; the essential purpose was still to return home.[943]

281. Use of driving for purposes connected with the motor trade may be excluded,[944] although the exclusion may be qualified so that cover is provided while the vehicle is merely in the custody or control of a motor trader for the purposes of repair, that is, so long as it is not being driven by someone other than the insured or a permitted driver.[945] A case may arise when the purposes of a journey are mixed. For example, an insured covered for social, etc. purposes but not for business purposes might be travelling to a business meeting followed by a social dinner. In *Seddon v. Binnions*,[946] the view of the trial judge was that there was a mixed purpose; the father

---

940. *See supra* . This decision was followed in *Killick v. Rendall* [2000] Lloyd's Rep. IR 581, construing a similar term in a personal accident policy, and in *Caple v. Sewell* [2001] EWCA Civ 1848, [2002] Lloyd's Rep. IR 626, a marine case.

941. [2004] EWCA Civ 1491, [2005] Lloyd's Rep. IR 289.

942. Which under the policy included travelling to and from work.

943. The insured in fact killed one of the passengers and pleaded guilty to a charge of manslaughter, but this was not criminal conduct of the sort that altered the essential purpose of the journey; *see* the comments of Brooke L.J. at [19].

944. As in *Browning v. Phoenix Assurance Co. Ltd.* [1960] 2 Lloyd's Rep. 360, where a garage employee was authorized by the insured to drive his car in order to warm the engine oil before it was drained at the garage. It was held that the insurers were not liable in respect of an accident that occurred when the employee was driving the car for pleasure the day after the oil had been drained, although the principal ground for the decision was that the employee was not a permitted driver in this respect. It was also clear that the car would not have been insured while the oil was being warmed.

945. *See* the Court of Appeal's construction of somewhat difficult terms to this effect in *Samuelson v. National Insurance Guarantee Corp Ltd* [1985] 2 Lloyd's Rep. 541. The actual decision was concerned with whether or not the insured vehicle was being driven by or in the charge of a person other than an authorized driver. It was made clear that once someone has completed his present journey, he is no longer in charge of the vehicle for insurance purposes. Thus, although the car had not been insured while being driven by a repairer on his way to collect spare parts, cover reattached once his journey was completed and the insured could recover for the theft of the car from where the repairer had parked it.

946. *See supra* .

was driving for social, etc. purposes in going home for lunch, not being an employee of his son and hence not strictly travelling from work, and for business purposes in taking his son's employee home. It was held, and the Court of Appeal confirmed this, that in this event the policy would not apply since the car was partly being used for an unauthorized purpose.

III. Conditions Regarding the Condition of the Insured Vehicle

282. Motor policies generally provide that the insurers are not to be on risk or liable when the insured vehicle is being driven in an unsafe or unroadworthy condition and/or if the insured fails to maintain the vehicle in an efficient or roadworthy condition. Such provisions may be drafted as exceptions to the risk or found under the heading 'conditions', in which case they may be warranties or conditions precedent. It is more common now for them to appear as conditions or warranties. In both cases, although the insurers will not be able to rely upon a breach as against an injured third party, because of the provisions of the Road Traffic Act which will be examined shortly, if they are warranties or conditions, they may well be able to recover from the insured, as damages for breach of condition, the money they have to pay to the third party.[947]

Application of the standard exception or condition has occasioned some difficulty. In *Barrett v. London General Insurance*,[948] it was held that, because of the verbal similarities, roadworthiness was to be interpreted in an analogous way to the standard requirement of seaworthiness in a marine policy. In a marine policy, seaworthiness is required only at the commencement of a voyage. The learned judge applied the same reasoning to a car journey in deciding that a car whose foot brake failed at the time of the relevant accident was not unroadworthy in the absence of proof that it was not working when the insured set out on his journey.[949] This reasoning was expressly disapproved by the Privy Council in *Trickett v. Queensland Insurance Co*,[950] though the exception in question there did not concern roadworthiness as such, but applied if the car was being driven in 'a damaged or unsafe condition'. The insured was involved in an accident at night at a time when the lights on his car were not working. It was held that this was sufficient to render the car damaged or unsafe. The knowledge of the insured was irrelevant, as was the question whether or not the lights were working at the beginning of the journey. The question was simply one of fact to be judged objectively.

More recently, it has been suggested that the marine analogy may be useful, but it appears unlikely that the decision in *Barrett* would be followed. The usual wording of this sort of exception is 'while the car is being driven', and this must include anything

947. Under s. 148(4) of the Road Traffic Act or, it seems, at common law: *National Farmers' Union Mutual Insurance Society v. Dawson* [1941] 2 KB 424.
948. [1935] 1 K.B. 238.
949. The judge may have been influenced by the fact that had the injured third party's claim arisen slightly later, the insurer would not have been able to take the point because of the imminent introduction of the statutory provisions which are now s. 148 of the Road Traffic Act 1988.
950. [1936] A.C. 159.

that happens during a journey and not just at the start of it.[951] In *Clarke v. National Insurance Corporation*,[952] a car intended to seat four people was driven with nine people in it. The Court of Appeal held that it was thereby rendered unroadworthy, although, with the normal number of people in it, it would have been quite safe. Unroadworthiness does not relate to just the mechanical condition of a vehicle, but can include any other relevant factors. In marine cases, overloading can render a ship unseaworthy, and the analogy was apt to this extent.

283. In the cases just discussed, the term in question was an exception and phrased in such a way that, fairly clearly, it should be properly read in a continuing objective sense. As noted above, modern policies tend to have replaced this exception by a condition or warranty requiring the insured to maintain the vehicle in a roadworthy or efficient condition. It has been suggested that these alternatives mean the same,[953] but it would seem that a term is both narrower and wider if phrased as a condition or warranty. It is narrower because, as a condition or warranty, it cannot be read wholly objectively. If a car's lights or brakes, for example, fail quite unexpectedly in the course of a journey, it may not be possible to say that the insured has failed to maintain the car in a roadworthy or efficient condition, whereas it can be said that the car is being driven in an unroadworthy condition. An insured's failure to maintain imports the notion of his knowing or being in a position where he ought to know that something is wrong, which requires the insurer to show more than a simple fact. This view is supported by the decision in *Conn v. Westminster Motor Insurance Association Ltd*,[954] where the insured should have known that his taxi's tyres were no good, as this was easily visible, but the same did not apply in relation to his braking system. However, a warranty as to roadworthiness is wider than an exception because there need be no connection between the breach of warranty and an accident which subsequently occurs. In *Conn's* case, as mentioned above, the insured's tyres on his taxi were so badly worn that there was no tread on them and they were illegal. It was held that this amounted to a breach of the obligation to maintain his vehicle in an efficient condition upon which the insurers could rely, even though the state of the tyres did not cause or contribute to the relevant accident.[955]

§3. Third Parties' Rights under the Road Traffic Act

284. As well as making some insurance compulsory, as we have already seen, the Road Traffic Act 1988 interferes with the contractual rights of insurers for the benefit of third parties to whom the insured is legally liable. The 1988 Act has now been supplemented by additional protection for third parties introduced pursuant to

951. *Clarke v. National Insurance Corp* [1963] 2 All E.R. 375 at 377.
952. *Supra*.
953. Sellers J. in *Brown v. Zurich General Accident and Liability Insurance Co* [1954] 2 Lloyd's Rep. 243 at 246.
954. [1966] 1 Lloyd's Rep. 407. *See also Lefevre v. White* [1990] 1 Lloyd's Rep. 569 and *Amey Properties Ltd v. Cornhill Insurance plc* [1996] C.L.C. 401.
955. Note though that this is now required under the Insurance Act 2015 (*see* para. 127).

the Fourth EC Directive, as explained below.[956] Because this additional protection was introduced without amending the provisions of the Act, we will explain the provisions of the Act first and then consider the additional rights.

Section 148(1) provides that, where a certificate of insurance has been delivered to the policyholder, so much of the policy as purports to restrict the insurance of the persons insured by reference to any of a list of specified matters is of no effect as regards insurance required under section 145. This invalidates certain terms in policies regardless of their exact legal status, i.e., whether they are warranties, conditions or exceptions. Section 148(2) lists the matters as follows:

(a) the age or physical or mental condition of persons driving the vehicle;
(b) the condition of the vehicle;
(c) the number of persons that the vehicle carries;
(d) the weight or physical characteristics of the goods that the vehicle carries;
(e) the times at which or the areas within which the vehicle is used;
(f) the horsepower or cylinder capacity or value of the vehicle;
(g) the carrying on the vehicle of any particular apparatus;
(h) the carrying on the vehicle of any particular means of identification other than any means of identification required to be carried by or under the Vehicle Excise and Registration Act 1994.

In most respects the sorts of warranties, conditions or exceptions avoided by section 148(1) are clear. For example, conditions or exceptions relating to roadworthiness, etc. will be of no effect; they fall within (b) above. A breach of warranty in a proposal form as to the value or size of engine of a vehicle will fall within (f). However, a condition requiring the insured to use all care and diligence to avoid accidents and prevent loss is not covered by the list,[957] and a limitation as to use is always effective as against third parties,[958] unless it relates to the use of a private vehicle under car-sharing arrangements.[959] This list is a relic from the original legislation which is curious because, if a term is enforceable by an insurer, the third party will have recourse against the MIB, as will be seen below. As has already been noted, section 148(4) entitles the insurer compelled to pay the third party, but who would otherwise have avoided liability, to recoup this money from the insured.

285. Section 148(5) invalidates other breaches of condition by an insured so far as the third party is concerned. The conditions covered are those providing that no liability shall arise under the policy, or that any liability so arising shall cease, in the event of some specified thing being done or omitted to be done after the happening of the event giving rise to the claim. This clearly covers a breach by the insured of a condition regarding notice or particulars of loss, and it must also cover an admission of liability in breach of the standard conditions.[960] Section 148(6) allows insurers to insert in their policies provisions allowing them to recover from the insured money

956. *See* para. 274.
957. *National Farmers' Union Mutual v. Dawson* [1941] 2 K.B. 424.
958. *Jones v. Welsh Insurance Corporation* [1937] 4 All E.R. 149.
959. *See* s. 150.
960. *See* Part III, Ch. 4.

which they have had to pay to a third party only by virtue of subsection (5). There is no automatic right given to insurers as there is under section 148(4), although it must be arguable that insurers would have that right in restitution, as there is a general principle that a claimant compelled by law to make a payment discharging the defendant's liability to a third party can recover that sum from the defendant.[961]

I. Insurer's Duty to Satisfy Judgments

286. The key provision so far as third parties are concerned is section 151. In effect, provided that a certificate of insurance has been delivered to the insured[962] and a third party has obtained a judgment against any person insured by the policy, the whole of the judgment, in respect of liability for death or bodily injury, and up to GBP 1,200,000 of it in respect of liability for damage to property, must be satisfied by the insurer, notwithstanding that the insurer may be entitled to avoid or cancel, or may have avoided or cancelled, the policy.[963] Further, this obligation applies in respect of persons not insured by a policy, for example, persons not within the category of permitted drivers or even a thief of the vehicle,[964] except that, in respect of liability for death or personal injury, it does not apply if the third party was allowing himself to be carried in or upon the vehicle knowing or having reason to believe that the vehicle had been stolen or unlawfully taken.[965] Although it was held[966] that this covers the situation where a third party passenger possessed sufficient information to afford him good reason to believe that the vehicle had been stolen or unlawfully taken, it is submitted that this is too broad a construction of the statute in the light of the approach taken by the ECJ.[967] In all cases, any term in a policy that purports to restrict its operation by requiring a driver to hold a licence to drive is invalid.[968] In order for a person to claim against an insurer under section 151, it is not necessary to identify the driver of the vehicle as long as the vehicle can be identified by description, namely its registration

961. *See* Goff and Jones, The Law of Restitution, Ch. 14.
962. But, as noted *supra* in para. 257, this requirement of delivery of a certificate has been eroded by the decision in *Motor and General Insurance Co v. Cox* [1980] 1 W.L.R. 1443.
963. Section 151(1), (2), (5) and (6). The award that must be satisfied includes costs and interest awarded. Where a property damage judgment exceeds GBP 1,200,000, s. 151(6)(b) provides as to how the insurer's exact liability is to be assessed.
964. In this situation the insurer can recover the amount paid to the third party from the driver or from the insured who caused or permitted the use of the vehicle: s. 151(8). As to the meaning of permission in this context, *see Lloyd-Welper v. Moore* [2004] EWCA Civ 766, [2004] Lloyd's Rep. IR 730. However, this does not apply when the insured is also a victim who has recovered damages from the driver and that judgment has been satisfied by the insurer: *Wilkinson v. Fitzgerald* [2009] EWHC 1291 (QB).
965. Unless he did not realize this until after the journey commenced and could not reasonably be expected to have alighted from the vehicle: s. 151(4).
966. *McMinn v. McMinn* [2006] EWHC 827 (QB), [2006] Lloyd's Rep. 802.
967. *See* especially *Candolin v. Vahinkovakuutusosakeyhtio Pohjola* Case C-537/03 [2006] Lloyd's Rep. IR 209 construing national legislation in the light of Art. 2(1) of the second Directive and Art. 1 of the third Directive.
968. Section 151(3).

number, and the date of the accident.[969] Where an insurer is liable to indemnify a person not insured by the policy, section 151(8) provides that it can recover the amount paid to the third party from the driver or from an insured who caused or permitted the use of the vehicle. This does not apply when the insured is a passenger in the vehicle and also a victim, as the insurer's obligation to satisfy a judgment in his favour and then automatically have the right to recover that back under the subsection is incompatible with the provisions of the Second Directive protecting third parties who are passengers.[970] The opinion of the ECJ to this effect was applied by the Court of Appeal in *Churchill Insurance Co Ltd v. Wilkinson*,[971] ruling that the subsection had to be read as requiring any recovery to be proportionate and determined on the basis of the circumstance of the case. As we shall see, an alternative route to using section 151 for third parties is now available in certain circumstances.

287. The insurer's obligation is qualified, however, by the provisions of section 152, in four respects:

(1) It arises only where the insurer was given notice, formally,[972] of the proceedings against the insured before or within seven days of their commencement.[973]
(2) It is not exercisable where execution of a judgment has been stayed pending an appeal.
(3) It does not apply if the insured's policy was cancelled before the relevant accident, either by mutual consent or under a term in the policy, and the certificate of insurance was surrendered or the insured made a statutory declaration that it was lost or destroyed within fourteen days of the cancellation, or within the same period the insurer commenced proceedings in respect of the failure to surrender the certificate.
(4) It does not apply if the policy was obtained by non-disclosure or misrepresentation of a material fact and the insurer, within three months of the commencement of the proceedings against the insured, obtains a declaration of the court to this effect, and the third party receives notice of the action for a declaration and the particulars of the non-disclosure or misrepresentation within seven days of its being commenced.[974]

The fourth qualification does not remove the insurer's right to avoid for non-disclosure or misrepresentation, but it limits the effectiveness of that right. However, it appears strictly not to include a discharge from liability for breach of warranty, for example,

969. *Cameron v. Hussain* [2017] EWCA Civ 366.
970. *Churchill Insurance Co Ltd v. Wilkinson, Evans v. Equity Claims Ltd* Case C-442/10.
971. [2013] Lloyd's Rep. IR 137.
972. *Herbert v. Railway Passengers Assurance Co* [1938] 1 All E.R. 650. A solicitor's letter to the insurers stating merely that the third party is being advised to issue proceedings is not sufficient to satisfy the requirement: *Harrington v. Link Motor Policies* [1989] 2 Lloyd's Rep. 310, but the notice does not have to be in writing or take a specific form: *Desouza v. Waterlow* [1999] R.T.R 71. *See also Wylie v. Wake* [2001] R.T.R. 291 and *Nawaz v. Crowe Insurance Group* [2003] EWCA Civ 471, [2003] Lloyd's Rep. IR 471.
973. This includes a counter claim by an injured defendant against an insured claimant, where appropriate: *Cross v. British Oak Insurance Co* [1938] 2 K.B. 167.
974. The third party has the right to be a party to this action.

by virtue of a misstatement on a proposal form warranted to be true. Section 152(2) refers expressly to the insurer's right to avoid apart from any provisions contained in the policy, meaning only the general right to avoid given by the common law or equity.[975] Warranties arise from express provisions. Thus, an insurer can avoid liability for breach of warranty as against the injured third party, without using the section 152 procedure, unless of course, the warranty relates to one of the matters in section 148(1), in which case the breach cannot be relied on at all. However, the cases have not always been too accurate in distinguishing non-disclosures, misrepresentation and warranties, and what appears strictly to be a breach of warranty has been treated as a misrepresentation or non-disclosure.[976]

Materiality is defined for the purposes of section 152 in the usual way,[977] namely, 'of such a nature as to influence the judgment of a prudent insurer in determining whether he will take the risk and, if so, at what premium and on what conditions'.[978] In addition, by statute it is not enough to show non-disclosure or misrepresentation of such a material fact. The insurer must also show that he himself was induced by the non-disclosure or misrepresentation to issue the policy as section 152(2) requires that the insurer show that the policy was obtained by non-disclosure or misrepresentation.[979] Section 152 has been amended to reflect the statutory reforms made by the Consumer Insurance (Disclosure and Representations) Act 2012 and the Insurance Act 2015.[980] If insurers are liable under section 151 to satisfy a judgment awarded to a third party, but could have avoided liability as between themselves and the insured, but chose not to do so, they can recover from the insured the amount paid to the third party.[981]

288. By section 153, the fact that the insured goes bankrupt or dies insolvent or, if a company, goes into liquidation, administration or receivership, does not affect the liability of the insured in respect of compulsory insurance, notwithstanding anything in the Third Parties (Rights Against Insurers) Act 1930.[982] In other words, the sections in the Road Traffic Act regarding the third parties' rights continue to apply, but otherwise section 153 incorporates the statutory assignment of the 1930 Act.

II. The Alternative Right to Sue Insurers

289. There is an alternative way in which third parties may proceed, introduced by the European Communities (Rights against Insurers) Regulations 2002.[983] These regulations implement part of the EC Fourth Directive, but in fact go further than that

975. *Merchants' & Manufacturers' Insurance Co v. Hunt* [1941] 1 K.B. 295.
976. *Merchants' & Manufacturers' Insurance Co v. Hunt, supra* ; compare *Zurich General Accident v. Morrison* [1942] 2 K.B. 53 which did concern a pure non-disclosure.
977. *See* para. 102.
978. Section 151(9)(6).
979. *Zurich General Accident v. Morrison, supra* .
980. *See* s. 11(3) of the Consumer Insurance (Disclosure and Representations) Act 2012 and s. 21(4) of the Insurance Act 2015.
981. Section 151(7).
982. As to this Act, *see* Part III, Ch. 4.
983. SI 2002/3061, in force from 19 Jan. 2003, but, it seems, irrespective of the date on which the accident occurred.

Directive requires. The critical point is that, subject to the requirements explained below, a third party may proceed directly against the insurers without first having to obtain a judgment against the negligent driver, although the insurers will of course be able to defend the claim on the basis that the driver was not in fact liable in tort. The regulations provide that an 'entitled party' can, without prejudice to his right to issue proceedings against the insured person, issue proceedings against the insurer, which 'shall be directly liable to the entitled party to the extent that he is liable to the insured person'.[984] An entitled party is someone who is a resident of the UK or any other EEA Member State,[985] so, for example, a tourist from outside Europe will not be able to use this right.

In addition, the entitled person must have a cause of action in tort against an 'insured person', which arises out of an accident caused by or arising out of the use of a vehicle on a road or other public places in the UK.[986] For these purposes an insured person is a person insured under a policy fulfilling the requirements of section 145 of the 1978 Act.[987] The requirement for an 'accident' is not one that appears anywhere else in the compulsory motor insurance requirements. Theoretically it could limit the application of the right, or at least raise the issue of whether or not a deliberate or reckless running down could be regarded as an accident, which would require a decision as to whether an event was to be looked at from the point of view of the insured driver or the victim.[988] In practice it seems unlikely to matter, since under the regulations the victim has no better rights than the insured, and it is clear that, on public policy grounds, the insured would not be entitled to an indemnity in such a case.[989] In contrast, public policy would not prevent an action brought under section 151 of the 1988 Act. There are other limits to this right, in contrast to the position under section 151. While, the restrictions in section 148 would also apply to an action brought under the Regulations, there is no other restriction on the insurer's contractual rights. There is no right under the Regulations to sue in respect of a tort committed by someone not insured under the policy nor when the insurance has actually been cancelled. In the latter case, section 151 will still apply if the insured is in possession of the certificate of insurance.

III. Information Regarding Insurance

290. The final aspect of the compulsory insurance requirements requires the driver against whom a claim is made in respect of damage compulsorily insurable is under a duty, on the demand of the third party, to give him information as to whether or not he was insured and, if so, such details of his insurance as are specified in his certificate of insurance.[990]

984. Regulation 3(2).
985. Regulation 2(1).
986. The vehicle must be normally based in the UK.
987. *See* para. 253.
988. *See* the discussion of the word 'accident' at para. 235.
989. *See* Ch. 12.
990. Section 154.

§4. Third Parties' Rights Against the MIB

291. The provisions just examined concerning third party rights under the Road Traffic Act have given rise to very few reported cases in recent years. This probably illustrates their relative unimportance since the MIB was established. In 1937, a Committee[991] recommended that a central fund be established to protect the victims of road accidents who received no compensation despite the protection afforded by the Road Traffic Act. Obviously the Act could not cover the situation of the driver who did not have insurance cover, nor was it really relevant when an insurer went into liquidation. Furthermore, as has been seen, there are occasions when an insurer can rely on terms in the policy to avoid liability to the third party despite provisions in the Act. Finally, the statute cannot of necessity protect the victim of an untraced or 'hit and run' driver. In this last respect, the Cassel Committee did not consider it practicable to give such victims' rights against the fund and this remained the position until 1969, although they did have a discretionary entitlement before then.

It was probably fears of possible nationalization of motor insurance business that led the motor insurers to conclude, on 31 December 1945, the first agreement between their creation, the MIB and the Minister of Transport. It is a condition of authorization to transact motor insurance business that the insurer is a member of MIB Ltd,[992] and the MIB agreements are now required by EC law.[993] UK residents injured in an accident within the European Economic Area[994] now have a statutory right to claim from the MIB pursuant to the Consolidated Motor Insurance Directive[995] in the situations covered by the MIB agreements.[996]

There are two agreements between the MIB and the Secretary of State. What will be hereafter referred to as the first MIB agreement is now dated August 2015, is entitled 'Compensation of Victims of Uninsured Drivers' and applies to accidents occurring on or after 1 August 2015; it has been supplemented by a supplementary agreement dated March 2017. This replaced the agreement dated August 1999, which itself replaced one dated December 1988. All agreements are in substance the original 1945 agreement with a number of amendments,[997] generally made to ensure compliance with EU law. As a result the conditions and exclusions under the 2017 agreement are fewer than under any of the earlier agreements. The second agreement, dated March 2017, is entitled 'Compensation of Victims of Untraced Drivers' and replaced earlier agreements dating from 1969, 1972, 1996 and 2003. The brief account of these agreements given here is based on the latest agreements, although cases will arise

991. The Cassel Committee, Cmnd 5528, paras 151–168.

992. Section 145(5), Road Traffic Act 1988.

993. Under the second Motor Insurance Directive.

994. And other countries that are party to the 'Green card' scheme for mutual recognition of motor insurance.

995. *See* the Motor Vehicles (Compulsory Insurance) (Information Centre and Compensation Body) Regulations 2003, SI 2003/37.

996. In the case of an accident outside the UK, the MIB has the right to claim indemnity from the insurers or its equivalent in the appropriate country.

997. Although the 1999 agreement introduced in particular more onerous procedural requirements than either of the earlier agreements contained.

under earlier versions for some time to come. More specialist works should be consulted for the detail.

I. The First MIB Agreement

292. This provides, in essence, that if a person injured or killed in a road accident, or whose property is damaged therein, obtains a judgment in respect of a liability that should have been insured against, and if that judgment is not satisfied in full within seven days, the MIB will satisfy it. Thus, the agreement covers the case of the uninsured driver, the driver without effective insurance and the driver whose insurer is unable to indemnify him, although in the latter case the compensation will normally be paid under the FSCS,[998] and the MIB will be in effect exempt. However, where a claim is made in respect of property damage, the MIB's liability is limited to GBP 1.2 million.

The MIB is not liable for any claim, or part of a claim, where the claimant has received, or is entitled to receive or demand payment or indemnity from any other person, including an insurer, other than the Criminal Injuries Compensation Authority. In the context of property damage claims, this is likely to apply in respect of damage to the claimant's vehicle recovered under his own insurance and in respect of damage to other properties that was separately insured. As far as personal injury claims are concerned, it might be argued that it is only compensation received from the FSCS or possibly social security payments that are likely to be relevant. It does not seem appropriate to take account of money received by the claimant (or his dependents) under a personal accident or life insurance policy, which is not taken into account when tort damages are assessed. Payments received under, for example, a medical insurance policy, which are assessed on an indemnity basis, will be deductible.

Different procedures operate depending upon whether or not the driver was insured, but his insurer was able to avoid liability.[999] If this is so, that insurer normally acts as agent for the MIB, although the latter pays the claim. Only where there is no insurance or the insurer is not known is the claim made directly to the MIB.

293. Under the 2015 agreement, the MIB was not liable in respect of vehicle damage claims where there was no contract of insurance in force and the claimant knew or had reason to believe this was the case and was not liable in respect of any claims arising out of an incident of terrorism. However, these exceptions have been removed under the 2017 supplementary agreement. The MIB remains excluded from liability as regards certain passenger claims and situations where the insurer is entitled to recover from its own insured under s. 151(8) of the Road Traffic Act. There are a number of preconditions to the MIB's liability. These require an application in such form, accompanied by such signatures and declarations, giving such information and accompanied by such documents as the MIB may reasonably require and prescribe the formalities that a claimant must comply with in terms of pursuing a legal claim against the uninsured driver.

998. *See* Part I, Ch. 7.

999. For example, by reason of a breach of a limitation of use or a successful plea of non-disclosure or misrepresentation.

II. The Second MIB Agreement

294. This agreement is necessarily much more complex than the first, because there will of course be no judgment against a tortfeasor for the MIB to satisfy. A number of requirements must be satisfied by an applicant for an award, including:

(1) The applicant must be unable to trace the person responsible for the death, injury or damage or a person partly so responsible.
(2) The death, injury or damage must have been caused in circumstances such that on the balance of probabilities the untraced person would have been liable to the applicant in damages.
(3) That liability must have been one required to be insured against under the 1988 Act; this is assumed in the absence of evidence to the contrary.
(4) The application must be made in writing within three years of the accident for personal injury claims (nine months for property damage claims).

The amount of compensation awarded to the applicant is assessed on the same basis as a court would assess damages in a tort action, except that the MIB does not award damages for loss of earnings in so far as they have been paid by the applicant's employer.

There are special provisions dealing with the cases where an untraced driver was only partly to blame for the accident. Here the applicant may be required to obtain judgment against the known driver or the known principal of an unidentified driver, or the applicant may have obtained such judgment without being required to do so. If this judgment is not satisfied at all within three months, the MIB awards an amount equal to the untraced person's contribution to a full award, namely, that proportion which a court would have awarded if proceedings had been taken against all the tortfeasors. If this judgment is only partly satisfied within three months, the MIB awards an amount equal to either the unsatisfied part of the judgment or the untraced person's contribution, whichever is the greater. If the applicant has not obtained, and is not required by the MIB to obtain, judgment against the known driver, and has not received any payment as compensation from any such person, the amount the MIB awards is an amount equal to the untraced person's contribution to a full award.

295. The conditions precedent to the liability of the MIB include: (1) that the applicant gives all such assistance as the MIB reasonably requires to enable any necessary investigation to be carried out; (2) if required, that the applicant must take all reasonable steps to obtain judgment against any person or persons in respect of their liability to the applicant; this is subject to his being indemnified against costs by the MIB; and (3) if required, that the applicant must assign to the MIB, or their nominee, any judgment obtained by him; if this produces a surplus over what the MIB paid the applicant, the MIB is accountable for this after deducting the reasonable expenses of the recovery of the sum for which the judgment was given. If required to do so, the applicant must furnish a statutory declaration concerning the facts and circumstances upon which his claim is based.

Part V. Insurance of the Person

Chapter 1. Workman's Compensation and Occupational Disease

296. An employee injured at work has, broadly speaking, the right to claim compensation from the state, regardless of questions of fault, under the social security legislation. This replaced workmen's compensation, which was an important class of insurance business for many years.[1000] If the employer, or someone for whom he is responsible, is at fault, then the injured employee also has a right of action in tort, either in negligence, or for breach of statutory duty. If the employer is not insured, or inadequately insured, then this right is clearly worthless. Some notorious instances of employers being without cover led to the enactment of the Employers' Liability (Compulsory Insurance) Act 1969.

§1. Employer's Liability (Compulsory Insurance) Act 1969

I. Compulsion to Insure

297. An employer carrying on any business in Great Britain must insure and maintain insurance under one or more approved policies with an authorized insurer against liability for bodily injury or disease sustained by his employees, which arises out of, and in the course of, their employment in Great Britain, in that business.[1001] However, such an employers' liability policy is not required to cover risks that must be insured under the Road Traffic Act.[1002] Thus, in practice, although an employers'

1000. The workmen's compensation legislation, the social security legislation and the employers' liability compulsory insurance legislation have some features in common, and in particular they all use the phrase 'out of and in the course of employment' which is discussed below. Generally speaking decisions on that phrase in one context are valid authorities in one of the other contexts, and some such cases are cited below.

1001. Employer's Liability (Compulsory Insurance) Act 1969 (hereinafter 'the 1969 Act'), s. 1(1). The Act must be read along with the implementing Regulations, now the Employers' Liability (Compulsory Insurance) Regulations 1998, SI 1988/2573, as amended by SI 2004/2882, SI 2008/1765 and SI 2011/686, hereafter referred to as 'SI 1988/2573'.

1002. SI 1988/2573, Sch. 2, para. 14.

liability policy could cover such risks, this is not now likely. An employers' liability policy, and the underlying tort claim, is transferred on the sale of a business under the Transfer of Undertakings (Protection of Employment) Regulations 2006.[1003]

In *BAI (Run-Off) Ltd v. Durham*,[1004] the Supreme Court held that section 1 requires an employer to insure against liability for disease caused during the period of the policy, even if the disease manifests itself only later. It did not matter whether the policy referred to injury or disease 'sustained' or injury or disease 'caused' during the policy period. In the test cases that were the subject of the litigation, some policies had one form of wording and others the other form, but the Court was adamant that the phrases had to be given a purposive construction, that is in the light of the requirement for employers to insure against their liability in contexts where, as in the present case which concerned exposure to asbestos, the symptoms of disease manifested themselves years later than the time of exposure. This very important decision, the effect of which was to ensure the benefit of insurance to employees whose employers had the 'sustained' policy wordings, is probably to be confined to situations where liability insurance is compulsory, rather than applying to, for example, public liability policies that use the 'sustained' wording.

Out of and in the course of employment covers two principles. 'In the course of employment' means that 'the accident must arise when the employee is doing what a man so employed might reasonably do during a time during which he was employed and at a place where he may reasonably be during that time to do that thing'.[1005] Therefore, employees travelling to and from work are not in the course of their employment, even if travelling in vehicles provided by their employers, unless their terms of employment oblige them so to travel.[1006] Even an accident at work is not necessarily in the course of employment. A policeman playing football for his force in a match against another force at the force sports ground was held not to be covered for state compensation when he was injured during the match even though participation was expected of him.[1007] The Court of Appeal rejected the argument that 'in the course of employment' includes matters reasonably incidental to employment, except where the accident occurs at the place of work during an interruption, for example, for a tea break. If an employee is injured outside his strict hours of work, this will not necessarily be in the course of employment. A reasonable period at the beginning and end of work will usually be included.[1008]

The other limb of the formula, namely, 'out of employment', is somewhat looser. Essentially it requires a causal connection between the employment and the accident.

1003. *Martin v. Lancashire County Council* [2000] Lloyd's Rep. IR 665.

1004. [2012] UKSC 14, [2012] 1 W.L.R. 867.

1005. Lord Loreburn in *Moore v. Manchester Liners Ltd.* [1910] AC 498 at 500–501.

1006. *Vandyke v. Fender* [1970] 2 QB 292. Compare *Paterson v. Costain & Press (Overseas) Ltd.* [1979] 2 Lloyd's Rep. 204 and note, however, that in an industrial injury benefit case, the test of obligation to travel has been held inapplicable: *Nancollas v. Insurance Officer* [1985] 1 All ER 833. It may be therefore that when the opportunity arises in a dispute on an employers' liability policy, the courts will adopt the view of the *Nancollas* case that there is no overriding principle concerning whether or not travel is in the course of employment.

1007. *R v. National Insurance Commissioner,* ex parte *Michael* [1977] 1 WLR 109.

1008. *See* , e.g., *R v. National Insurance Commissioner,* ex parte *East* [1976] ICR 206.

It will not give rise to any problems in the employers' liability insurance field, because, if an employer has been adjudged or has agreed to be legally liable in tort to an employee, a necessary precondition of the insurer's liability, it must follow that the liability of the employer arose out of the employee's employment.

298. An approved policy must not contain provisions rendering the insurer's liability conditional upon a number of matters but these are prohibited only if they are conditions precedent to liability under the policy, either generally (i.e., as warranties)[1009] or in respect of a particular claim (i.e., as conditions precedent).[1010] Thus it is perfectly permissible to have conditions that are not precedent to liability, but merely give the insurer the right to claim damages for breach. This is confirmed by Regulation 2(3): a policy can expressly provide for the insured to pay the insurer any sums that the insurer is liable to pay and which have been paid to employees.

The conditions prohibited are those 'providing that no liability shall arise or liability shall cease':

(a) 'in the event of some specified thing being done or omitted to be done after the happening of the event giving rise to a claim under the policy'.

This covers such matters as failure to give notice or particulars of loss in time and unauthorized admissions of liability:

– 'unless the policyholder takes reasonable care to protect his employees against the risk of bodily injury or disease in the course of employment'.

The courts have interpreted conditions in liability policies generally requiring the insured to take reasonable care as applicable only if an employer is more than merely negligent,[1011] so the prohibition makes little, if any, change to the general law:[1012]

– 'unless the policyholder complies with the requirements of any enactment for the protection of employees against the risk of bodily injury or disease in the course of their employment';
– 'unless the policyholder keeps specified records or provides the insurer with or makes available to him information therefrom'.

299. Cover must extend to an amount of GBP 5 million for any one occurrence,[1013] and a certificate of insurance must be displayed at every place of business where persons are employed.[1014]

1009. As to warranties, *see* para. 118.
1010. As to conditions precedent, *see* para. 129.
1011. *See* para. 58.
1012. Even recklessness would not entitle an insurer to avoid liability, it is suggested, if it relies merely upon a condition to take reasonable care, for such a condition is prohibited. However, a condition expressly providing that recklessness debars liability would arguably be enforceable.
1013. SI 1988/2573, reg. 3.
1014. The 1969 Act, s. 4(1).

II. Scope of Insurance

300. Employer's liability policies are contracts of indemnity[1015] and are governed by the general principles of insurance applicable to fire and other indemnity policies. The question of whether a particular workman is the employee of the insured for the purposes of an employer's liability policy may give rise to difficulty especially where a workman is employed and paid by one employer, but is temporarily working for another. The general test for the purposes of liability is not who employs the workman, but 'who has at the moment the right to control the manner of execution of the acts of the servant'.[1016]

III. Exceptions

301. Section 3 of the 1969 Act exempts certain employers altogether from the requirement to insure. Basically these are certain local government councils, nationalized industries and any employer specifically exempted by regulations. The first set of regulations[1017] list a number of other public bodies that are exempted. More recent regulations[1018] exempt any employer that is a company with only one employee who owns 50% or more of the issued share capital in that company.

IV. Enforcement

302. Enforcement of the 1969 Act is effected by first ensuring the display of certificates of insurance, second permitting inspections of certificates and policies, and third by criminal penalties.[1019] Section 4(1) requires insurers to issue certificates in the form prescribed in the Regulations, and Regulation 5 requires these to be displayed at any place of business where an employer employs any person whose claims may be the subject of indemnity under the insurance. Employers must produce their certificates, or copies, to an officer of the Health and Safety Executive on being served with notice to do so.[1020] In addition, any inspector authorized by the Secretary of State can demand to inspect any policy of employers' liability insurance on reasonable notice.[1021]

The directors of a company that has failed to insure as required by the Act are not personally liable for damages in tort for breach of statutory duty.[1022]

1015. *Dunbar v. A & B Painters Ltd.* [1986] 2 Lloyd's Rep. 38.
1016. *Mersey Docks and Harbour Board v. Coggins & Griffiths (Liverpool) Ltd.* [1947] AC 1.
1017. SI 1971/1933, SI 1974/208 and SI 1981/1489.
1018. The Employers Liability (Compulsory Insurance) Amendment Regulations 2004 SI 2882.
1019. As to the penalty, *see* s. 5 of the 1969 Act.
1020. Section 4(2) and SI 1988/2573, reg. 6.
1021. Section 4(2) and SI 1988/2573, reg. 7.
1022. *Richardson v. Pitt-Stanley Ltd.* [1995] 1 All E.R. 460.

Chapter 2. Personal Accident and Bodily Injury

§1. General

303. Personal accident policies, under which benefits are payable in the event of personal injury or death arising from an accident, are relatively common in the UK, but they have occasioned difficulties of interpretation.[1023] The word 'accident' is itself difficult to define precisely; in the context of an accident policy the word is usually contained in phrases such as 'injury by accident', 'accidental injury' or, 'injury caused by accidental means', which all connote an unexpected occurrence. It is therefore difficult to improve on Lord MacNaughten's definition; he said that an accident is 'an unlooked for mishap or an untoward event which is not expected or designed'.[1024] No intended event can therefore be described as accidental from the point of view of the person responsible for it, nor can any naturally occurring event. The latter would appear to encompass disease, but death or injury as a result of disease may be covered, if some accidental event gives rise to the disease.[1025] One way, which is commonly adopted by insurers, of qualifying the protection offered by a personal accident policy is expressly to provide for an exception if, for example, the insured wilfully exposed himself to needless peril. This is considered below. First, we examine the meaning of the word 'accident' and other standard phrases used to describe the risk.

304. If the insured takes a deliberate risk, then any injury resulting from it is unlikely to be held to be accidental. In *Candler v. London & Lancashire Guarantee & Accident Co*,[1026] a Canadian case, the insured balanced himself on a hotel patio coving thirteen floors above the street, in order to demonstrate to a friend that he had not lost his nerve. Unfortunately, he fell and was killed. This was held not to be an accident. If, however, the insured did not intend to expose himself to deliberate risk, the death would, prima facie, be covered. In *Marcell Beller Ltd. v. Hayden*,[1027] the plaintiff company insured their employees against death consequent upon 'accidental bodily injury' being the sole cause. An employee, driving under the influence of alcohol,[1028] drove too fast when approaching a corner, crashed and was killed. It was argued for the insurers that his death was not an accident, because it was a reasonably foreseeable consequence of his deliberate act when voluntarily intoxicated. This

1023. There can also in theory be problems of determining the proximate or real cause of an accident. These were adverted to in para. 67, *supra* . In practice insurers avoid these issues by providing that injury or death must result directly or indirectly from an accident which must be the exclusive cause of loss, independently of all other causes; *see Jason v. Batten* [1969] 1 Lloyd's Rep. 281.

1024. *Fenton v. Thorley & Co. Ltd.* [1903] AC 443 at 448.

1025. *Sinclair v. Maritime Passengers Assurance Co.* (1861) 3 E & E 478.

1026. (1963) 40 DLR (2d) 408.

1027. [1978] QB 694.

1028. The permitted legal limit for driving in the UK is 80 mgs of alcohol per 100 millilitres of blood. Most people are incapable of dealing with an emergency at 150 mgs; this employee had 261 mgs!

argument was rejected by the trial judge, who said: 'It seems to me that a clear distinction can be made between cases where the predisposing cause, although it leads to the taking of risks, itself involves risk which was neither deliberately run, nor actually appreciated.' Whilst one may have sympathy with the result in this case, the reasoning sits uneasily with other decisions, particularly those involving voluntary intoxication, which hold that the results of recklessness are not accidental,[1029] and it gives subjective intention an importance not generally recognized in this area of UK law.[1030]

I. Bodily Injury

305. Insurance companies have always experienced difficulty in defining the risk that they are prepared to take in an accident policy. For some time a common definition has been 'bodily injury caused by violent, accidental, external and visible means'. This definition may well have retained its popularity because of a remark by Cozens-Hardy, M. R., who said that 'it is open to doubt whether this does not exempt the company upon every occasion that is likely to occur'![1031] Bodily injury will usually be of an obvious kind but it is not necessary that there should be any outward and visible sign of the injury. Dilation of the heart has been held to amount to bodily injury,[1032] and the fact that injury and death occur at the same moment will not prevent the clause from coming into operation.[1033] Disease may amount to bodily injury if it has been caused by accident.[1034]

II. Violent Means

306. The element of violence may often be as evident as the bodily injury; the insured may, for example, be bitten by a dog,[1035] knocked down by a train[1036] or merely slip and fall.[1037] It may not, however, be so obvious, and the phrase 'violent means' has been held to be the antithesis of 'without any violence at all'.[1038] The phrase seems to include almost any external cause of injury such as drowning[1039] or the inhalation of gas.[1040]

1029. For example, *DPP v. Majewski* [1977] AC 443.
1030. *See* , e.g., *Glenlight Shipping Co. Ltd. v. Excess Insurance Co. Ltd.* [1983] SLT 241.
1031. *Re United London & Scottish Insurance Co., Brown's claim* [1915] 2 Ch 167 at 170.
1032. *Re Scarr & General Accident Assurance Corp.* [1905] 1 KB 387.
1033. *Trew v. Railway Passengers Assurance Co.* (1861) 6 H & N 839.
1034. *Fitton v. Accidental Death Insurance Co.* (1864) 17 CB 122.
1035. *Mardorf v. Accident Insurance Co.* [1903] 1 KB 584.
1036. *Lawrence v. Accidental Insurance Co.* (1881) 7 QBD 216.
1037. *Hopper v. Accidental Death Insurance Co.* (1806) 5 H & N 557.
1038. *Hamlyn v. Crown Accidental Insurance Co.* [1893] 1 QB 750.
1039. *Trew v. Railway Passengers Assurance Co., supra* .
1040. *Re United London & Scottish Insurance Co.* [1915] 2 Ch 167.

III. Accidental Means

307. This phrase has given rise to difficulties of interpretation. Until recently it was thought that English law did not follow the literal interpretation of the phrase and refused to distinguish between means and results. So, in *Hamlyn v. Crown Accidental Insurance Co.*,[1041] where the insured stooped forward to pick up a marble and in doing so wrenched his knee, it was held that as the insured did not intend to wrench his knee, it must have been caused by accidental means. The Court of Appeal seemed to reject the argument that if the 'means', in other words, the prior act of the insured was a deliberate act, the insured was not covered. However, an argument along these lines has prevailed in the intervening years in decisions in some other jurisdictions, including a leading American case,[1042] and it was adopted by the Court of Appeal in the decision in *Dhak v. Insurance Company of North America (UK) Ltd.*,[1043] where recovery was denied in circumstances where the insured died from asphyxiation due to vomiting while under the influence of alcohol; she had drunk in order to control severe back pain. This must now represent the prevailing English view, but it is submitted that the earlier English approach is to be preferred.[1044]

IV. External and Visible Means

308. The word 'external' is meant to encompass anything that is not 'internal'[1045] and refers to the cause of the injury, not the injury itself. An insured who stoops to pick up a marble and wrenches his knee is therefore injured by external means, as in the *Hamlyn* case, as is one who suffers death by drowning. This may be contrasted with disorders that arise within the body, such as senility, or certain types of disease. 'Visible means' really adds nothing to 'external means', since it has been held that any cause which is external must be visible.[1046]

1041. *Supra.*

1042. *Landress v. Phoenix Insurance Co.* 291 US 491 (1933); there was a strong dissent here by Cardozo J. who said: 'The attempted distinction between accidental results and accidental means will plunge this branch of the law into a Serbian bog.'

1043. [1996] 1 Lloyd's Rep. 632. *See also* the analysis of *Hamlyn* in *De Souza v. Home and Overseas Insurance Co. Ltd.* [1995] LRLR 453 (1990).

1044. Some jurisdictions have rejected the distinction between means and results: *see* , e.g., the Scottish Court of Session cases of *Glenlight Shipping Ltd. v. Excess Insurance Ltd.* 1983 SLT 241 (where the earlier Scottish decision in *Clidero v. Scottish Accident Insurance Co.* (1892) 19 R. 355 was ignored) and *MacLeod v. New Hampshire Insurance Co Ltd* [1998] SLT 1191, the decision of the High Court of Australia in *Australian Casualty Co. Ltd. v. Federico* (1986) 66 A.L.R. 99, the Canadian case of *Tracey-Gould v. Maritime Life Assurance Co.* (1992) 89 D.L.R. (4th) 726, and the decision of the New Zealand Court of Appeal in *Groves v. A.M.P. Fire & General Insurance Co. (N.Z.) Ltd.* [1990] 1 NZLR 122.

1045. *Hamlyn v. Crown Accidental Insurance Co., supra* .

1046. *Ibid.*

V. Wilful Exposure to Needless Peril

309. As already mentioned, a common way for insurers to qualify the cover provided by personal accident policies is to insert express exceptions, and a standard one provides that no benefit is payable if death or injury results from wilful exposure to needless peril (except in an attempt to save human life). It has been held by the Court of Appeal[1047] that such an exclusion has to be construed in a manner consistent with and not repugnant to the purpose of the policy; to construe it so as to deprive the insured of benefit whenever his intentional acts had exposed him to a substantial risk would severely restrict the scope of the benefit. In order to avoid liability, the insurers must show that the exposure to needless peril was wilful, not merely that intentional acts done by the insured resulted in his being exposed to such peril. In the case, the insured had been drinking with his fiancée and friends. He got out of the car in which they were travelling, which was being driven by his fiancée, and arranged to get back in over a bridge. As a joke, when the insured approached the car, his fiancée drove slowly forward. The insured stepped on the rear bumper. Not realizing the danger, the fiancée accelerated and steered the car from one side of the road to another. The insured fell off and suffered head injuries from which he subsequently died. It was held that the insured's representatives were entitled to recover under the policy in question; his impulsive response to a practical joke was not wilful exposure to needless peril, falling short of deliberate risk taking or recklessness of injury of which he was mindful.

1047. *Morley v. United Friendly Insurance plc.* [1993] 1 Lloyd's Rep. 490.

Chapter 3. Private Health Insurance

§1. Scope of Private Health Insurance

310. Increasing pressure on an already overburdened National Health Service has meant that private health insurance has greatly increased in popularity in the UK over recent years. The policies available generally aim to provide the insured with an indemnity against the costs of medical treatment necessitated by unforeseen injury or illness.[1048] Most insurance companies offer cover both to individual subscribers and to members of a group scheme, usually operated by an employer. The policy may be extended to cover eligible dependants, i.e., a spouse and children.

311. Private health insurance was traditionally underwritten by exclusion or restriction, following the obtaining of medical evidence from the proposer's doctor. These policies are, however, increasingly being sold via the medium of direct mail, and to encourage the take up rate, there is no medical underwriting at the point of purchase. Such policies therefore frequently include clauses that provide for a general restriction regarding the treatment of pre-existing conditions, so that payment is not made towards such treatment if a pre-existing condition recurs within two years of the start of the policy.

§2. Exclusions

312. Private health insurance in the UK is designed to provide cover for insurable acute conditions. Benefit is not therefore paid for normal maternity, although pregnancy complications can be covered, routine dental treatment, although some commercial companies do offer such cover, and 'nature' cures. Other exclusions are more often than not written into policies, for example, cosmetic treatment and routine sight testing, and psychiatric treatment, geriatric treatment and alcohol/drug abuse treatment may all be subject to limitations.

1048. There are also hospital cash schemes, which offer a fixed, tax-free amount for every night the insured spends in a hospital bed. This is available whether the patient is undergoing private, or 'free' NHS treatment. Eligibility to join a scheme may be subject to a maximum age, but once accepted, renewal is usually possible at any age.

Chapter 4. Life Insurance

§1. Regulatory Framework

313. Companies wishing to conduct life insurance business in the UK must be authorized under, and comply with, the provisions of the Financial Services and Markets Act 2000 or be authorized in another EEA State and be selling directly or through a UK branch.[1049] For a number of years, the sale and marketing of most forms of life insurance[1050] was regulated together with other types of investment,[1051] quite separately from the limited regulation of general insurance. However, when the selling of general insurance also became statutorily regulated, the two regimes converged to a large extent, although the rules for life insurance are found in the general COBS made by the FCA rather than the Insurance Conduct Business of Sourcebook that governs general insurance. The principal effects of the regime relating to most life insurance contracts are that it can be sold only by tied agents, who can market only the policies of their principals, or by completely independent intermediaries. In contrast with the position regarding most other forms of investment, life insurance can be sold by 'cold-calling', that is, without prior appointment, but the price for this is that the insured purchaser has cancellation rights which are described below. One of the most hotly debated issues concerning the marketing of life insurance has been the question of disclosure of the commission earned by independent intermediaries. This is now regulated by COBS 6.4.[1052]

§2. Categories of Life Insurance

314. There are a number of categories of life insurance traditionally available in the UK and as has been seen, the regulatory requirements will differ to some extent depending on that form. A fundamental point is the contrast between pure life insurance, that is where the contract will pay a fixed sum of money only on the death of the life insured, and other types of life insurance. The latter will incorporate an element of variation into the sum insured, the amount payable on death being dependent upon the performance of the investments into which the premiums have been placed; in this event, the insurance is generally referred to as linked life insurance, that is insurance linked to investment. In addition, there will invariably be an endowment element, that is to say the insurers agree to pay money if and when the life insured reaches a stated

1049. *See* Part I.

1050. Those excluded were essentially pure life insurance, short-term life insurance and single premium life insurance. These are still regulated separately (and with general insurance) under the modern scheme.

1051. Under the Financial Services Act 1986 and then, until 2005, under the Financial Services and Markets Act 2000.

1052. The full detail can be found at http://www.fca.org.uk.

age; this money could be a fixed sum or it could be a periodical payment, often known as an annuity.[1053]

Types of life insurance can also be distinguished by whether or not insurance is term-based or whole-life. Term insurance covers the risk of death within an agreed period of years and is relatively inexpensive because the period will expire before the life insured reaches the 'usual' age of death. Within the broad category of term insurance there are sub-variations, particularly the decreasing term policy and the convertible term policy. The decreasing term policy reduces the sum insured over the period of the insurance and is often used in conjunction with a mortgage on a home where the debt secured by the mortgage will decrease in amount over the period. A convertible term policy gives the insured the option to convert to whole-life insurance without the need for further medical evidence of good health.

Whole-life insurance is, as the description implies, simply insurance that provides cover until the life insured dies, provided of course that the premiums are paid.

The different classifications described are not mutually exclusive. So, for example, it is possible to have pure life insurance or linked life insurance with an endowment element that in either case is term-based or whole-life.

§3. Formalities and Cancellation Rights

315. Because the life insurance contract is a long-term contract, and because individuals may be persuaded by high pressure salesmanship to enter into contracts which may not be entirely appropriate for them, the law has for some years provided for a cooling off period, that is policyholders are given a period within which they can change their minds and cancel an already legally binding contract without penalty.[1054] In addition, the prospective insured must be supplied with a great deal of information. The content is required by the EC Life Directives, as are cancellation rights, but the scope of the latter, made under the 2000 Act, is greater than EC law requires.

316. The requirements for pre-contractual disclosure[1055] apply to contracts entered into by a UK or EC company or a member of Lloyd's which constitute the carrying on in the UK of long-term business which is not reinsurance business or the provision in the UK of long-term insurance.[1056] Before entering into such a contract the insurer must provide the prospective insured with the following information in writing:

1053. Much-debated issues in fairly recent years have been questions arising concerning the value of endowments, especially when they are linked to mortgages used to purchase houses and concerning the value of bonuses. Problems at one very large insurer led to litigation concerning the duty of the directors when allocating bonuses: *Equitable Life Assurance Society v. Hyman* [2000] 3 WLR 529.

1054. These rules were introduced originally in the UK on the recommendation of the Scott Committee on Property Bonds and Equity Linked Life Assurance, 1973, Cmnd 5281 and have their equivalent in hire purchase and consumer credit legislation.

1055. These are contained in the FCA's Conduct of Business Sourcebook (COBS 13).

1056. They thus catch insurance sold from an establishment in the UK and insurance sold directly from another EC State.

(a) the name of the undertaking and its legal form, the name of the EEA State in which the head office and, where appropriate, the agency or branch concluding the policy is situated and the address of the head office and, where appropriate, of the agency or branch concluding the policy;
(b) a definition of each benefit and option;
(c) the term of the contract and the means by which it may be terminated;
(d) the method of paying premiums and the duration of the payments;
(e) the method of calculating bonuses and the distribution of bonuses;
(f) an indication of surrender and paid-up values and the extent to which these values are guaranteed;
(g) an indication of the premiums for each benefit;
(h) in respect of unit-linked policies, a definition of the units and an indication of the nature of the underlying assets;
(i) the arrangements with respect to the period within which the policyholder may cancel the contract;
(j) the tax arrangements applicable to the policy;
(k) the arrangements for handling complaints;
(l) the law applicable to the contract where the parties do not have a free choice or, where they do have a choice, the law which the insurer proposes to choose.

In addition to the disclosure of information before the contract is entered into, there are requirements for disclosure of information by the insurer during the contract. These apply to the same categories of insurers and primarily require the disclosure in writing of any changes to most of the information described above. In addition, if the policy provides for the payment of bonuses, information in writing as to the amount of bonuses which has become payable must be given once a year.

317. Notice of the right to cancel in the prescribed form, and the prescribed form of notice of cancellation must be sent to the insured. The right to cancel[1057] can be exercised up to thirty days after the insured receives the notice of the right.[1058] Notice of cancellation operates to rescind any concluded contract or to withdraw any offer not yet accepted. Any money paid by the insured must be returned to him.

§4. Assignment of Life Policies

318. The fact that life insurance policies are a valuable piece of property, normally attracting a surrender value after the payment of a number of premiums means that they can be sold or otherwise disposed of or used as security, features which are assisted by the fact that the requirement of insurable interest exists only at the date the policy is effected.[1059] Many dealings of this sort with life policies will in law be assignments, regarding which there are a number of special rules. The description 'assignment' covers any case where the insured disposes entirely of his interest in the policy, whether by way of sale, gift or mortgage. If a policy is used as security, some of the statutory

1057. Notice of which is deemed to be served when posted.
1058. Thus, if no notice of the right to cancel is sent, the right to cancel always exists.
1059. *See* para. 79.

formalities as to assignment may be used even where the insured does not dispose entirely of his interest.

I. Assignment as Mortgage

319. If a transaction with a life policy appears to be an absolute assignment, but in reality is a mortgage as security for a debt, the mortgagee, the insured, is entitled to redeem the mortgage on repayment of the debt and recover his policy, notwithstanding any provision to the contrary. In deciding whether or not a deal with a life policy is an outright assignment or a mortgage, the court will look at the surrounding circumstances and parole evidence is admissible. For example, in *Murphy v. Taylor*,[1060] a policy for GBP 999 was assigned for a consideration of GBP 144. The evidence showed that the assignor in fact borrowed the latter sum from the assignee. The latter later recovered GBP 600 from the insurer. It was held that the substance of the transaction was that of a mortgage to secure a debt. Therefore, after allowing for the debt of GBP 144, the assignor was entitled to redeem the mortgage and recover from the assignee the remainder of the GBP 600 that he had recovered from the insurer.

320. The rule allowing the insured to redeem what is in substance a mortgage of a life policy is part of the general law relating to mortgages whereby clogs or fetters on the equality of redemption or equitable right to redeem are void. An interesting example in the insurance context is the decision in *Salt v. Marquess of Northampton.*[1061] X borrowed GBP 10,000 from an insurer and secured this by a charge on his reversionary interest in certain property. In addition, he agreed to pay the premiums on a policy for GBP 34,000 taken out by the insurers against the possibility of the interest not vesting. It was agreed that if X paid off the loan before the interest vested, the policy would be assigned to him, but if he died before payment and besting, the policy would belong to the insurers. The latter event occurred. It was held that, despite the agreement, the transaction was in substance a mortgage, and the personal representatives of X were entitled to redeem and recover the proceeds of the policy, after deducting the loan and interest.

II. Statutory Assignment

321. Prior to the Policies of Assurance Act 1867, the assignment of a life policy was not recognized by the common law. Although equity always permitted such assignments, the assignee could only sue to enforce the policy if he joined the assignor in the action, and an insurer could not obtain a good discharge against payment from the assignee alone. The 1867 Act permits legal assignments so that the assignee of a life policy can, if the requirements of the Act are compiled with, enforce it in his own name. Furthermore, a life policy is itself a chose in action,[1062] one of the forms of intangible personal property recognized by the common law, so that an alternative

1060.(1850) 1 IR Ch R. 92.
1061.[1892] A C 1.
1062.*Re Moore* (1878) 8 Ch D 519.

procedure for assignment lies under section 136 of the Law of Property Act 1925. In addition, an assignment that is incomplete according to statutory requirements may well still be valid as an equitable assignment.

There is one essential difference between the two statutory procedures. Under the 1867 Act, an assignment is valid if it is of the assignor's whole interest in the policy or of merely a part of it, by way of mortgage. Under section 136, an assignment must be absolute, that is it must be of the assignor's whole interest. Therefore, a mortgage whereby the whole interest in a life policy is charged can be effected under section 136, but not one whereby only part is charged.

An assignment under the 1867 Act must be in the form prescribed in the Schedule to the Act or in words with a similar effect and it must be endorsed on the policy or contained in a separate instrument.[1063] Written notice of the assignment must be given to the insurer at its principal place of business.[1064] An assignment under section 136 must simply be in writing but again notice must be given to the debtor, that is the insurer. In neither case is the consent of the insurers necessary, but a condition in the policy making it non-assignable is effective to prevent a legal assignment, although it cannot prevent an effective equitable assignment.[1065]

322. In most cases, therefore, the statutory procedures are alternative devices for achieving the same result. Even if one of the statutory procedures is not complied with, an assignment may be effective in equity as has been noted. This may be because there was a failure to give notice to the insurer,[1066] because there was merely an agreement to assign, or because the policy was simply delivered to the assignee, for example, as security. If there have been more than one purported assignments of the same policy, well-established rules as to priority apply.[1067] Briefly, a legal assignee has priority over anyone except an earlier equitable assignment of which he has notice or an earlier legal assignment. Equitable assignments generally rank in order of creation, except that the first such assignee to give notice to the insurers will take priority over any prior assignments of which he had no notice. If there is any doubt as to who is entitled to the policy monies, in this or any other context, the insurer may pay them into court under the Life Assurance Companies (Payment into Court) Act 1896.[1068]

§5. Trust of Life Policies

I. Family Arrangements

323. It may frequently be argued that the insured under a life policy established a trust of the policy for the benefit of another. This will normally arise only on an own life policy. If such a trust can be shown to exist, it has two distinct advantages. The

1063. Section 5.
1064. Section 3.
1065. *Re Turcan* (1888) 40 Ch D 5.
1066. For example, *Williams v. Thorp* (1828) 2 Sim 257.
1067. *See* , further, *MacGillivray on Insurance Law*, paras 25-087–25-098.
1068. *See MacGillivray on Insurance Law*, paras 25-059–25-068.

first is that on the death of the life insured, the monies will belong to and go directly to the beneficiary, thus avoiding and not being counted as a part of the insured's estate. Second, if the insured becomes bankrupt, the beneficiary can claim the policy without it being subject to the claims of the insured's creditors, provided that the trust itself was not created in order to defraud creditors.[1069]

324. The easiest way to establish such a trust is under the provisions of section 11 of the Married Women's Property Act 1882, although this section is limited in its application. Under it, a policy effected on his or her own life by a married man or woman, and expressed to be for the benefit of his or her spouse and/or children, creates a trust in favour of the spouse and/or children, and the money payable under the policy does not form part of the insured's estate. Section 11 also applies to insurances effected by civil partners.[1070] The section applies only to policies effected by a married man or woman (or a civil partner) on his or her own life. Thus, for example, a policy by a father on the life of his son, even if legal, which is doubtful, cannot fall within section 11.[1071] If the section does apply, the insured is a trustee and must therefore act with respect to the policy in the best interests of the beneficiaries. For example, if he has an option to surrender the policy, that may properly be exercised only in the interests of the beneficiaries; it is not exercisable in order to defeat the trust, and if the policy is surrendered, the money received will probably be held for the ultimate benefit of the beneficiaries.[1072]

Section 11 applies to any policies securing benefits payable on the death of the life insured, including an accident policy covering only death by accident[1073] and an endowment policy providing for payment if the insured dies before the expiry of the stated period.[1074] If the policy names the beneficiary or beneficiaries, then the latter acquire an immediate vested interest in it. In *Cousins v. Sun Life Assurance Society*,[1075] a wife was the named beneficiary of a policy effected by her husband whom she predeceased. It was held that the policy monies belonged to the wife's estate, even though the husband had remarried. Divorce does not of itself change any rights under a section 11 policy, but that these can be varied as part of a general settlement of property rights under general family law legislation. If the policy does not name the beneficiaries but is merely expressed to be for the benefit of the insured's wife and children, for example, the beneficiaries have only a contingent interest, and only those people who fit the description on the death of the life insured will be entitled to benefit.

325. If section 11 is inapplicable, then establishing a trust of a life policy used to require proving an exception to the doctrine of privity of contract, whereby a third party to a contract could not enforce it even if it was made for his benefit,[1076] but this will not apply in respect of policies taken out after the Contracts (Rights of Third

1069. Insolvency Act 1986, ss 423–425; proviso to Married Women's Property Act 1882, s. 11.
1070. Civil Partnership Act 2004, s. 70.
1071. *Re Engelbach* [1924] 2 Ch. 348.
1072. *Re Fleetwood's Policy* [1926] Ch. 48.
1073. *Re Gladitz* [1937] Ch. 588.
1074. *Re Ioakimidis' Policy Trusts* [1925] Ch. 403.
1075. [1933] Ch. 126.
1076. *Beswick v. Beswick* [1968] A C 58.

Parties) Act 1999 came into force.[1077] In addition, it is a well-established principle of trusts law that a person will not be regarded as having declared himself a trustee of property in the absence of words showing a clear intention to do so.[1078] Quite apart from these points, many of the cases dealing with trusts of life policies reveal other deficiencies in the law relating to life insurance. If A effects a policy on his own life for the benefit of B, there are no problems if a trust is created, and provided that B's name is inserted in the policy.[1079] However, often the point arises because it appears that A has effected a policy on B's life for the benefit of B. A must therefore have an insurable interest in the life of B,[1080] quite apart from whether or not there is a trust in B's favour. Many of the policies in the relevant cases took a form which it appears is quite common, whereby a parent insures the life of his child for the latter's benefit. Whether or not such a policy is lawful must be open to great doubt, as a parent does not usually have an insurable interest in the life of his child.[1081] The question is rarely raised in this context, usually because the insurer will have already handed over the money, so that the sole question is whether A or B is entitled to it, and insurers who did raise it would attract unfavourable publicity. Nevertheless, the point should be recognized as a consequence of the narrowness of the law governing insurable interest, and perhaps also as a factor which should encourage the court to find a trust. If this is so, the position is not so much A insuring B's life for the benefit of B as A acting for B in insuring B's life, perhaps because, as a minor under the age of 18, B is unable to do so himself.

The cases appear to reveal more willingness latterly to find that a trust has been created, but two things are clear.[1082] First, the mere fact that A takes out a policy which is expressed to be for the benefit of B or on behalf of B does not constitute a trust for B. Second, the mere fact that the policy provides that the policy monies are to be payable to B does not create a trust in favour of B. For example, in *Re Engelbach*,[1083] a father proposed 'for his daughter' an endowment policy whereby she was to receive GBP 3,000 if she should reach the age of 21. If she died before then, her father was entitled to recover the premiums paid. It was held that the father's estate, on his death, was entitled to the GBP 3,000 when the daughter became 21, since there was not sufficient evidence to create a trust.[1084]

326. However, if, in a case of this sort, the 'beneficiary' is, in fact, paid the insurance money, he will normally be entitled to keep it, even if there was no trust in his favour. The only situation where this would not be the case is if the policy compels the conclusion that he was to receive it merely as a nominee or agent for the insured.[1085]

1077. On 11 May 2000. There may, though, be other reasons, e.g., avoiding tax, for seeking to establish a trust.
1078. Example, *Jones v. Lock* (1865) 1 Ch. App. 25.
1079. Life Assurance Act 1774, s. 2; *see* para. 73.
1080. Life Assurance Act 1774, s. 1; *see* para. 73.
1081. *Halford v. Kymer* (1830) 10 B & C 724.
1082. Plowman J in *Re Foster* [1966] 1 W L R 222 at 227.
1083. [1924] 2 Ch. 348.
1084. *See also Re Sinclair* [1938] Ch. 799. Strictly the policies in both these cases must have been illegal for lack of insurable interest, as already explained.
1085. *Re Schebsman* [1944] 1 Ch. 83.

A court is most unlikely to conclude this nowadays, unless the wording of the policy compels it, so that if in fact the insurer pays the 'beneficiary', the result is a useful way around the decisions just discussed.

327. Modern policy wordings and more modern cases show in any event a greater willingness to find a trust. In *Re Webb*,[1086] a father took out policies on the lives of his two children. He was described as 'the grantee' and in the proposal form as wishing to effect insurance 'on behalf of and for the benefit of the person … named as the life assured'. Each policy provided:

(1) that on the child's death at or after the age of 21, the money would be paid to his representatives, and, on his twenty-first birthday, all the father's interest in the policy would cease; until then the father had power to surrender, assign and otherwise deal with the policy, and the father would recover the premiums paid if the child died before the age of 21;
(2) that if the father, having paid all the premiums due, died before the child reached 21, the policies would remain in force until the child's twenty-first birthday.

The father did die before the children were 21, and the question was whether the policies that survived by reason of the term mentioned belonged to his estate or to the children. It was held that they belonged to the children, having been effected by the father on trust for them; there was more than a mere taking out of a policy for the benefit of another as in the earlier cases. The terms of the policies were sufficient to establish a trust, especially that providing that the father's interest in them would cease completely when the children were 21 and that providing that the policy monies themselves were never payable until the children reached the specified age, thus making it clear that the father had no interest in these. This seems sound, since such provisions are inconsistent with the father or nominal insured having the whole beneficial interest in the policy. A beneficial interest must lie elsewhere, that is with the children, and hence there must be a trust. *Re Webb* was followed in *Re Foster*,[1087] where the policy was not quite in the same form. It provided that upon the child becoming 21, the rights vested in the father (the grantee) to surrender or charge the policy until the child reached the age were to be vested in the child. It was held that the fact that these rights were vested absolutely in the child at 21 was inconsistent with the father thereafter retaining any beneficial interest, so that although this latter point was not expressly spelt out, as in *Re Webb*, it was necessary impliedly provided, and the same result followed.

As a result of these cases, it appears likely nowadays that the court will strive to find a trust where policies are taken out for children, not least because it avoids any insurable interest problems. In effect, therefore, the children in these cases were insuring their own lives through a trustee. At all times, the trustee must act in accordance with the responsibilities surrounding that position. For example, although he will probably until a stated age have the right to surrender or assign the policy, he can properly do so only if it is in the best interests of the child. When the latter reaches the specified age, he has full powers over the policy and, if the trust still exists, will be able to

1086. [1941] Ch. 225.
1087. [1966] 1 W L R 222.

terminate it.[1088] He will also, if necessary, be able to enforce it through the trustee, but he will be able to enforce it directly only if he becomes legal owner or if there is a new agreement arising by virtue of his paying and the insurer accepting from him the premiums due.

II. Group Insurance

328. The trust question has hitherto been considered solely in the context of family arrangements. The other equally common area where the same problems can arise is that of group insurance policies, for example, taken out by an employer on the lives of his employees or a group of them for the benefit of the latter. The circumstances may make it clear that the employees are beneficiaries under a trust, as in *Bowskill v. Dawson (No. 2)*,[1089] where the employer entered into a trust deed with the trustee company, which effected the policy for the employees. There were clear references to the fact that any sums received by the trust company where to be held on trust for the employees and the court had no difficulty in holding that the latter were therefore beneficiaries under the trusts of the deed. By contrast, there were no such references in *Green v. Russell*,[1090] where an employer, called the insured, effected a group accident policy for the benefit of his employees named in a schedule to the policy. The policy expressly provided that the insurer was entitled to treat the insured as absolute owner and was not bound to recognize any equitable or other claim or interest in the policy. In the light of this, it was held that the employees had no legal or equitable claim to the policy, in spite of the fact that one of the employees covered, or rather his widow, had received a sum of money paid under the policy. There was clearly no basis for implying a trust on the authorities already mentioned.[1091] It seems likely in practice that group policies of this nature are not effected always with terms that would enable the court to find a trust.

1088. *Saunders v. Vautier* (1841) Cr & Ph 240.
1089. [1955] 1 Q B 13.
1090. [1959] 2 QB 226.
1091. It must therefore be doubtful whether the policy was strictly legally enforceable, as the employer may not have had an insurable interest in the lives of his employees, or at least not to the extent of the amount each employee was insured for.

Chapter 5. Pensions

329. Although there is a state pension scheme in operation in the UK, it is inadequate provision for retirement for those individuals who have had anything other than very limited earning capacity during their working lives. It has become, therefore, increasingly common for individuals to make their own pension arrangements, either by joining an occupational pension scheme, administered by their employer on their behalf, or by purchasing their own individual pensions contract. Both are subject to generous tax concessions, making them even more attractive.

330. Insurance plays a limited role in personal pensions, i.e., the element of true insurance is limited, even though insurance companies presently command a virtual monopoly in the provision of personal pensions. The real basis of any pensions is savings, at least until retirement age is reach. Then the funds available from personal pensions may be used to purchase annuities, which are genuine insurance contracts.

331. Occupational pension schemes can be divided broadly into two groups – those that are self-administered, that is under the control of the employer and administered by trustees appointed by the employer, and those which are insured.[1092] The latter have their assets managed by insurance companies. Contracts on offer can be divided into four groups: deferred annuities; deposit administration; controlled funding; and managed funds. The latter is the most modern and is much like a unit trust, except that it is operated by the insurance company. Controlled funding is declining in popularity; current concern is therefore directed at the two main types of contract, deferred annuities and deposit administration.

332. A deferred annuity contract usually involves an agreement that, in return for a fixed sum paid now, an annuity will be purchased at a fixed time in the future with whatever sum is standing to the credit of the contract at that time. The insurance company is therefore on risk only at that time; until then the fund may gain interest at a fixed rate (guaranteed) or at a variable rate (with profits).

333. A deposit administration contract involves the payment of regular sums to the insurer by the employer in order to create a pool of money out of which, at the appropriate time, an annuity is purchased and assigned to a member of the fund.

Risks, such as they are, remain with the employer until the annuity is purchased, and the principal element of insurance, the 'death in service' benefit, is usually insured by a separate policy.

334. The provision of pension benefits in funded schemes would be prohibitively expensive in the UK without some form of tax relief. The granting of such relief has been made progressively easier over recent years, with considerable relaxation of the rules with effect from April 2006.

1092. Pension funds under employers' control are now subject to regulation under the Pensions Schemes Act 2017.

Part VI. Social Security

335. Persons living in the UK may receive income during periods of disability from any combination of the following: Statutory Sick Pay (SSP) from their employer, some form of benefit provided by the state, which is basically funded from general taxation, and/or a pension following early retirement. Neither SSP nor other state benefits provide adequate protection against the loss of earning power for those with anything other than relatively low earnings, and there is therefore a strong case for individuals to effect one or more of several insurance options available to compensate for long-term disability. This Part outlines such options; it does not examine the state system of social security in the UK.[1093]

§1. Permanent Health Insurance

336. Permanent Health Insurance (PHI) is available for both employed and self-employed persons and is typically payable if 'the insured is totally unable by reason of sickness or accident to follow his/her occupation and is not following any other occupation'. In relation to the security provided, PHI premiums are low. Cover is usually limited to 75% of earnings and ceases when a pension becomes payable. PHI policies are available both to individuals and to groups, for example, employees of a common employer.

Exceptions common to almost all insurers are typically war risks, and recently, AIDS. Most insurers exclude sickness, etc. arising from self-inflicted injuries, participating in crime and alcohol and drug abuse and racing (other than athletics) and aviation (other than being a passenger on a commercial airline) are normally standard exclusions. The absence of a standard exclusion clause does not automatically mean that full cover is available in all circumstances. Most proposal forms include a question on hazardous activities, so that in the event of an untrue answer the insurers will be able to avoid liability.[1094] Further, individual acceptance terms may include a specific restriction on cover, or require an extra premium.

337. It is possible to obtain a combination of PHI and family income benefit, which provides an income to a claimant and will continue to a predetermined age, in the event of his or her earlier death; such policies are becoming increasingly common in the UK.

338. It is normally provided that any purported assignment of a PHI policy terminates the cover, and some insurers go so far as to state that assignment will not be recognized. It is unlikely that such provisions are fully effective. The object of them is both to protect the insurer from claims difficulties arising with third parties, and to

1093. The leading text is Wikeley, Ogus and Barendt, *The Law of Social Security*.

1094. Either for breach of warranty or for misrepresentation; *see* Part II.

protect the insured from his or her creditors. It is perceived that a claimant whose total disability income is to be taken over by creditors will not recover as quickly as one who is financially self-sufficient. However, while it may be possible to prohibit assignment of a policy itself, it is unlikely that assignment of the benefit under a policy can be forbidden. These are legally two separate matters, as was explained in Part II, Chapter 1.

§2. Critical Illness Insurance

339. Critical Illness Insurance (CII) is sometimes referred to as 'dread disease' insurance. It provides a lump sum in the event of the insured suffering a specific medical condition as defined in the policy, and surviving for a limited period. Lump sum CII can be seen as a replacement for, or, more typically, a supplement to, PHI. CII is available for both the employed and the self-employed. There is at present no agreed list of medical conditions covered by insurers, but some, for example, invasive cancer, coronary disease, renal failure, and paralysis, are typically covered by all insurers, and most cover a common list of critical conditions.[1095] Many contracts in the individual market have no ceasing age, and offer cover throughout life. Benefit is normally limited to four times the insured's annual salary, subject to a maximum of GBP 500,000. Exclusions are in general the same as those for PHI.[1096]

§3. Personal Accident and Sickness Insurance

340. The principal legal considerations concerning personal accident and sickness insurance were considered earlier,[1097] but as it is an alternative form of private social security, it merits brief further consideration here. The main advantage to the insured of this type of contract, compared with PHI, is one of cost, and the availability of substantial lump sum payments. The main disadvantage is that personal accident insurance is invariably an annual contract, and the insurer is not obliged to invite renewal if there is a material change in the insured's circumstances. The principles of law applying to these contracts, for example, the duty of disclosure, the requirement of insurable interest, etc. are the same as for any contract of life insurance.[1098] Personal accident policies are prima facie not contracts of indemnity. They generally undertake to pay a fixed stated benefit if an insured event occurs, for example, the loss of a limb. Polices that pay, for example, a proportion of earnings in the event of disability ought to be regarded as indemnity contracts, but there is no authority in point.

1095. For example, stroke, organ transplant, permanent brain damage, leukaemia, loss of independent existence.

1096. *See supra*.

1097. *See* Part V, Ch. 2 *supra*.

1098. *See* Part II, Ch. 4 *supra*.

Part VII. Insurance Intermediaries

Chapter 1. Law of Establishment and Supervision

341. There is a wide variety of insurance intermediaries in the UK, although there are only two fundamental types for both life and other business – 'tied' agents and independent intermediaries. Tied agents will be employed by or under another exclusive contractual arrangement with one insurer. Independent intermediaries include brokers and other agents who may use title such as 'insurance consultant' or 'insurance adviser'. They may also include people whose insurance role is part-time and incidental to their principal occupation, such as motor dealers, solicitors, mortgage lenders, travel agents and estate agents. A special category is the Lloyd's broker, through whom only can a policy be taken out with a Lloyd's Underwriter.[1099]

342. The wide variety of types of insurance intermediary raises important questions concerning their suitability and qualifications, and how to respond with the conflicts of interest that may arise[1100] and has led over the years to a number of different mechanisms for their regulation. Apart from a statutory scheme for the registration of persons calling themselves insurance brokers,[1101] which was repealed in 2000, the oldest form of regulation is of intermediaries advising on life insurance. These were covered by the scheme introduced under the Financial Services Act 1986, which was then replaced by the Financial Services and Markets Act 2000. Independent intermediaries selling most forms of long-term insurance must be authorized by the FCA, and an insurer is directly liable for the acts and omissions of one of its appointed representatives.[1102] The Authority has made detailed rules governing these intermediaries, which are contained in the CBS.

343. For a relatively short period, intermediaries involved in general insurance business were regulated by a self-regulatory system,[1103] but, with some exceptions, in particular for those involved in large risks[1104] and reinsurance they too came within the jurisdiction of what is now the FCA when the Insurance Mediation Directive

1099. This was a rule of custom, enshrined in statute: Lloyd's Act 1982, s. 8(3).
1100. For example, where insurance is sold on a commission basis, the intermediary may well try to persuade the client to accept the policy that pays him the best rate of commission, rather than that which is best suited to the client's needs.
1101. Under the Insurance Brokers Registration Act 1977.
1102. Financial Services and Markets Act 2000, s. 39(3).
1103. Under what was called the General Insurance Standards Council.
1104. As to these, *see* para. 43.

(IMD),[1105] which sets minimum standards across Europe for the sale and administration of both general and life insurance, was implemented in 2005.[1106] One most important consequence is that all complaints against insurance intermediaries are now within the jurisdiction of the FOS.[1107] The IMD is due to be replaced by the Insurance Distribution Directive (IDD) by 23 February 2018, and it will clearly be implemented in the UK by that date notwithstanding the expected departure from the EU in 2019 and, it is presumed, will continue to apply thereafter except perhaps as regards the provisions on freedom of services and establishment. The other major impact of the IDD is that it extends the scope of regulation to most insurance 'distributors'. These include claims managers and ancillary insurance intermediaries, as well as insurers that sell directly to customers, although in the UK the latter are in general already subject to the same regulation as insurance intermediaries.

344. In many respect the requirements concerning intermediaries are the same as those that apply to insurers, as described in Part I. The detail is to be found in the Principles for Business and the ICOBS produced by the FCA, and, so far as concerns the competence of individuals, the Fit and Proper Test for Approved Persons part of the High Level Standards part of the Handbook. ICOB draws a distinction between retail customers and commercial customers. Retail customers are natural persons acting for purposes outside their trade, business of profession. Commercial customers are any other persons, although small businesses do receive some extra protection as regards product disclosure and advice. They key requirements of ICOBS are as follows.[1108] They are required to disclose a number of matters, including their name and address, that they are included in the Financial Services Register and their complaints procedure (including mention of the FOS). They must also disclose whether they give advice on the basis of a fair analysis of the market or are under a contractual obligation to conduct business exclusively with one or more insurers or that they are not under such an obligation nor do they give advice on the basis of a fair analysis of the market. If they do not advise on the basis of a fair analysis of the market, they must inform customers that the latter have the right to request the name of each insurer with which they may and do conduct business. Before the conclusion of an initial contract with a consumer, intermediaries must state whether they are giving a personal recommendation or information. This must all be disclosed clearly, accurately and comprehensibly in a 'durable medium' before conclusion of an insurance contract, unless customers require immediate cover or the contract is made by telephone, in which case oral disclosure suffices. Intermediaries must disclose their fees (or the basis for calculating them) before the customer incurs liability to pay them or before conclusion of the contract, whichever is earlier. Commercial customers have the right to be told of the commission that intermediaries receive.

1105. 2002/92/EC.

1106. The Directive was implemented by the Insurance Mediation Directive (Miscellaneous Amendments) Regulations 2002, SI 2004/1473 and the Financial Services and Markets Act 2000 (Regulated Activities) (Amendment) (No. 2) Order 2003, SI 2003/1476, which came into force in January 2005.

1107. *See* para. 24.

1108. There are additional requirements for protection policies, which are essentially term life policies and payment protection policies.

Chapter 2. Insurance Intermediaries and the Insurance Contract

345. The insurance transaction where an intermediary is involved is governed by the principles of agency law.[1109] Several questions of importance arise; what is the relationship between principal and agent; when is a principal bound to a third party via the acts of his agent; when is an agent's knowledge reputed to his principal; and perhaps most importantly of all, whose agent, in law, is the agent – that of insured, or insurer.

§1. Relations Between the Principal and Third Party

346. A principal is bound by any of the acts of his agent if the act is within the agent's actual or apparent (or ostensible) authority. A principal is also bound by any unauthorized act of his agent that he later ratifies.

I. Actual Authority

347. Actual authority may be express or implied. Express authority raises no problems; if the principal appoints an agent to negotiate and contract with a particular person on particular terms. The agent has express authority to that effect. Implied authority will arise if, in all the circumstances, it must be the position that the agent has actual authority, even if it is never conferred on him by express words. If, for example, an insurer gives his agent blank cover notes, he impliedly authorizes him to effect binding temporary insurance contracts,[1110] and, the continuing adoption by the insurer of temporary oral contracts entered into by its agent will confer implied authority on that agent.[1111] The insured as principal may also confer implied authority. In *Zurich General Accident and Liability Ins. Co. Ltd. v. Rowbury*,[1112] brokers were instructed to effect a policy in respect of the insured's forthcoming journey to France. The brokers mistakenly inserted into the proposal form that the insured's destination was Paris, when it was, in fact, Nice. The insured attempted to repudiate the policy on the grounds of his mistake, but he was held bound by the broker's actions – he had given them authority to negotiate the proposal without any specific instructions as to destination.

Under general agency law, a principal whose identity or even existence was undisclosed at the time of the contract, may sue upon a contract made by an agent of his with actual authority. This principle can apply to insurance situations where the

1109. Detailed guidance on the UK law of agency can be found in *Bowstead and Reynolds on Agency*.
1110. For example, *Stockton v. Mason* [1978] 2 Lloyd's Reports 430.
1111. *Murfitt v. Royal Insurance Co.* (1922) 38 TLR 334.
1112. [1954] 2 Lloyd's Rep. 55.

existence of the true insured is undisclosed,[1113] although it seems likely that it will apply in relatively special circumstances, for example, situations of co-insurance.[1114]

II. Apparent Authority

348. Apparent authority arises when the principal, by words or conduct, holds out his agent as having particular authority. The essence of apparent authority is estoppel; if the principal makes a representation as to the authority of his agent, and the third party relies on this representation, then the principal is estopped from denying this authority, and is bound to the third party.[1115] If an agent is appointed to a particular position, then he will have apparent authority to bind his principal in respect of all the usual as is which someone in that position has authority to do. It is irrelevant that the agent actually is not authorized to do some of those usual acts, unless the third party is aware of this, in which case there can be no reliance.[1116]

Someone who holds the position of inspector in an insurance company will probably be regarded as having apparent authority to vary the terms of a proposal form.[1117] The payments of premiums to an agent will bind the insurer, if the agent is held out to have the authority to receive them.[1118] An agent held out as having authority to make alterations in a policy or to waive a breach of condition will bind the insurer.[1119] As stated earlier, blank cover notes give the agent implied actual authority to effect binding temporary insurance, but even if this is expressly forbidden by the insurer so that actual authority cannot be found, the agent in such a situation will have apparent authority. However, an agent will never, it seems, have apparent authority to bind the insurer by the issue of a formal policy,[1120] nor can an agent of the insurer bind his principal as to the meaning of construction of a policy. However, this is because the representation is one of law, and in general, these, unlike representations of fact, are not binding, rather than because of any lack of authority.

III. Ratification

349. If an agent acts outside the scope of his authority, whether actual or apparent, the principal is not, prima facie, bound by that act. Provided the agent was acting as an agent however, and the principal was in existence and identifiable at the time of the act, then the principal may ratify the unauthorized act. The effect of ratification is

1113. *See* the decisions in *National Oilwell (UK) Ltd. v. Davy Offshore Ltd.* [1993] 2 Lloyd's Rep. 582 and *Siu Yin Kwan v. Eastern Insurance Co. Ltd.* [1994] 1 All ER 213.

1114. As in the *National Oilwell* case. The *Siu Yin Kwan* case was a rather special case on the facts. For a full discussion of these decisions, *see* Birds [1994] JBL 386.

1115. *See* , e.g., *Freeman and Lockyer v. Buckhurst Park Properties* [1964] 2 QB 480.

1116. *Wilkinson v. General Accident Fire & Life Assurance Corp. Ltd.* [1967] 2 Lloyd's Rep. 182.

1117. *Stone v. Reliance Mutual Insurance Society Ltd.* [1972] 1 Lloyd's Rep. 469.

1118. *Kelly v. London and Staffordshire Fire Insurance Co.* (1883) Cab & E 47.

1119. *Wing v. Harvey* (1854) 5 De GM & G 265.

1120. *Stockton v. Mason* [1978] 2 Lloyd's Rep. 430.

as if the agent has always been authorized, but it is not possible, in non-marine insurance, to ratify after a loss has occurred. Thus, in *Grover & Grover Ltd. v. Matthews*,[1121] where a broker effected without authority a renewal of the insured's policy, the insurer was held not liable, on the grounds that the insured's purported ratification was after the occurrence of his loss. It is strongly arguable, however, that this case was wrongly decided.[1122]

§2. Imputing the Agent's Knowledge

350. Of particular importance in the context of insurance are the rules whereby, in certain circumstances, the knowledge of an agent is imputed to his principal. In such cases the agent is usually the agent of the insurer, and the insured is seeking to rely upon imputed knowledge. The issue will normally arise when the insurer makes allegations against the insured of non-disclosure of material facts. The insured will claim that the insurer is deemed to know them because they were known to the agent, and an insurer will be deemed to have the knowledge of his agent if that knowledge is acquired when the agent is acting within the scope of his actual or apparent authority. Thus it is, crucial to this issue that the agent is, in law, the agent of the insurer and not the insured. Knowledge has been imputed to the insurer in cases concerning non-disclosure,[1123] breach of condition or warranty,[1124] and waiver.[1125] However, knowledge will not be imputed where the insured has signed a proposal form with inaccurate information, even though the inaccuracy results from the action of the agent completing the form who knew the truth.[1126] It has also been held that the knowledge of one branch of insurers, which dealt with an earlier application for insurance, was not imputed to another branch of the same insurers dealing with a later application.[1127] The knowledge of an agent is never imputed when the agent is acting in fraud of the principal.[1128]

1121. [1910] 2 KB 401.

1122. Because it conflicts with other authority; *see* the *dictum* in *Waters v. Monarch* (1856) 5 E & B 870; and *Trident General Insurance Co. Ltd. v. McNeil Bros Pty. Ltd.* (1988) 165 CLR 107 where the *Grover* case was regarded as wrong by the Australian courts, but ratification failed for other reasons; *Grover* was similarly disapproved of in *National Oilwell (UK) Ltd. v. Davy Offshore Ltd.* [1993] 2 Lloyd's Rep. 582. Ratification after loss has occurred is possible in marine insurance; *see* *Williams v. North China Insurance Co.* (1876) 1 C.P.D. 757.

1123. *Woolcott v. Excess Ins. Co.* [1979] 1 Lloyd's Rep. 231.

1124. *Wing v. Harvey, supra* .

1125. *Ibid.*

1126. *Newsholme Bros. v. Road Transport & General Insurance Co.* [1929] 2 KB 356. *See infra* para. 360.

1127. *Malhi v. Abbey Life Assurance Co. Ltd.* [1994] C.L.C. 615.

1128. *P.C.W. Syndicates v. P.C.W. Reinsurers* [1996] 1 Lloyd's Rep. 241; *Group Josi Re v. Walbrook Insurance Co. Ltd.* [1996] 1 Lloyd's Rep. 345; *Deutsche Ruckversicherung A.G. v. Walbrook Insurance Co. Ltd.* [1996] 1 All E.R. 791.

§3. Relationship Between Principal and Agent

351. If, for some reason, a principal cannot enforce a contract against a third party or he is liable to a third party because of the unauthorized acts of his agent, he may well have a remedy against the agent. Equally the relationship of principal and agent is a fiduciary one and duties arise as a result. For example, the insurer bound by a contract which he could have avoided for non-disclosure had his agent not known the non-disclosed facts and his knowledge been imputed to the insurer, can sue the agent for damages, being the amount of money which he has had to pay the insured.[1129] Similarly, if an agent acts beyond his actual authority, but the insurer is liable by virtue of the principles of ostensible authority, the insurer will have a damages remedy against the agent.

It is more likely in practice, however, that it is the insured seeking a remedy against his agent, commonly, but not necessarily, his broker. In this context, it is usual and convenient to split up the heads of liability into two; that arising by virtue of the fiduciary relationship between the insured and his agent, and the duties of care and skill required of an agent.

I. Fiduciary Duties

352. A fiduciary relationship carries with it strict duties, in particular the overriding one that the fiduciary, the agent, must not put himself into a position where his own interests do or may conflict with his duties to his principal.[1130] This means, *inter alia*, that he must not act for another in a matter relating to his principal without full disclosure to and the consent of his principal. It used to be standard practice for Lloyd's brokers to act for the underwriter in certain matters, despite the fact that, as was mentioned earlier, they are in law agents of the insured. This practice was condemned in *Anglo-African Merchants v. Bayley* [1131] as clearly constituting a breach of fiduciary duty, unless the insured consented. Shortly afterwards the point arose again in *North and South Trust v. Berkeley*,[1132] where a claim by the insured was investigated by assessors instructed by the brokers. Their report was handed to the brokers who showed it to be underwriters, but refused to let the insured have sight of it or know what it contained. They were thereupon sued by the insured who relied upon the earlier decision as establishing that the brokers had acted in breach of duty. The judge again condemned the practice of brokers acting for both parties and held that what had been done was a breach of duty, but, apart from admitting the possibility of a claim for damages by the insured, which was not, in fact, sought, he refused to give the insured the remedy they did seek, namely, an order for delivery of the documents. This is rather curious, although it was expressly stated that a remedy would be available in future cases.

1129. *Woolcott v. Excess Ins. Co., supra* .
1130. Example, *Boardman v. Phipps* [1967] 2 AC 46.
1131. [1970] 1 QB 311.
1132. [1977] 1 WLR 470.

II. Duties of Care and Skill

353. In respect of the duties of care and skill, there is no doubt that an agent such as a broker owes a duty to his client, the insured, to take reasonable care and skill and this is potentially an important head of liability. It should be noted that the insured's cause of action is in damages for breach of duty in contract or tort. If what the insured is claiming is in effect the damages he has to pay to an injured third party, for example, this relates only to the measure of the broker's liability. The claim is not in respect of damages for personal injury, so that the relevant limitation period is six years, not three years.[1133]

354. In advising his client with whom to insure, the broker must take due care. In *Osman v. J. Ralph Moss*,[1134] the defendant brokers recommended to the plaintiff that he effect a motor policy with an insurer already well known in insurance circles to be in a serious financial situation and which in fact was subsequently wound up, leaving the plaintiff uninsured. As a result, the plaintiff was convicted of driving without insurance and involved in an accident for which he was liable, with no insurer to foot the bill. The plaintiff was of Turkish origin and had difficulty in reading and understanding English. The only warning the defendants gave him was a letter asking him simply to insure elsewhere. It was held that the defendants were liable in damages for the amount he was fined and the damages he had to pay the third party. What is not completely clear is how much turned on the fact that the plaintiff was not really literate in English, so that the letter that the defendants sent could not possibly have been enough to satisfy the duty they owned him. The decision does not actually hold that a broker must always expressly warn his client of the impending insolvency of his insurer, if he is aware or ought to be aware of this, and there are passages in the judgments referring to the particular position of the plaintiff. It is suggested that brokers ought to be under a duty at all times to all classes of insured to advise and warn about particular insurers, not just as to their financial stability but also as to the suitability of particular policies and their general record in treating their insured's, for example, as to their generosity in paying claims. It seems clear that a broker who fails to warn the insured of any special terms incorporated on renewal is negligent.[1135] There is clearly a duty to obtain effective cover,[1136] to warn the insured about the insurer's particular terms[1137] and to explain terms that might result in the insured being under-insured.[1138]

355. Another instance of negligent advice arose in *Cherry Ltd. v. Allied Insurance Brokers Ltd.*[1139] Here the defendants had been the plaintiff's brokers for some fifty years, but the plaintiffs became dissatisfied and proposed to put their business elsewhere. As a result, they wished to cancel all their policies held through the defendants well before their renewal date, and they instructed the defendants to seek to do so. The

---

1133. *Ackbar v. Green* [1975] QB 582.
1134. [1970] 1 Lloyd's Rep. 313.
1135. *Mint Security Ltd. v. Blair* [1982] 1 Lloyd's Rep. 188.
1136. *FNCB Ltd v. Barnet Devanney (Harrow) Ltd* [1999] Lloyd's Rep. IR 459.
1137. *Harvest Trading Co. Ltd. v. Davis Insurance Services* [1991] 2 Lloyd's Rep. 638.
1138. *JW Bollom & Co Ltd v. Byas Mosley & Co Ltd* [2000] Lloyd's Rep. IR 136.
1139. [1978] 1 Lloyd's Rep. 274.

defendants cancelled most of the policies but advised the plaintiffs that the particular insurer concerned would not accept cancellation of the plaintiff's consequential loss policy. The plaintiffs having effected a new policy of this sort thereupon cancelled it to avoid being doubly insured. Subsequently, however, that first insurer did agree to a cancellation of the original policy, but the defendants failed to advise the plaintiff of this. The latter then suffered loss for which, because both policies had been cancelled, they were uninsured. It was held that the defendants were negligent in failing to advise the plaintiffs of the first insurer's cancellation and were liable in damages for the amount which the plaintiffs would have recovered from their insurer had they been insured.

356. Several cases have been concerned with the broker's position in respect of the duty of the insured to disclose material facts and not to make misrepresentations. This is obviously a crucial area as the insured who is dealing with a broker will not, in practice, have any direct communication with his insurer, and thus the exact nature of the broker's duty with regard to advising his client about such matters is vital. If the broker fails to ask the insured questions about facts that he, the broker, knows are material, he will be liable in damages to the insured if the insurer subsequently avoids liability. In *McNealy v. Pennine Insurance Co,*[1140] the brokers who knew that the insurers refused to issue motor insurance to persons with certain occupations, including that of part-time musician which their client was, were held under a duty to the insured to ask him whether or not he was affected by this. Having failed to do so, they were liable in damages when the insurer repudiated its liability to the insured. It would seem to follow that the same result would apply if the broker actually knows of material facts which he fails to disclose to the insurer.

If the broker is unaware of material facts, and there are no special circumstances as in *McNealy* requiring him to quiz the insured, it appears unlikely that the court would hold that the broker was under a duty to warn the insured of his duty of disclosure. In *Warren v. Sutton,*[1141] the plaintiff, who held a motor policy, was going on holiday to France with a friend whom he wished to share the driving with him and arranged through his brokers for the friend to be covered under his policy. However, the latter had an appalling driving record with several convictions, none of which was disclosed to the insurer, so that the latter was able to avoid the policy and not pay in respect of an accident that occurred in France. The broker actually said to the insurer that there were 'no accidents, convictions or disabilities' when the extension was being arranged. On this basis, the majority of the Court of Appeal held the broker liable to pay damages. He had made a false representation to the insurance company in breach of his duty to the plaintiff. If, however, the broker had not made the representation, and the reason for the insurer's repudiation had simply been non-disclosure by the insured of which the broker was unaware, it appears that the result would have been the other way. This supports the view that the court would not hold a broker under a duty to warn the insured of his duty of disclosure in the abstract. Further support can perhaps be found in another Court of Appeal decision on a related point. In *O'Connor v. Kirby,*[1142] the plaintiff insured his car through the defendant broker who incorrectly answered a

1140. [1978] 1 Lloyd's Rep. 18.
1141. [1976] 2 Lloyd's Rep. 276.
1142. [1972] 1 QB 90.

question on the proposal form relating to the garaging of the car; the insurer subsequently avoided the policy for breach of warranty. The plaintiff sued the broker for failing to complete the form properly. It was held that he was not liable, as the plaintiff had signed the form containing the mistake and was solely responsible because it was his duty to see that the information therein was correct. It may be that this reasoning is suspect in the light of the consideration that the insured dealing with a broker does place great reliance on the latter. It is thought that the reasoning of Megaw L.J., to the effect that a broker who completes a proposal form does owe a duty to the insured to take reasonable care that its contents are correct but that in the circumstances the broker had fulfilled that duty since the mistake was at most due only to a slip or misunderstanding and the broker had given the form to the insured to check, is better. That this is a better ratio seems to be supported by the more recent decision in *Dunbar v. A & E Painters Ltd.*[1143] Here brokers who inserted incorrect answers on a proposal form were held liable in damages since it was shown that the answers required fell especially within the broker's knowledge. However, it seems likely that this last factor is crucial. If the broker is not in possession of the relevant information, primary responsibility in respect of body non-disclosure of material facts and the answering of questions seems to fall on the insured rather than the broker.[1144]

However, later cases indicate a different view, influenced by the introduction of rules made with statutory authority. In *Jones v. Enrivoncom Ltd*,[1145] the judge, after citing the relevant provisions of the Insurance: CBS, summarized the broker's duty with regard to the proposer's duty of disclosure as requiring that he must: (a) advise his client of the duty to disclose all material circumstances; (b) explain the consequences of failing to do so; (c) indicate the sort of matters which ought to be disclosed as being material (or at least arguably material); and (d) take reasonable care to elicit matters which ought to be disclosed but which the client might think it not necessary to mention.

357. If a broker is liable in damages to the insured, the measure of damages will, as has been seen, usually be that sum which the insured would have recovered from the insurer had the latter been liable. If the breach of duty by the broker is a failure to effect insurance at all, the question has arisen whether it is open to him to say that even if he had obtained the cover, the insurer would still not have been liable, and hence he should not be liable, because of some breach by the insured. The point arose neatly in *Fraser v. Furman*,[1146] where the broker had failed in his duty to effect employer's liability cover for the plaintiff. The broker argued, however, that the insurer would not have been liable for the loss that subsequently occurred, because the plaintiff would have been in breach of a condition in the policy to take reasonable precautions to avoid loss. The Court of Appeal held that the broker was liable for the full amount of loss suffered by the plaintiff. Even if the defence would have been available to the insurer, which was doubted,[1147] the fact was that in the circumstances the insurer in question would not have repudiated liability. Therefore, the question depends on the

1143. [1986] 2 Lloyd's Rep. 38.
1144. *See also Kapur v. JW Francis & Co* [2000] Lloyd's Rep. IR 361.
1145. [2010] EWHC 759 (Comm), [2010] Lloyd's Rep. IR 676. *See also Synergy Health (UK) Ltd v. CGU Insurance plc* [2010] EWHC 2583 (Comm), [2011] Lloyd's Rep. IR 500.
1146. [1967] 1 WLR 898.
1147. As only recklessness on the part of the insured will amount to a breach; *see* para. 58.

likely attitude of the insurer rather than the strict point as to whether, in fact, the insurer would have been legally liable.[1148]

§4. Whose Agent, in Law, Is the Agent?

358. This area is of great practical importance, but there is a degree of uncertainty surrounding it. This was recognized by the Law Commissions as part of their review of pre-contractual disclosure and representations and the Consumer Insurance (Disclosure and Representations) Act 2012 includes rules to assist in determining the exact status in law of insurance intermediaries.[1149] As a general rule, the agent under the direct employment or control of the insurer is the agent of the insurer, but he may not always be so.[1150] For most purposes all other agents, including Lloyd's brokers,[1151] are the agents of the insured, but some recent cases have regarded brokers in a particularly close relationship as the agent of the insurer.[1152] This element of uncertainty is most acute regarding the position of brokers, and their relationship with the parties to the insurance contract. If the broker is the agent of the insured, then his knowledge of certain matters pertaining to the contact should not logically be imputed to the insurer. Nor, if he purports to act for the insurer, should the insurer be bound by those actions. Two recent cases have decided the contrary, however. In *Stockton v. Mason*,[1153] the insured, through his wife, instructed his brokers to transfer his existing motor policy from a Ford Anglia to an MG Midget. An employee of the broker sanctioned this for a temporary period. The previous policy covered the driving of the car by any authorized person, and the insured assumed that the transferred policy would carry the same terms. The insured's son, whilst driving the vehicle, negligently injured a third party, and the brokers claimed that the cover for the MG was restricted to the insured only. The issue was whether the injured plaintiff could sue the insurers, in tort, for damages, which depended upon whether the insurers were bound by the oral statement of the broker's employee regarding the transfer of the policy. A strong Court of Appeal held them bound, Lord Diplock stating: 'A broker in non-marine insurance has implied authority to issue on behalf of the insurer, or, enter into, *as agent for the insurer*, contracts of interim insurance … it seems to me quite unarguable that in saying, "Yes, that will be alright Mrs Mason", the brokers were acting as agents for the insurance company and not merely acknowledging an order or request by Mrs Mason to negotiate a contract

1148. But the position may be different if the insurance which the broker should have effected would have been void: *Thomas Cheshire & Co. v. Vaughan Bros & Co.* [1920] 3 KB 240. If in fact the insured is virtually uninsurable, the damages payable by the broker are likely to be reduced: *O & R Jewellers v. Terry* [1999] Lloyd's Rep. IR 436.

1149. *See* para. 109.

1150. *See* , e.g., *Newsholme Bros. v. Road Transport & General Insurance Co.* [1929] 2 KB 356, discussed below.

1151. *McNealy v. Pennine Ins. Co. Ltd.* [1978] 2 Lloyd's Rep. 18; *Roberts v. Plaisted* [1989] 2 Lloyd's Rep. 341; *Winter v. Irish Life Assurance plc* [1995] 2 Lloyd's Rep. 274.

1152. *Stockton v. Mason supra* ; *Woolcott v. Excess Ins. Co. supra* . This will never be the case in respect of Lloyd's brokers.

1153. *Supra.*

on her husband's behalf.'[1154] In *Woolcott v. Excess Insurance Co. Ltd.*,[1155] it was clearly assumed beyond argument by the Court of Appeal that knowledge of the broker as to a material fact should be imputed to the insurer.

359. Whilst these decisions are welcome as according with the reality of the situation, particularly from the viewpoint of the insured, a note of caution should be sounded. It is likely that the principles of these cases will be applicable only where there was a close relationship between the broker and the insurance company, the former being actually authorized to conclude at least interim contracts of insurance. Whether, in the case of an agent without actual authority from the insurer, an insured can rely on the principle of apparent authority must be in doubt, following a line of authority of which *Newsholme Bros v. Road Transport & General Insurance Co.*[1156] is the leading case.[1157] This case was concerned with the common situation of the agent filling in the proposal form for the contract of insurance, on the insured's behalf. The agent was employed by the insurer to canvass for proposals, but he was not authorized to effect insurance, whether permanent or temporary. Incorrect answers relating to the previous losses were warranted to be true, on the proposal form filled in by the agent, even though the agent knew them to be false.[1158] The Court of Appeal refused to impute his knowledge to the insurer, and Scrutton L.J., who delivered the leading judgment, gave two reasons for the decision. First, if the agent filled in the form at the request of the proposer, then he must be acting as the agent of the proposer. Second, if the proposer signs the proposal form, knowing what it is, and is negligent in doing so, then he cannot hope to escape the consequences of his negligence by claiming that the agent is not his agent, but the agent of the insurer.

The latter point is unquestionably correct as regards the signature and is strictly in accordance with the law governing the signature of documents. However, it appears that, as regards the agency point, the court was most impressed with the fact that the agent did not have actual authority from the insurer to fill in proposal forms.[1159] This, with respect, cannot be regarded as conclusive. The fact that this agent was armed with proposal forms and must have frequently completed them should, arguably, have conferred on him apparent authority on which the insured could rely. Equally, if the agent does, at some point, become the agent of the proposer, then the presentation of the form is only an offer to contract, and at some stage later the correct knowledge of the agent could be imputed to the insurer if the facts warrant it. *Newsholme*, however, remains the governing authority in this area, and strictly correct. Whether the decision is fair is a separate matter.

360. Finally, it falls to be considered whether, at any time during the transaction to contract, the agent can be the agent of both the insurer and the insured. It appears from the decisions in two recent cases that he can, at least so far as Lloyd's brokers

1154. *Ibid.*, at 431–432.
1155. *Supra.*
1156. *Supra.*
1157. *See also Winter v. Irish Life Assurance plc* [1995] 2 Lloyd's Rep. 274.
1158. This aspect cannot apply now because of the statutory provisions described in.
1159. The position may be different where the agent is actually authorized: e.g., *Stone v. Reliance Mutual Insurance Society* [1972] 1 Lloyd's Rep. 469.

are concerned.[1160] If the principle applies generally, then the agent must owe both fiduciary duties and duties of care and skill to both his principals. Whilst the latter will be unlikely to cause problems, there must be a potential conflict regarding the former. As a general rule 'fully informed consent apart, an agent cannot lawfully place himself in a position in which he owes a duty to another which is inconsistent with his duty to his principal'.[1161] If the 'another' is also his principal then it is not difficult to envisage situations where the agent's duties will be in constant conflict. It is perhaps unfortunate that so much uncertainty surrounds the role of intermediaries in the insurance transaction – almost all insurance businesses in the UK is conducted via agents, and the legal technicalities have important repercussions for the consumer.

1160. *Anglo-African Merchants v. Bayley* [1970] 1 QB 311; *North & South Trust v. Berkeley* [1971] 1 WLR 470. So the courts have been prepared to imply terms so that insurers are entitled to necessary information and documents in the hands of the brokers: *Goshawk Dedicated Ltd v. Tyser & Co Ltd* [2006] EWCA Civ 379.

1161. *Ibid.*, 484–485. *See also Callaghan and Hedges v. Thompsons* [2000] Lloyd's Rep. IR 125.

Part VIII. Reinsurance

§1. Definition and Nature of Reinsurance

361. No English authority provides a wholly satisfactory definition of reinsurance. There is however a working definition, which is borrowed from US law and followed by the English courts, namely that a reinsurance contract is one whereby, for a consideration, one agrees to indemnify another, wholly or partially, against loss or liability incurred by reason of a risk which the latter has assumed under a separate and distinct contract as the insurer of a third party.[1162]

The reinsurance contract is a separate contract from the contract of original insurance, and may be subject to different systems of law.[1163] It follows therefore that there is no privity of contract between the reinsurer and the original insured;[1164] thus reinsurance is distinguished from double insurance. It is neither an assignment nor a transfer of the original insurance business from one insurer to another,[1165] nor is it a relationship of partnership or agency between insurers.[1166] It is not a species of liability insurance.[1167] Reinsurance is essentially an independent contract of indemnity insurance, and is therefore subject to the general binding principles and rules of law relating to all indemnity insurances, such as the principles of utmost good faith and subrogation, and the rules relating to insurable interest and illegality. It is worth noting however that not all forms of reinsurance are necessarily contracts *of* insurance; some treaties may be no more than standing offers to reinsure, if, and when, business is ceded, and it is therefore more accurate to classify these agreements as contracts *for* insurance rather than contracts *of* insurance.

1162. *Stickel v. Excess Insurance Co. of America* 23 NE (2d) 839, Ohio 1939. For the House of Lords' views, *see Forsikringsaktieselskapet Vesta v. Butcher (No. 1)* [1989] A.C. 852 at 908 and *Wasa International Insurance Co. Ltd v. Lexington Insurance Co.* [2009] UKHL 40, [2009] 3 W.L.R. 575.

1163. *Citadel Insurance Co. v. Atlantic Union Insurance Co.* [1982] 2 Lloyd's Rep. 543.

1164. *See* , e.g., *Re Norwich Equitable Fire Assurance Society* (1887) 3 TLR 781.

1165. *Re Lancashire Plate Glass Fire & Burglary Insurance Ltd.* [1912] 1 Ch. 35.

1166. *Home Insurance Co. v. Victoria Montreal Fire Insurance Co.* [1907] AC 59.

1167. *Wasa International Insurance Co. Ltd v. Lexington Insurance Co.* [2009] UKHL 40, [2009] 3 W.L.R. 575.

§2. Reinsurance Categories and Terminologies

362. Difficulties can arise when trying to determine the precise meaning of reinsurance terminology. Differences of opinion exist as to the meaning of particular terms or descriptions of business, even when the term is in common use. Some of the basic categories and terminologies are examined in the following text, but reference should be made to a specialized text for more detail:[1168]

(1) Terminologies:

- *Reinsurance and Retrocession*: Reinsurance is properly limited to describe reinsurance of primary insurance, whilst retrocession strictly refers to the reinsurance of a contract of reinsurance. The reinsurer is then the 'retrocedant', who cedes his liability to a further reinsurer, called the 'retrocessionaire'. The distinction is not, however, always observed in practice.[1169]
- *Cession, Acceptance and Retention*: Risks are 'ceded' by the reinsured and 'accepted' by the reinsurer. Ceded risks are called 'cessions', which has a meaning separate from its common meaning as a term of assignment. Typically, the reinsured will reinsure only part of the risk; his retained interest is referred to as the 'retention'.[1170]

(2) Categories:

- *Facultative reinsurance*: In its simplest form, facultative reinsurance involves the reinsurance of one sole risk, but it can involve reinsurance of a series of related original policies. What is essential is that the reinsurer and reinsured are free to choose whether to accept, and cede, any particular risk.
- *Treaty Insurance*: Treaty insurance proceeds via an agreement between reinsured and reinsurer that all risks of the class of business specified by the treaty and accepted by the reinsured *must* be ceded to the reinsurer, who, in turn, is bound to accept them.[1171] The oldest treaty to be judicially decided upon is probably that in *Re Norwich Equitable Fire Assurance Society*,[1172] where the court referred to it as an agreement of agency, although it was accepted that the original insured had no contractual relationship with the reinsurer, in common with all reinsurance agreements.

1168. For example, Butler & Merkin, *Reinsurance Law*; Carter, *Reinsurance* (2nd ed.); Golding, *The Law and Practice of Reinsurance* (4th ed.). A concise summary can be found in *MacGillivray on Insurance Law* Ch. 34 (12th ed.).

1169. *See* , e.g., *Commonwealth Insurance Co. of Vancouver v. Spinks* [1983] 1 Lloyd's Rep. 67. A retrocession agreement is often described as a reinsurance, but a reinsurance agreement would not normally be called a retrocession.

1170. A retention is sometimes reinsured separately; equally, there may be a term that it will not be reinsured at all. Such a term has been held not to be a warranty – *Great Atlantic Insurance Co. v. Home Insurance Co.* [1981] 2 Lloyd's Rep. 219.

1171. *See* the analysis in *The Beursgracht (No. 1)* [2001] 2 Lloyd's Rep. 602.

1172. (1887) 3 TLR 781.

- *Open cover reinsurance*: This is an arrangement set up by a broker or other intermediary who declares the particular risk to be covered and the name of the proposed reinsured to the reinsurers, thereby creating privity of contract between reinsured and reinsurer. Open cover provides a means for a reinsurer to enter the market, and for a reinsured to be certain of his cover before entering into the contracts of primary insurance. It is arguable that these are not, of themselves, contracts *of* insurance – rather, they are agreements which create individual contracts of insurance when the reinsured, or intermediary, makes use of the facility available to him for reinsurance, and when declarations are made and policies issued.[1173]

§3. Formation of the Contract of Reinsurance

I. The Slip

363. The formation of the contract of reinsurance is occasionally difficult to analyse, but, provided that there is a clear intention to create legal relations and the transaction is of a commercial nature, the court will certainly be prepared to recognize the creation of a contractual relationship. If the reinsurance constitutes a contract of marine insurance however, the court cannot dispense with the requirement that such a contract be embodied in a policy.[1174]

Reinsurance contracts may be formed by a conventional offer and acceptance during correspondence. They are not infrequently however formed by the reinsurer initialing a 'slip', presented to him by the broker acting for the reinsured. Unless the slip is qualified in some way, or is circulated with the express intention of obtaining only a quotation, then the slip contains the contract of insurance.[1175] Usually the slip will require the production of a policy; if it does not, then the slip will be referred to as a reinsurance slip policy.[1176]

In both insurance and reinsurance, a slip is generally treated the same way, but there are at least two respects in which they differ. First, the reinsurance slip often creates contractual relations between a number of reinsureds and reinsurers, so that in a composite transaction each reinsured is put into privity with each reinsurer.[1177] Second, the slip may be initialed before the primary insurance contract is concluded, so that the reinsured is not known at that stage. The early definitions of reinsurance, which

1173. This analysis is supported by decisions which have held that marine insurance treaties are 'contracts *for* insurance' within the Stamp Acts, e.g., *Home Marine Insurance Co. v. Smith* [1898] 2 QB 351.

1174. Marine Insurance Act 1906 ss 22–24; *see* para. 178. *See Commonwealth Insurance Co. v. Groupe Spinks* [1983] 1 Lloyd's Rep. 67 at 83.

1175. *General Accident Fire & Life Assurance v. Tanter* [1984] 1 Lloyd's Rep. 58 at 69.

1176. For example, *Balfour v. Beaumont* [1984] 1 Lloyd's Rep. 272.

1177. *See* , e.g., *General Accident Fire & Life Assurance v. Tanter, supra* .

required both the reinsurer and the reinsured to be in existence at the time of the formation of the reinsurance contract,[1178] are now clearly outmoded.[1179]

II. Disclosure

364. The pre-contractual duty in reinsurance is the same as in primary insurance,[1180] whether the contract is one of marine or non-marine insurance, but the duty was reformulated in market terms as an obligation to ensure that the presentation of the risk proposed is fair and substantially accurate,[1181] a formulation that is now enshrined in the Insurance Act 2015. In practice reinsurance is often offered to reinsurers on the basis of limited information in the expectation that the reinsurers will either accept the business on the faith of the summary, or will ask further questions,[1182] but the reinsurer is entitled to assume that the summary is fair and accurate, and will be held to have waived the requirement of further disclosure only if a prudent insurer would have been sufficiently put on notice by the summary that the picture it represented was incomplete.[1183] A reinsurer will be expected to be aware of the general course of losses affecting the market in which he operates, but not particular circumstances affecting only limited groups of insureds within that market.[1184] He is not required either to carry in his head information which had no interest for him at the time he acquired it.[1185]

365. As discussed earlier, insofar as a reinsurance treaty is not strictly a contract of insurance, it may be thought that the duty of disclosure should not apply. In *Glasgow Assurance v. Symondson*,[1186] however, the submission that the duty was inapplicable to open cover reinsurance was rejected, and in *Berger v. Pollock*,[1187] a similar submission in respect of open cover for marine insurance was also rejected. This must be correct; the doctrine of *uberrima fides*, which underlies the duty of fair presentation, is as applicable to contracts of reinsurance as it is to contracts of primary insurance[1188] and should be as applicable to reinsurance treaties as it is to facultative reinsurance. The reinsurer subscribing to a treaty is binding himself to offer an indemnity in the future

1178. For example, per Lord Mansfield in *Delver v. Barnes* (1807) 1 Taunt 48 at 51.
1179. As to the relationship between the slip and a policy, *see* *HIH Casualty and General Insurance Co Ltd v. New Hampshire Insurance Co* [2001] Lloyd's Rep. IR 596 at 616–622.
1180. *See* paras 99–103.
1181. *Container Transport International v. Oceanus Mutual Underwriting Association (Bermuda) Ltd.* [1984] 1 Lloyd's Rep. 476 per Kerr LJ at 497.
1182. *Ibid.*
1183. *Ibid.*, at 511.
1184. *North British Fishing Boat Insurance Co. v. Starr* (1922) 13 Ll L R 206, at 210.
1185. *London General Insurance Co. v. General Marine Underwriters Association* [1921] 1 KB 104.
1186. (1911) 16 Com Cas 109.
1187. [1973] 2 Lloyd's Rep. 442 at 459–460.
1188. Because a contract of reinsurance is in the nature of a contract of insurance, and the reinsurer has the same defences open to him, as regards liability, as are available to the reinsured in his capacity as primary insurer; *see* *China Traders Insurance Co. v. Royal Exchange Assurance Corp.* [1898] 2 QB 187.

in respect of the risks covered by the treaty, which must be ceded to him. He should therefore be entitled to the benefit of full disclosure before committing himself.

366. In facultative reinsurance, the duty of fair presentation exists up to the time that the reinsurer binds himself to take the risk. In treaty insurance, it is clear that the duty exists up to the conclusion of the treaty, but it may not persist in the cases where the reinsurer is bound to take the risks ceded, as there is then no opportunity for him to exercise his judgment upon those risks.[1189] If, however, a treaty or open cover allows the reinsurer the right to query, and/or refuse risks under it, then the duty of fair presentation and the principle of good faith will continue throughout the contract.[1190]

The test of materiality in reinsurance contracts will follow the guidelines set down in authorities on original insurance.[1191] In facultative reinsurance those facts which are material to the reinsured will be equally so to the reinsurer. Clauses in the primary insurance which are unusual enough to be unexpected should be disclosed.[1192] It has been held in treaty reinsurance that certain facts, including that the treaty must result in a loss to the reinsurer, were not material;[1193] no expert evidence was called however, and it may be that such facts would be held to be material today.

III. Misrepresentation

367. A misrepresentation may arise in a number of ways in reinsurance contracts. The reinsured may fail to pass on material facts received from the insured,[1194] or he may fail to check information received which proves to be false.[1195] Alternatively, it can arise when a representation by the primary insured is passed on by the reinsured, either expressly, or because of an incorporating clause in the reinsurance contract which adopts a warranty of certain facts given in the primary contract.[1196]

IV. Illegality

368. The general principles of illegality apply to reinsurance contracts as they do to primary insurance contracts. If, therefore, the primary insurance is itself illegal when effected, then any subsequent reinsurance of it will also be tainted with the same illegality, and will be void.[1197] This is despite the fact that the reinsureds may have

1189. *See* the comments of Kerr, J., in *Citadel Insurance Co. v. Atlantic Union Insurance Co.* [1982] 2 Lloyd's Rep. 543, at 548.
1190. *The Litsion Pride* [1985] 1 Lloyd's Rep. 437.
1191. *See* Part II, Ch. 4.
1192. *Property Insurance Co. v. National Protector Insurance Co.* (1913) 108 LT 104; the requirement was waived in this particular case by a term in the original insurance.
1193. *Glasgow Insurance Co. v. Symondson* (1911) 16 Com Cas 109.
1194. *Equitable Life Assurance Society v. General Accident Insurance Corp.* (1904) 12 SLT 348.
1195. *Highlands Insurance Co. v. Continental Insurance Co.* [1987] 1 Lloyd's Rep. 109.
1196. *Australian Widow's Fund Life Assurance v. National Mutual Life Association of Australia* [1914] AC 634.
1197. *Re London County Commercial Reinsurance Office Ltd.* [1922] 2 Ch. 67.

paid out under the primary insurance; they will not be able to recover the sums insured nor the premiums they themselves have paid to the reinsurers.

Illegality may occur at the level of the original contract, or at reinsurance, or both, and the illegality will have an effect upon the enforceable rights between the original insured and his insurer, and those between the reinsured and his reinsurer.

§4. Construction of Reinsurance Contracts

369. The reinsurance contract is normally contained in the slip, which, usually, is carefully worded by people with experience of the current market terms. It can be difficult however, to state with certainty the intention of the parties from the wording of the slip alone. It is therefore customary to adduce expert evidence to assist the court in construing a contract of reinsurance, even if no customary usage is contended for.[1198]

370. Standard market terms and common insurance terms are often incorporated by reference into reinsurance contracts. Two different types of incorporating provisions can be distinguished: first, the incorporation of standardized terms into a particular contract, and second, the incorporation of a term in the underlying contract of insurance into the reinsurance contract.

In determining whether a particular standard term is to be incorporated, the court will first attempt to establish the intentions of the parties. If there is a clear intention to incorporate the term, then it will be held to be so, provided that it is not inconsistent with the remaining terms of the reinsurance. If compliance with a term is, or might be, impossible for the reinsured, then it has been held that such a term cannot have been intended to be incorporated.[1199] By contrast, standardized terms of primary insurance annexed to, and clearly expressed to be incorporated into, a contract of reinsurance, have been held to be incorporated, even though they related to obligations which had to be performed by the primary insured.[1200]

371. A common feature of reinsurance contracts is the incorporation of terms of the underlying contract of insurance, achieved by such provisions as 'all terms, clauses, and conditions as original',[1201] or, if there are no such words, then the reinsured may warrant that the terms and conditions in both the primary and reinsurance contracts should be the same. The courts will not however, allow a literal application of the incorporating provision to produce inconsistency or ambiguity, if, for example, the incorporation of terms in the primary insurance contradicts express terms in the reinsurance.[1202]

1198. The admissibility of such evidence has been doubted – *Barlee Marine Corporation v. Mountain* [1987] 1 Lloyd's Rep. 471; *cf. Phillips v. Dorintal Insurance Co.* [1987] 1 Lloyd's Rep. 482.

1199. *Home Insurance Co. of New York v. Victoria Montreal Insurance Co.* [1907] AC 59.

1200. *Forsikringsaktieselskapet Vesta v. Butcher* [1986] 2 Lloyd's Rep. 179; affirmed [1988] 1 Lloyd's Rep. 19.

1201. *Pine Top Insurance Co. Ltd. v. Union Italiana Anglo-Saxon Reinsurance Co. Ltd.* [1987] 1 Lloyd's Rep. 476. This may cause difficulties of interpretation: *see HIH Casualty and General Insurance Ltd v. New Hampshire Insurance Co* [2001] Lloyd's Rep. IR 596.

1202. *Australian Widows v. National Mutual Life* [1914] AC 634.

If the original insurance contains an unusual term, then the reinsurer is not bound by it unless it is well known and in common use.[1203] This is supported by the fact that, in respect of such a term, the parties will not intend that it should be incorporated. It has also been held if it *is* intended that such a term should be incorporated, then it should be subject to the duty of disclosure,[1204] although it is, of course, possible to waive this duty, if, for instance, the reinsurance contract contains a clause which incorporates terms and conditions 'without notice'. This type of clause will, in practice, be unusual.

§5. The Proper Law of Insurance and Reinsurance Contracts

372. The term 'proper law' is here used in the sense of the system of law by which the parties intended the contract to be governed, or, where their intention is neither expressed, nor to be inferred from the circumstances, the system of law with which the transaction has its closest and most real connection.[1205] Reinsurance and primary insurance may be intended to apply to the same risk on the same terms, but that each be governed by different systems of law. In *Citadel Insurance Co. v. Atlantic Union Insurance Co. SA*,[1206] facultative reinsurances were placed with a Greek reinsurer by a Canadian reinsured, via both British and US brokers. The reinsurance slips were prepared and initialled in London, by the reinsurer's London agents. At first instance it was held that the reinsurance transaction had no substantial connection with English law; London had been used as a forum for the transaction purely as a matter of convenience. This was overruled by the Court of Appeal, however, this court regarding the facultative mechanisms as the very substance of the transaction. The governing law of the reinsurance contract was held to be English law, and not the law of the original insurance. The Court of Appeal also rejected a submission that a reference to reinsurance terms 'as original' meant that the intention of the parties must have been that the reinsurance and underlying insurance be governed by the same system.

Incorporating provisions may however have a bearing on the choice of governing law to ensure uniformity of interpretation. In *Vesta v. Butcher*,[1207] the reinsurance contract was formed in London, and under normal criteria, as outlined above, would have been governed by English law. The contract incorporated a number of terms from the underlying insurance, which was governed by Norwegian law, and certain of these terms would be construed differently under the two systems. It was held that the incorporated terms must remain subject to Norwegian law, whilst the remainder of the reinsurance contract should be governed by English law. This 'hybrid and admittedly unorthodox' solution was considered to be the only way to implement the presumed intention of the parties that the relevant clauses should have the same effect in both contracts. In the important House of Lords' decision in *Wasa International Insurance*

1203. *Martin v. Nippon Sea and Land Insurance Co.* (1898) 3 Com Cas 168.
1204. *Property Insurance Co. v. National Protector Insurance* (1913) 108 LT 104.
1205. *See* Dicey & Morris, *The Conflict of Laws* (10th ed.) at 747.
1206. [1982] 2 Lloyd's Rep. 543.
1207. [1988] 1 Lloyd's Rep. 19.

Co. Ltd v. Lexington Insurance Co.,[1208] where the reinsurance contract was governed by English law, whereas the underlying insurance was governed by the law of the US State of Washington, it was held that the duration of the reinsurance contract, and thus the liability of the reinsurers, was governed by English law. The fact that US law had extended the duration of the liability of the insurers under which they were liable to indemnify their insured against the liability of the latter, did not bind the reinsurers.

Problems can therefore arise where insurance and reinsurance agreements, subject to differing proper law, seek to define their respective coverages. The solution is probably the prudent adoption of express choice of law clauses.

1208. [2009] UKHL 40, [2009] 3 W.L.R. 575.

Part IX. Taxation of Insurance

373. Tax law in the UK is highly complex. For the purposes of rules of particular importance to insurance, which is all that this Part is concerned with, there are four aspects of taxation which merit consideration. In respect of income tax, which is obviously a tax on a person's income from employment, self-employment and investment, there are special rules applying in respect of life insurance and pensions. Tax on a person's income is payable under one of a number of schedules as laid out in the Income and Corporation Taxes Act 1988. Capital Gains Tax (CGT) applies whenever a person disposes of a capital asset at a gain or profit and is of some importance in insurance generally. Inheritance tax is a tax on the transfer of wealth generally on death and there are some important considerations concerning the availability of life insurance to mitigate the consequences of inheritance tax. Finally, there is the tax payable on insurance premiums.

§1. Income Tax

I. Life Insurance

374. Qualifying life insurance policies[1209] entered into before 14 March 1984 attract tax relief in respect of the premiums paid, at a rate of 12.5% of those premiums. This relief was abolished for any policy effected after 14 March 1984, but policies existing at that date continue to attract the relief, provided that the terms of the policy are not altered to any great extent, nor an entirely new policy entered into.[1210] Relief on qualifying policies is effected by the taxpayer deducting the allowable percentage from his premium before paying it to the insurance company. The insurer therefore receives the premiums net of tax, and recovers the tax deducted from the Inland Revenue. The upper limit for relief is GBP 1,500 or one-sixth of the taxpayer's total annual income, whichever is the greater. This relief applies also to premiums paid under personal accident and permanent health policies which have a life insurance element.

II. Private Health Insurance

375. Premiums paid under a private health insurance policy are not tax deductible, unless the subscriber is aged 60 or over when the policy is effected. If the premiums

1209. Income and Corporation Taxes Act (ICTA) 1988, Sch. 15, para. 1.
1210. Finance Act 1984.

are paid by the insured's employer on his behalf, then the insured will be taxed on the cost to the employer of providing this benefit. This is so if the insured is either a director of the company or a 'higher paid' employee.

III. Personal Accident Insurance

376. Any lump sum received under a personal accident policy is normally treated as income for income tax purposes. Benefits received under a permanent health policy are taxed under Schedule D Case III,[1211] but, by concession, benefits are free of tax until they have been received for a full fiscal year. If, as is more usual, the benefit is paid to the employer, who in turn pays the employee an equivalent amount of salary, then this salary is taxed just as any other income. The amount paid to the employer is taxed as a trading receipt but this is cancelled out by the relief available on the salary payments to the employee.

IV. Pensions

377. Taxation rules for pensions are complex and ever changing; they may be briefly summarized as follows. Income received from occupational pension schemes is taxed under Schedule E. If the scheme is an 'approved' scheme, then the contributions made by the employee are tax deductible, up to a maximum of 15% of salary. Employee contributions to a relevant statutory scheme are likewise deductible. The taxpayer will not be charged to tax on the cost to his employer in respect of any contributions made by the employer into either of the above. For those individuals who can afford it, making the maximum permitted payments into a pension scheme is a valuable aid in reducing his income tax bill.

Personal pension schemes, provided they are approved by the Inland Revenue, also attract tax relief. Contributions made by a member are tax deductible up to a maximum of 17.5% of his net taxable earnings for the tax year. This maximum is raised for contributors over the age of 35, rising to a maximum of 40% for those aged 61 and over. Any contribution made by the taxpayer's employer will not be taxable as an emolument. Again, individuals should make the maximum payments they can afford into the scheme, to reduce their income tax liability.

§2. Capital Gains Tax

378. CGT was first introduced in the UK by the Finance Act 1965. Its purpose was simple. Income tax was, and still is, a tax on income. Before the introduction of CGT therefore, any profit made by a taxpayer on the disposal of a capital asset escaped tax. Since the introduction of CGT, however, whenever a taxpayer makes a chargeable

1211. This Schedule taxes all income received from annuities, and all annual payments: ICTA 1988, s. 18(3).

gain on the disposal of a chargeable asset, then he will be charged to CGT, subject to the deduction of any allowable exemptions and reliefs.

The legislation relating to CGT was consolidated in the Taxation of Chargeable Gains Act (TCGA) 1992, and CGT plays an important role in the taxation of insurance. A capital sum is often received under-insurance policies, for example, when an insured asset is lost, or destroyed by fire, or when a lump sum is received in connection with a life insurance policy. All of these may be subject to CGT, depending upon circumstances.

I. Disposal of Rights under a Policy of Insurance

379. If an insurer disposes of his rights under an insurance policy, then the disposal is exempt from CGT, and this is so whether the risks insured relate to property or not. The disposal of rights by an insured however is not usually exempt; any chargeable gain is taxable if the rights relate to assets which would themselves be chargeable if disposed of.[1212] This does not apply to life insurance policies, or deferred annuity contracts however; disposals of the rights in either are exempt from CGT, unless the person making the disposal is not the original beneficiary under the policy, and acquired the rights for a consideration in money or money's worth.[1213] Where the exemption applies, the occasion of the payment of the sums insured (including the transfer of investments directly to the policyholder), is treated as a disposal of rights, as is the first instalment of a deferred annuity, and the occasion of the surrender of a policy under a deferred annuity contract. The application of this main principle will therefore effectively exclude from CGT the great majority of life insurance policies and deferred annuity contracts, because it exempts the proceeds in the hands of the original beneficial owner.

In addition, by virtue of section 237 TCGA, no chargeable gain accrues on the disposal of any rights in:

- any allowance, annuity or capital sum paid under a superannuation scheme established solely for persons (and their dependants) in a trade, profession or employment;
- an annuity which is not granted under a deferred annuity contract;
- unsecured annual payments under a covenant.

II. Loss or Destruction of an Asset

380. Any sum received under a policy covering the risk of any damage to, or the loss or depreciation of, assets, is a sum derived from those assets,[1214] notwithstanding that the rights under the policy may, or may not, be assets in their own right.[1215] The receipt of the capital sum when the asset is lost or destroyed is treated as a disposal

1212. TCGA 1992, s. 204(1).
1213. *Ibid.*, s. 210.
1214. *Ibid.*, s. 204(2).
1215. *See supra* .

of that asset and is therefore subject to CGT.[1216] It would however be unfair to a taxpayer if the insurance monies he receives to replace his asset should be diminished by tax; therefore, if he applies the money wholly in replacing his asset within one year of receiving it, then no CGT is charged.[1217] If, however, he is able to replace his asset for less than the money received, then the excess is effectively subject to CGT.[1218]

If the asset is not wholly lost or destroyed, but merely damaged, then the taxpayer may claim that there is no disposal of it on receipt of the capital sums insured, provided that the sums are wholly applied in restoring the asset, or wholly applied except for a part of them which is considered small compared to the total value of the asset.[1219] The word 'small' is not defined in the Act, but the Inland Revenue take it to mean no more than 5%. Where less than 95% of the sum received is applied in restoration, then the part not so applied is treated as a capital gain and taxed accordingly.

§3. Inheritance Tax

381. Most countries impose some kind of wealth tax and the UK is no exception. Inheritance tax is both a tax on a deceased's property passing under a will or on intestacy, and it is a tax on certain gifts made during the donor's lifetime.[1220] Life insurance has always been a valuable tool in the tax planner's armoury, and this has continued since the advent of Inheritance Tax (IHT) in 1984. It is possible for instance, and indeed, advisable, to insure against one's 'death bill'. The policy should take the form of a trust, so that the proceeds go straight to the hands of the beneficiary, and are not taxed as part of the deceased's estate. The introduction of IHT brought with it the Potentially Exempt Transfer (PET). Basically, gifts made during a donor's lifetime will not be taxed, provided the donor lives for seven years after making them; the risk that a PET may become chargeable can be insured against. As the value of the gift is fixed at the date of transfer, the maximum IHT liability, (assuming that the rates are not retrospectively increased) will be known. Some kind of decreasing seven-year term insurance will therefore be appropriate and such insurance can be taken out both by the donor and the donee.

I. 'Asset-Freezing' Arrangements

382. There were two main types of asset-freezing arrangements – inheritance trusts and PETAs (Pure Endowment, Term Assurance), and insurance plays a large part in both of them. However, the Finance Act 1986 passed rules which destroyed many of the benefits offered by both inheritance trusts and PETA plans, so much so that these plans have now been withdrawn from the market. Any contract entered into

1216. TCGA 1992, s. 22(1)(a).
1217. *Ibid.*, s. 23(4).
1218. *Ibid.*, s. 23(5).
1219. *Ibid.*, s. 23(1).
1220. For the detailed rules relating to the principles of Inheritance Tax, the reader is referred to specialized texts; e.g., Whitehouse & Stuart-Buttle, *Revenue Law – Principles and Practice*.

before 18 March 1986, however, will be generally unaffected by the legislation, so that brief consideration below is still thought justified. The formation of the contract date is a matter for general contract law;[1221] if a contract can be shown to have existed on 18 March 1986, however, then the payment of further premiums into it will not affect the tax position. There is one area of possible danger, however, section 103 of the Finance Act 1986 prevents the deduction of artificial debts on death, and this section may eventually operate to tax the gift-type of inheritance trust discussed below.

A. Inheritance Trusts

383. The inheritance trust ensures that the value of a particular asset owned by the taxpayer is frozen at a particular moment so that any increase in value belongs to the beneficiary. It was generally essential that the taxpayer survived the creation of the trust by several years, if any significant IHT advantage was to be secured. The trust is created with an interest in possession, the donor being obliged to name his beneficiary at the outset, and the donor becomes one of the trustees. The trustees are given a power to appoint away the fund to the settlor or his spouse, up to two years after the settlor's death. The exercise of such a power does not lead to the imposition of IHT, because of an exception in the Inheritance Tax Act 1984 (IHTA).[1222] If the power to terminate the interest is not exercised, and the property ultimately vests in the interest in possession beneficiary, then, again, there is no liability to IHT.[1223] Inheritance trusts involve investment in a single premium life insurance bond which produces no income; almost invariably these are unit-linked policies. They are not qualifying policies,[1224] so no question of income tax relief on premiums arises, but any capital gains or income accruing on the underlying investments will be taxed only in the hands of the insurance company.

B. PETA Plans

384. PETA plans achieve a tax saving even if the individual dies immediately after making the transfer. They involve the taxpayer entering into two separate life insurance policies. The first is a single premium endowment policy in which 99% of the investment is made. No sum is ever likely to be paid on this policy as it is always subject to a contingency which is impossible to satisfy. The second, linked policy is a single premium term insurance purchased with the remaining 1% of the investment. Despite this small amount, the maturity value of the policy is equal to the value of the units into which the endowment premium is invested. So long as the taxpayer does not satisfy the contingency (and he will not), then the value of the units at the date of death is payable. This term policy has no surrender value and is settled on a named beneficiary.

1221. *See* Inland Revenue Press Release, 18 Mar. 1986.
1222. Section 53(3)–(5).
1223. IHTA 1984, s. 53(2).
1224. *See* para. 373, *supra* .

II. Modern Arrangements

385. As well as the two plans mentioned above which are increasingly of historical interest only, there are other insurance based schemes which offer a considerable IHT saving. A combination of a whole-life policy and an annuity policy, for instance, works well. The arrangement involves a purchased life annuity (which results in a capital sum leaving the taxpayer's estate) whose annuity instalments are used to pay the annual premiums on a whole-life insurance policy which is held on trust for the intended beneficiaries (so that the proceeds do not form part of the deceased's estate). For this arrangement to avoid IHT, however, the policies must be shown to be independent; this is best achieved by the taxpayer entering into each contract with a separate, unconnected insurance company.

§4. Insurance Premium Tax

386. The Finance Act 1994 introduced a new form of indirect taxation affecting insurance.[1225] The purpose is simply to raise revenue for the government, insurance premiums being a relatively straightforward and lucrative target. There are two rates, namely a standard rate of 6%, increased to 9.5% from November 2015, and a higher rate of 20% for travel insurance and some insurance for vehicles and domestic and electrical appliances.

Most long-term insurance is exempted from the tax, as is reinsurance, insurance for commercial ships and aircraft and insurance for commercial goods in international transit. Premiums for risks located outside the UK are also exempt, but they may be liable to similar taxes imposed by other countries. The tax is collected from insurers but the cost is borne by insureds.

1225. The detail is in the Insurance Premium Tax Regulations SI 1994/1774 as amended.

Part X. Risk Management and Prevention

387. All individuals and organizations constantly practice risk management in that they make decisions and take steps to control the risks to which they are exposed. Once the risks are identified and evaluated, various handling methods can be employed. No matter how good a firm's loss control programmes, however, some losses will occur, and provision needs to be made for financing them, either from the firm's own resources, (risk retention), or, most commonly, by transferring the loss to another party, usually an insurer.

§1. Self-Insurance

388. Risk retention is often called self-insurance, but this is, in fact, a misnomer, as there is no transfer of the risks involved. Even if the organization establishes its own captive insurance company to underwrite some of the risks, it is still in the same position, except that part of the risk may be the subject of reinsurance. The main reason for carrying part of one's own risk is cost; a firm should not, however, lose sight of the ancillary benefits of insurance, such as expert claims handling, nor should it underestimate the impact of several small losses during a single accounting period. Another disadvantage of risk retention is that there are no tax concessions for a contingency fund set up to handle the loss, unlike insurance premiums, which are tax deductible.

§2. Risk Transfer

389. The most important mechanism for risk transfer is insurance. In return for a known, or determinable, premium, the insured transfers to the insurer the risk of losses which may be uncertain both as to timing, and amount. Some risks *must* be insured under UK law, either because of compulsory insurance legislation,[1226] or because of contract terms.

390. By insuring, an insured can obtain more than financial security. In many classes of non-life business insurers frequently carry out surveys which enable them to make recommendations to their clients as to how to reduce risks, which may then qualify for a reduction in premium. Help is also available following losses. Loss adjusters can often help in salvaging operations in connection with large-scale property losses, and many firms prefer, from the standpoint of public and industrial relations,

1226. For example, as regards motor vehicle and employers' liability insurance; *see* Part IV and Part V, Ch. 1.

to have claims handled by their insurer's officials; expert claims handling services are now an important feature of liability insurances.

§3. The Insurer's Handling of Risk

391. An insurer manages risk via the terms of the contract. There are three different types of contract term, namely warranties (or conditions), exceptions and terms descriptive of the risk; the most important of these is the warranty. For example, a sea voyage may carry insurance from Dover to a port on the French coast in July (description of risk), Calais excepted (exception), in a ship equipped with cold storage facilities (warranty). The legal nature of all these types of term has been considered earlier in this work, but a brief resumé in the context of this Part is appropriate.

Warranties limit the risk, and so limit the burden of the insurer's cover, which is conditional, first upon the payment of the premium by the insured, and second, on the risk covered being no more than expected when the premium was calculated, and being that risk described in the contract. Exceptions clearly limit the risk, therefore they have a function similar to warranties. Their effect is different, however; if an exception is ignored, then cover is suspended whilst the exception operates, but if a warranty is breached, cover will be automatically terminated if the contract so provides.[1227] This difference in consequence arises from a difference in concept. Both exceptions and warranties provide against the possibility that the risk is, or will be, different from that expected, but the exception concerns a temporary difference, whilst the true warranty concerns a change or difference that is permanent,[1228] or gives rise to the possibility of such a change. Terms descriptive of the risk may not always be relevant to the risk of loss, but if they are so relevant, then they will usually be treated as warranties.[1229] An example is that of a two-storey property insured against fire – the erection of a third storey would be a breach of warranty of description.

392. Other obligations assumed by the insured are also designed to limit loss and expense to the insurer, for example, claim conditions, such as notice provisions and the duty of co-operation. These are not warranties, but are inserted into the contract expressly to limit the insurer's loss once a claim arises. Such conditions have been described as 'incidental to the subject-matter of the insurance – made with a view to fence round and protect the rights of an insurer, so as to enable him to require satisfactory evidence of, or to make due enquiry concerning, the facts upon which his liability depends'.[1230] They do not, therefore, limit the scope of the insurer's main promises, for example, cover and payment on loss, but are designed to make those promises less difficult and less expensive to perform. Breach of a claims condition will not normally entitle the insurer to repudiate the contract, but it may entitle him to repudiate liability for that particular loss.

1227. This is no longer automatic as a matter of general law, but in a commercial contract the relevant provisions of the Insurance Act 2015 can be excluded.
1228. *De Maurier (Jewels) Ltd. v. Bastion Insurance Co. Ltd.* [1967] 2 Lloyd's Rep. 550.
1229. *Yorkshire Insurance Co. v. Campbell* [1917] AC 218; *Sillem v. Thornton* (1854) 3 El & Bl 868.
1230. *Lancashire Insurance Co. v. Inland Revenue Commissioners* [1898] 1 QB 353 per Bruce, J., at 359.

Selected Bibliography

1. General Books on Insurance Law

Birds, J. *Birds' Modern Insurance Law.* 10th edn. Sweet & Maxwell, 2016.

Birds, J. *Encyclopedia of Insurance Law*, first published 1983, updated by looseleaf supplement. Sweet & Maxwell.

Butler, J.S. & R.M. Merkin. *Reinsurance Law.* Sweet & Maxwell, Looseleaf, 1986.

Clarke, M. *Law of Insurance Contracts.* Informa, Looseleaf.

Regulation of Insurance in the United Kingdom, Ireland and EU. Sweet & Maxwell, Looseleaf, 1982.

McGee, A. *The Modern Law of Insurance.* 3rd edn. LexisNexis, 2011.

Merkin, R.M. *Colinvaux's Law of Insurance.* 11th edn. Sweet & Maxwell, 2017 (and supplements).

Birds, J., B. Lynch & S. Paul, *MacGillivray on Insurance Law.* 13th edn. Sweet & Maxwell, 2015 (and supplements).

Rose, F.D. (ed.), *New Foundations for Insurance Law.* Stevens, 1987.

2. Books on Intermediaries

Henley, C. *The Law of Insurance Broking.* 2nd edn. Sweet & Maxwell, 2003.

3. Books on Specific Types of Insurance Law

Bennett, H. *The Law of Marine Insurance.* 2nd edn. Oxford University Press, 2006.

Cannon, M. & B. McGurk. *Professional Indemnity Insurance.* Oxford University Press, 2010.

Clarke, M.A. *The Law of Liability Insurance,* Informa, 2013.

Enright, I. & D. Jess. *Professional Indemnity Insurance Law.* 2nd edn. Sweet & Maxwell, 2007.

Gilman, J.C.B., et al. *Arnould's Law of Marine Insurance and Average.* 18th edn. Stevens, 2013.

Jess, D.C. *The Insurance of Commercial Risks: Law and Practice.* 4th edn. Sweet & Maxwell, 2011.

Margo, R.D. *Aviation Insurance.* 4th edn. LexisNexis, 2013.

Merkin, R. & J. Stuart-Smith. *The Law of Motor Insurance.* Sweet & Maxwell, 2004.

Roberts, H. *Riley on Business Interruption and Consequential Loss Insurance and Claims.* 9th edn. Sweet & Maxwell, 2011.

Rose, F. *Marine Insurance: Law and Practice.* 2nd edn. Informa.

4. Books on Insurance Practices and Markets

Clayton, G. *British Insurance,* 1970.

Cockerell, H.A.L. *Lloyd's of London: A Portrait.* Woodhead-Faulkner, 1984.

Index

The numbers here refer to paragraph numbers.

Made in the USA
Monee, IL
18 October 2026

66041415R10142